Chakra Healing and Karmic Awareness

Keith Sherwood is an internationally known teacher and healer whose ability to see and remove energy blockages and karmic energy has been instrumental in transforming the lives of his students and clients. He is the founder of onewholelove.com, and the publisher of *Inner Awareness Magazine*. He is the author of *Chakra Therapy* and *The Art of Spiritual Healing*, books that have appeared in more than twelve languages. Sherwood has taught in North America, Europe, South Africa, and India for more than twenty years. In addition, he lectures and conducts seminars on four continents and appears regularly on radio and television in the cities where he works. He writes for a number of magazines, including *Psychology Today, Esotera, Connections, Bres,* and various other international publications.

Chakra Healing and Karmic Awareness

KEITH SHERWOOD

Llewellyn Publications
St. Paul, Minnesota

First Edition
First Printing, 2005

Book design and editing by Connie Hill
Cover background copyright © 2005 Brand X Pictures
Cover design by Lisa Novak
Interior illustrations by Llewellyn Art Department

Llewellyn is a registered trademark of Llewellyn Worldwide, Ltd.

Library of Congress Cataloging-in-Publication Data
Sherwood, Keith.
    Chakra healing and karmic awareness / Keith Sherwood — 1st ed.
        p.   cm.
    Includes glossary and index.
    ISBN 0-7387-0354-0
        1. Chakras. 2. Healing—Miscellanea. 3. Karma. I. Title.

    BF1442.C53S54   2005
    131—dc22   2005043599

Llewellyn Worldwide does not participate in, endorse, or have any authority or responsibility concerning private business transactions between our authors and the public.

All mail addressed to the author is forwarded but the publisher cannot, unless specifically instructed by the author, give out an address or phone number.

Any Internet references contained in this work are current at publication time, but the publisher cannot guarantee that a specific location will continue to be maintained. Please refer to the publisher's website for links to authors' websites and other sources.

Llewellyn Publications
A Division of Llewellyn Worldwide, Ltd.
P.O. Box 64383, Dept. 0-7387-0354-0
St. Paul, MN 55164-0383, U.S.A.
www.llewellyn.com

Printed in the United States of America

Contents

Part Two — Protecting Yourself
Chapter Six: 85

Chapter Seven: 109

Chapter Eight: 127

Chapter Nine: 137

Chapter Ten: 147

Part Three — Expanding Yourself
Chapter Eleven: 159

Part One

Knowing Yourself

Chapter One

Better than ruling this world, better than attaining the realm of the gods, better than being lord of all the worlds, is one step taken on the path to nirvana.

—Dhammapada, vs. 178

Introduction

The goal of every human being alive today—whether they can articulate it or not—is to find within themselves a state of unconditional joy. Although this goal may appear to be illusive, the simple fact is that such a state exists within everyone, regardless of their physical, emotional, mental, or spiritual condition.

The state I'm speaking of is not something new waiting to be discovered, nor is it something that must be achieved through self-improvement or learned through a course of study. It is not reserved for the elect or for those who believe in some special doctrine. The state I'm speaking about exists *a priori* in the depths of each person. To actualize it, one must simply bring it into conscious awareness by going within and allowing it to emerge and radiate through spirit, soul, intellect, and body.

Unfortunately, for the vast majority of people alive today the goal of unconditional joy seems an impossible one to achieve. For far too many people, the human condition is one of suffering, pain, confusion, lack of self-control, and spiritual emptiness.

Let me assure you from the start that the goal can be achieved! There has always been a way home to the Self, the reservoir of unconditional joy and bliss, which emerges from the center of each human being. Many people before you have found it.

The way home has never been a secret, though it is not an easy one to follow. It leads inward through the levels of body, soul, intellect, and spirit to the source of unlimited energy and consciousness, the Self. However, by far the greatest obstacle to the experience of the Self and union with it are the attachments to the world created by karmic baggage—the dense, qualified energy carried from one lifetime to another in the human energy field. Karmic baggage not only limits awareness by creating attachment to the external world of phenomena (*maya*), it disrupts the transmission and transmutation of unqualified energy (*prana*) through the higher and lower mind and the human energy system. Prana can be considered the life force. In the macrocosm it serves as the foundation of the phenomenal universe, and in the microcosm it serves as the foundation of the higher and lower mind and the human energy system. Once the natural transmission and transmutation of energy through the microcosm, the human energy field, has been disrupted by karmic baggage, access to pleasure, human love, intimacy, and joy—which emerge from the Self—will be restricted.

What is Karma?

To get a sense of how karmic baggage—in the form of dense, qualified energy—disrupts access to joy, intimacy, love, and pleasure, one must first know what karma is and how it functions. The ancient Sanskrit word *karma* comes from the root *kri*, "to act," and it signifies an activity or action. Swami Shivananda declared that karma ". . . is a universal law that keeps up the inner harmony and the logical order of the universe."

In the west, karma has been defined as ". . . The cumulative effect of action." In a limited way this is true, although the great religions of the east go beyond this definition by describing karma in terms of both its structure and function. Jainism views karma as an aggregate of subtle matter that accumulates in the human energy system and veils the consciousness of the Self and everything that emerges from it, including bliss, joy, love, and pleasure.

According to this ancient religion, which stresses aestheticism, non-violence and reverence for life, karma has eight functional aspects:

- Karma obscures comprehension.

- Karma obscures awareness.

- Karma produces counterfeit feelings (emotions and sensations).

- Karma deludes a person (veils the truth).

- Karma is age determining.

- Karma defines personality by creating personas.

- Karma determines status and therefore psychic well-being.

- Karma disrupts personal power.

The first four aspects are obstructive, the remaining four are not, although they are Self-limiting since they obstruct the flow of unqualified energy (*prana*) through the human energy system.

In Vedanta—which is the foundation of Yoga and Tantra—karma is broken down in three ways, based on its effects. *Sancita karma* is the residue of actions performed in either the present or previous lives, which have already come to fruition. A person has the free will to overcome sancita karma, which manifests in the form of karmic baggage and/or physical weakness or disability. *Agami karma* is potential karma from actions which can be avoided, even though a compelling pattern already exists. *Prarabdha karma* is the residue of actions taken in this life, which have not yet come to fruition. A person is powerless to avoid the consequences or karmic effects that have accrued from these actions, although an enlightened master, by virtue of his or her detachment, will be less affected or not affected at all.

To anyone with a minimum of discernment it is clear that karma is far more complex than the abstract principle that guarantees you will reap what you sow. Karma is a force of nature that manifests will and intent and can be both Self-limiting and obstructive. It connects to their causes the effects of actions on all interpenetrating worlds and dimensions. Through its ability to create attachment it defines a person and limits his or her freedom. Much like gravity, the polarity that karma creates between the cause and its effect attracts a person to objects, phenomena, and living beings (based on past actions), and then, using qualified energy, binds them to the object, idea, feeling, or living being to whom they are attracted. The actual method by which karma does this will be explained in later chapters. For now, it is important to recognize that karma functions through the synergistic relationship of qualified energy and the individual mind and ego. Without the individual mind and ego to express and focus qualitative energy through intent and will, there would be no action or reaction on any dimension, nor would qualified energy be able to attach a person to objects, energetic fields, and/or beings in external environment.

Swami Shivananda affirmed that, "Any physical or mental action is karma(ic). Thought is Karma(ic). Reaction that follows an action is karma(ic). . . . Attraction, repulsion, gravitation, breathing talking, walking, seeing, hearing, eating, feeling, willing, desiring, thinking, and all the actions of the body, mind, and the senses constitute Karma(ic) activity. Karma includes both cause and effect" (*Practice of Yoga*, Shivananda, 189).

What is Karmic Baggage?

Karmic baggage is the total amount of qualified energy that has accumulated in a human being's energy field during this lifetime and previous incarnations. Since qualified energy exists in time-space, it has a structure and function, which are determined by fixed principles, regardless whether the qualified energy is located in the field of maya surrounding the higher mind (the world of spirit, intellect, soul), the lower mind (bodies of desire), the levels of the splenic chakras, the world of chakras, and/or the functions and aspects of mind.

Jesus the Nazarite recognized the considerable power and effect of karmic baggage and instructed his listeners not to sin in thought or deed. What he recognized, as did the masters of Yoga and Tantra, was that thoughts, emotions, and feelings are subfields of qualified energy. Swami

Sivananda expanded on this principle by declaring that "Every thought has got a weight, shape, size, form, color, quality, and power. Thoughts are like things . . . bitterness and sweetness . . . are in the mind. They are created by thought" (*Thought Power*, Swami Sivananda, 10–11).

In fact, each thought, action, emotion, feeling, and sensation can be seen as an energetic wave with distinct characteristics that a person may unconsciously radiate or deliberately project through the larger field of qualified energy—or become attached to—when a foreign wave enters his or her internal environment. Indeed, all actions, on both the subtle and physical dimensions, emerging from the individual mind and ego cause reactions by subfields (primarily living beings) of qualified energy within the collective field of maya.

The reactions caused by interacting subfields radiate in all directions, including in the direction from which the initial action originated. Like the original wave or projection, a reactive wave resonates within the same portion of the energetic spectrum as the original wave. When these reactive waves interact with one's energy field they can get stuck to layers of qualitative energy already present from past incarnations in the form of sediment. Once qualitative energy gets stuck, it becomes part of the host's karmic baggage and it will increase their karmic load and attachment to the external world. It is this kind of attachment that disrupts one's relationship to the Self (universal consciousness) and restricts one's access to bliss, love, intimacy, and pleasure.

Karmic baggage tends to accumulate in certain locations, including the auric fields that surround personal body space—the space on the higher and lower dimensions that corresponds to the space occupied by the physical-material body—personal body space—if an energy body has been ejected, or within an energy body that has been ejected. Note that the spirit, intellect, soul, and lower mind are composed of communities of energy bodies that function synchronistically.

Effects of Karmic Baggage

To a human being trapped in the individual mind and ego, karmic baggage can appear to have both positive and negative effects, but even what appears to be positive can attach a person to the external environment and restrict the free flow of prana. In the end, it is attachment of any sort that causes suffering. "All human beings are subject to attachment and the thirst for pleasure. Hankering after these, they are caught in the cycle of birth and death. Driven by this thirst, they run about frightened like a hunted hare, suffering more and more . . ." (*The Dhammapada*, vs. 341–2, 185).

The attachment caused by karmic baggage causes suffering by disrupting the flow of unqualified energy (prana) through the human energy system, which in turn obstructs access to the Self and inhibits self-awareness and self-expression.

Since it is unqualified energy that vitalizes all pleasurable, joyful, and blissful activities, any disruption in its ability to flow through the human energy system will result in the restriction of bliss, joy, and pleasure and/or the channeling of pleasure into unsavory activities.

The importance of pleasure, love, intimacy, and bliss in one's life cannot be overstated. The Yogic Sutras teach that an absence of any of these positive feelings will cause suffering. Indeed, negative sensations, feelings, emotions, and thoughts will flood one's internal environment and energy system whenever pleasure, intimacy, joy, and bliss are restricted and/or pushed out of conscious awareness.

Karmic Baggage on the
Spiritual Level

Any disruption in the transmission and transmutation of unqualified energy will disrupt a person's life on the spiritual level by disrupting their access to the Self (their source of bliss). This, in turn, will inhibit their ability to recognize and follow their dharma. The Dhammapada tells us, "There is no gift better than the gift of dharma, no gift more sweet, no gift more joyful. It puts an end to cravings and the sorrow they bring" (*Dhammapada,* vs. 354, 186).

One's individual spiritual path (dharma) is the route one takes home (inwardly, through the worlds of the lower and higher mind) to the Self. By following dharma one does what is appropriate by choosing only those actions that promote the flow of unqualified energy through the energy system. Actions that emerge from karmic baggage (which can counterfeit the functions of the higher and lower mind and the human energy system) create attachments, which in turn cause contraction. Contraction disrupts the flow of prana, and a lack of prana obstructs one's experience of the Self—and the bliss, joy, and pleasure that emerge from it.

Once one has been cut off from the conscious experience of bliss personal survival will overcome Self-realization as one's dominant paradigm. The individual mind and ego, which are composed of qualified energy, will supersede the influence of the higher and lower mind and energy system in one's day-to-day life. "Living in a spiritual desert" is a phrase often used to describe such a condition.

"Identifying the Self with the nonself (the individual mind and ego with the higher and lower mind), this is the bondage of man, which is due to his ignorance, and brings in its train the miseries of birth and death. It is through this that one considers this evanescent body as real, and identifying oneself with it, nourishes, bathes, and preserves it by means of (agreeable) sense objects, by which he becomes bound as the caterpillar by the threads of its cocoon" (*Viveka Cudamani,* Sri Sankara-carya, vs. 137, 51).

The accumulation of karmic baggage on the spiritual level can cause a host of collateral problems. It can disrupt boundaries (particularly the auric boundaries), inhibit the free flow of unqualified energy (prana, the kundalini-shakti, and the aprana), and disrupt the synchronistic functions of the community of energy bodies on the world of the spirit.

Spiritual consciousness is a function of unqualified energy on the spiritual level, and, like any form of energy, spiritual consciousness needs an energetic medium through which to move. Without sufficient unqualified

energy to serve as that medium, consciousness of the internal environment, on the spiritual level, will be restricted and individuals will find
themselves locked outside themselves, with a corresponding loss of bliss,
knowledge, and Self-awareness.

In extreme cases the excessive accumulation of karmic baggage can
create counterfeit personas. Counterfeit personas, on the spiritual level,
are self-contained personalities composed of qualified energy and subtle
matter that can intrude into personal body space and usurp the functions
of spirit, making it increasingly difficult to remain fully conscious on the
spiritual level.

In time, as karmic baggage accumulates and usurps the functions of
spirit, a person can fall prey to a counterfeit spirituality, supported by
counterfeit personas and counterfeit spiritual experiences. A counterfeit
spirituality is one that denies a human being's innate divinity and union
with the Self, and his or her a priori state of enlightenment.

The accumulation of karmic baggage can even create a fragmented
spirituality that discounts essential aspects of human nature or pits one
part of the individual mind and ego against another in a vain effort to
achieve counterfeit spiritual goals. Conflict of this sort is not only point-
less, it is essentially a subterfuge used by the individual mind and ego to
thwart a person's attempts to emancipate themselves from the suffocat-
ing control of karmic baggage.

Karmic Baggage on the
Mental Level

Any disruption in the flow of unqualified energy on the mental level
(world of intellect) will disrupt awareness, creativity, peace of mind, memory, and the normal balance of inductive and deductive reasoning. In fact,
once there has been a disruption in the transmutation and transmission of
unqualified energy, on the mental level it will become almost impossible to
go inward. Instead, one will find one's self trapped in the internal dialogue
(the incessant chatter of the individual mind and ego) and reactive to subfields and projections of qualified energy on the mental level.

Human awareness is a function of unqualified energy on the mental level, and, like any form of energy, awareness needs an energetic medium through which to move. Without sufficient unqualified energy to serve as that medium, awareness of the microcosm will become severely restricted and individuals will find themselves locked outside themselves on the mental level, with a corresponding loss of creativity, focus, intuition, and memory.

Given enough time, intellect—which is composed of the communities of energy bodies that function within the range of finite human awareness—will have its functions disrupted. It is the intellect that has the innate capacity to recognize and organize phenomena and objects in the external environment into a coherent structure, and it is the functions and aspects of mind associated with the intellect that enable a person to function cognitively and manifest their knowledge within this structure.

On the mental level, both unqualified energy and qualified energy containing information from the external environment make an impact on human awareness, and the higher and lower mind, particularly the intellect, processes this information. Karmic baggage can disrupt this process. The unfortunate individuals who have had their mental functions disrupted by karmic baggage will often feel like their mind has become foggy, or is racing out of control.

In extreme situations, when boundaries are weakened and enough qualified energy has been introduced into personal body space on the mental level, counterfeit personas can develop. Counterfeit personas, on the mental level, can be so compelling (badgering and nagging a person) that the unfortunate individual begins to think, and eventuality feel and behave, in anti-Self and/or antisocial ways. Given enough time, counterfeit personas, with the support of the individual mind and ego, can usurp the position and function of the bodies of intellect, particularly if they have been ejected from personal body space. In time, they can grow strong enough to compel a person to obsessively fulfill their needs and desires at their host's expense or the expense of other people with whom they associate.

Karmic Baggage on the
Emotional Level

Any disruption of unqualified energy on the emotional level (world of soul) will restrict one's ability to emote and/or express or even sense emotional energy.

Human emotion is a function of unqualified energy on the world of soul. Like any form of energy, emotion needs an energetic medium through which to move. Without sufficient unqualified energy to serve as that medium, emotions will be stifled and one's awareness of the internal environment on the world of soul will become severely restricted.

There are only four authentic emotions: anger, fear, pain, and joy. They are authentic because they emerge from the chakras deep within personal body space, in the world of soul. Anger emerges through the second chakra, fear through the third chakra, pain through the fourth chakra, and joy through the fifth chakra (for more about chakras and emotions see chapter twelve).

When prana is flowing properly through the human energy system and is not restricted by karmic baggage and/or attachment on the emotional level, the four authentic emotions will be expressed spontaneously without fear, and there will be a purging of the emotion as it is resolved through the facial musculature and the organs of expression—the mouth and the eyes.

Human beings have evolved the ability to express these four emotions by crying, yelling, screaming,, etc., as well as expressing them through their eyes and facial musculature. When an emotion is expressed spontaneously and is resolved, there will be a feeling of satisfaction indicating that the pent-up emotional energy has been purged and a healthy flow of unqualified energy through the human energy system has resumed. Karmic attachments, which block the movement of unqualified energy on the emotional level, rarely allow emotions to reach the third or final stage of this process, *resolution*.

Resolution is possible only after emotional energy has reached the organs of expression in the head and has been expressed through the voice, the facial musculature, and/or the eyes. Since the buildup of karmic baggage blocks the flow of emotional energy, the release of emotional energy is rarely complete and a residue of emotional energy is left behind. No amount of crying, screaming, or shouting after the fact will transmute this residual emotional energy and release it. Emotional energy that has not been expressed spontaneously will get stuck in the human energy system and become part of the karmic baggage of dense, qualified energy that is deposited in the auric fields surrounding personal body space on the emotional level.

In extreme cases, when there has been an inordinate buildup of karmic energy on the emotional level, one or more energy bodies can be ejected from personal body space. When energy bodies are ejected on the emotional level one may react by becoming more withdrawn or one may abandon their emotional life altogether and adopt counterfeit emotions, which are created by the qualified energy (karmic baggage) that has intruded into personal body space, or has been laid down as sediment on the dimensions of soul.

It is not uncommon in circumstances such as these for counterfeit emotional personas, created when qualified energy has intruded into personal body space, to collectively create a counterfeit will. A counterfeit will on the emotional level can be particularly dangerous because it can become obsessive-compulsive and weaken or disrupt an individual's self-control. Virtually all forms of violence and Self-destructive behavior owe their obsessive-compulsive quality to counterfeit will and the emotions expressed by counterfeit personas on the emotional level.

For some people, the loss of self-control and the buildup of counterfeit emotional energy can lead to patterns of addictive behavior. Anything from obsessive sexual activity, eating disorders, substance abuse, to relationship addictions can be traced back to the ejection of one or more energy bodies on the emotional level and the substitution for them of counterfeit will, emotions, and/or personas.

Karmic Baggage on the
Etheric Level

Feelings emerge from the etheric plane, which means they vibrate within a lower spectrum of frequencies than emotions, which emerge from the astral plane, the world of soul. Hence, feelings are denser and less precise than emotions. Some are so dense that they closely resemble physical sensations. In fact, many of the most common psychosomatic ailments and stress-related diseases endemic to modern civilization are etheric ailments caused by the accumulation of karmic baggage on the etheric level. Chronic fatigue syndrome, attention deficit disorder, chronic and acute depression, anxiety disorders, and panic attacks, as well as shortness of breath, back pain, and colitis are some of the more well-known ailments that are caused by the inordinate accumulation of karmic baggage on the etheric level.

Feelings and sensations are functions of unqualified energy on the etheric level, and, like any form of energy, feelings and sensations need an energetic medium to move through. Without sufficient unqualified energy to serve as that medium, awareness of the internal environment on the etheric level will be restricted, and individuals will find themselves locked outside themselves on the etheric level, with a corresponding loss of sensitivity, Self-awareness, and pleasure.

Karmic Baggage on the
Physical-Material Level

Sensations emerge from the physical-material level, which means they vibrate in a lower spectrum of frequencies than feelings. In fact, when the flow of unqualified energy on the physical-material level is disrupted by karmic baggage it will result in the loss of bodily sensation and pleasure. This can result in sexual dysfunction, such as impotence and premature ejaculation in men and orgasmic dysfunction in women. In fact, any type of aversion to normal sexual stimulation and pleasure can be traced back to the same root cause, a disruption in the transmission and transmutation of unqualified energy on the physical-material level.

Since karmic baggage can have a negative impact on stamina and strength, it can also have a disruptive effect on physical performance. By accumulating at strategic points in the physical-material body, karmic baggage can even create an environment conducive to injury. In fact, injuries can occur whenever the buildup karmic baggage compels one to compensate for added density on the physical-material level by making micro-movements that strain the body at its weakest points, the joints and points where tendons and cartilage meet. This added stress, particularly for athletes who demand top performance from their physical-material body, can cause serious injury.

When karmic baggage becomes too great a burden on the physical-material level a person may become angry and lash out at loved ones in a vain effort to gain some control over themselves and their energy system on the physical-material level. When verbal outbursts offer no relief, one's expression can become violent. Violent outbursts can be externalized or internalized or shift erratically between them both. The violence can be either passive or assertive. When it is passive it can be played out ritualistically through sado-masochistic sexual activities. When it is assertive it can become explosive and can be played out through sexual abuse or physical violence.

For those who internalize their anger, karmic baggage can give rise to a host of addictive patterns and behavior. Although most addictive behavior is the result of disruptions that take place on the etheric level, addictive patterns can be carried through to the physical-material level where they can disrupt the flow of sexual energy and prana. This, in turn, can disrupt the production of pleasure-producing compounds in the brain. The disruption of body chemistry can then lead to physical dependency, particularly if the afflicted persons are unable to control themselves and their immediate environment.

Karma and Culture

Karmic attachment should not be viewed exclusively as an individual or relationship problem. It must be viewed more broadly as a cultural problem. By shaping personalities and restricting access to the Self, karmic baggage and the attachment it causes have a collective effect on culture.

Since collective intent shapes the collective will of a culture, one can say that qualified energy (at least to some degree) is responsible for the creation of political, social, educational, and economic institutions, as well as class distinctions and social pressure—all of which can be used to restrict pleasure and inhibit access to intimacy, joy, and bliss.

It is an accepted fact that, within each culture, class distinctions and expectations that emerge as social pressure abound, and that people are expected to behave, think, and even feel in a way acceptable to their position in society. Indeed, in most cultures values are proscribed for people through the ongoing acculturation process, in a script adopted by the culture but shaped by karmic baggage. Each individual quickly learns that they must subordinate to some degree their individual will, and adapt to the script or suffer the consequences.

In one way or another the script gives life structure, but in most cases it is an ill-fitting structure. Hence, many people cannot naturally adapt to the script. This unfortunate minority is left with two choices, neither of which are satisfactory. The first is social ostracism. The second is the grudging acceptance of a set of values that will turn them into something unnatural—beings alienated from themselves and others, incapable of sustained intimacy, and antagonistic to their own dharma (life path).

With the loss of intimacy and empathy that takes place when dharma has been abandoned, one will end up identifying oneself and those around them as objects. As a result of this unnatural juxtaposition, Self-worth will become determined more by temporal, superficial values, such as physical beauty, material prosperity, and performance in sport, work, etc., rather than by the more lasting values of character, integrity, empathy, and wisdom.

With the goal of intimacy and dharma obscured by an avalanche of rules and expectations, duality (the concept of "I-thou") becomes enshrined as a self-perpetuating truth. As a result, everyone outside the individual mind and ego becomes the *other*. Even within the microcosm, a division takes place, which invariably leads to a loss of balance and Self-awareness. As a consequence, selfish desire, fear, and the need to control events both internally and externally become the dominant motivating force behind the actions of individuals, groups, and nations. As people begin to lose sight of their purpose (dharma) and substitute counterfeit goals supported by their culture for authentic ones supported by the Self, cataclysmic events in the private and public lives of people are set in motion that eventually force groups and whole nations to clash with one another in a vain attempt to control events, grow (often at each other's expense), or merely survive.

Who Do You Love?

The consequences of karmic baggage and the attachment it creates can be found to one degree or another in all the world's cultures and among all the world's people, regardless of their technological sophistication or cultural heritage. By their very nature, cultures support karmic attachment as part of their system of values, norms, and taboos, although it has been recognized by researchers that patriarchal cultures such as those in northern Europe and North Africa tend to be more repressive than those that are matriarchal. In fact, even in those that are the most permissive, such as the Jewish and Hopi cultures, there are rules and/or laws restricting the free radiation of unqualified energy. These rules often pit the will of the individual against the collective will of the group. Though rules are considered necessary for the common good, it is important to recognize that the unrestricted flow of unqualified energy is not the same as the unrestricted flow of qualified energy. It may be necessary for qualified energy and the actions that emerge from the individual mind and ego to be restricted. However, the restriction of unqualified energy, regardless of the justification, will always produce negative effects for the individual and the groups and institutions to which the individual belongs. In the final analysis, the suppression or sublimation of unqualified energy, rather that creating a more structured and orderly society, will create the very opposite. It will create a culture that undermines relationships and institutions and sows the seeds of future discontent and discord.

Indeed, the effects produced by the inordinate accumulation of qualified energy within the human energy field and the negative cultural influences that result from them makes it necessary to create a new paradigm as well as a new culture for individuals, relationships, and institutions. Only then will people find the joy and peace they seek within themselves, and loving relationships based on mutual trust and intimacy. When enough people have overcome the effects of their karmic baggage a new culture based on cooperation, shared responsibility, and Self-awareness will emerge. It will replace a world order that supports unsustainable cultures that are Self-limiting and antagonistic to shared intimacy and dharma.

What You Will Learn

The purpose of this book is to free you from the influence of karmic baggage and the attachment it has created. As you proceed you will learn how attachments caused by karmic baggage have influenced your personality (your individual mind and ego) and relationships, and how patterns created by attachment have infiltrated your belief system, disrupted your free will, and predetermined the course of your emotional, mental, and spiritual life.

Once you've learned how karmic baggage in the form of dense, heavy qualified energy has influenced you—and how you've compensated for it by developing behavioral, emotional, mental, and spiritual patterns—you will learn simple skills that will help you locate, identify, and release karmic baggage and the attachment it has created.

Chakra Healing and Karmic Awareness is more than a book. It is a step-by-step program designed to strengthen your boundaries, activate your chakras within personal body space, activate the minor energy centers in your hands and feet, activate the chakras above and below personal body space, enhance the flow of prana through your meridians, activate your splenic chakras, activate the aprana (which will be used to release karmic baggage and negative personas), and recollect and reintegrate your energy bodies and energetic vehicles if they've been ejected. In the process you will learn to stay centered in the higher mind and to follow your dharma by performing appropriate activity so that the Self can emerge into your conscious awareness and you can experience the childlike bliss that is your birthright.

As you study this book and begin to overcome the effects of karmic baggage and attachment, you will find that sharing your expanded awareness and inner strength and confidence with your partner, family, and friends becomes one of your greatest joys. As your life becomes more joyful and you courageously follow your dharma, you will find that the universe supports you in everything that you do and that pleasure, joy, intimacy, and bliss become a way of life for you and for those with whom you share your personal wisdom.

Chapter Two

. . . The Still is the master of unrest. Therefore the sage, traveling all day, does not lose sight of his baggage. Though there are beautiful things to be seen, he remains unattached and calm.

—Tao Te Ching, 26

Getting to Know Your Self

Though you may not be consciously aware of it, you and the Self—the singularity from which everything emerged—are one. In the process of overcoming karmic baggage your awareness of this unique relationship will grow until union with the Self becomes your moment-to-moment experience. Until then, it is important to get some idea of what the Self is, how it functions, and what union with the Self would be like.

Much has been written about the Self in Yogic, Tantric, Taoist, and Jainist literature. Before we proceed take note: the Self is is not an object of knowledge and has no defining qualities, so a precise definition of the Self is impossible. Furthermore, since spirit, intellect, soul, and lower mind, as well as the functions and aspects of mind, emerge from the Self, none of these fields of activity has the capacity to conceive or understand what the Self is, since the Self is their root cause or creator. The paradox this represents can be likened to the problem faced by beings in a dream who vainly try to conceive of their creator (the dreamer), to whom they owe their existence and in whose consciousness they exist and function.

Of course, it is an a priori fact, accepted by Yoga and Tantra and the great eastern religions, that you are already in union with the Self, whether you are consciously aware of it or not, and that the Self is the root of your spirit, soul, intellect, and body, as well as everything else in the phenomenal universe. But the Self does not correspond precisely to what you imagine yourself to be, or at least the self with whom you identify in your daily life. It would be more accurate to say that the Self is the foundation of what you are now and what you were before you became individuated and identified with the individual self, the part of you that is composed of the individual mind and ego. If you don't exactly understand what I'm getting at, you're in good company, because most of the world's sages, seers, theologians, and psychologists have had the same problem with the Self you may be having. The truth is that it is impossible to know the Self using the individual mind and ego.

You can only know the Self by having a direct experience of the Self, which means transcending the individual mind and ego at least temporarily.

Until you have a direct experience of the Self, however, you can satisfy your intellectual curiosity (and this can be quite useful) by learning how the phenomenal universe, including your self and the various aspects of your being, emerged from the Self and how the Self continues to influence everything on every world and dimension of the phenomenal universe.

The Functional Nature of the Self

The Self corresponds to the holy spirit in Christian nomenclature. In Yoga, it is referred to as *Atman*. Atman in Sanskrit means "that which cannot be doubled." The Self, or Atman, is functionally the same as the Singularity at the center of each human being, as well as the universal field from which the dualistic universe emerged. The Self is the source as well as the foundation of time-space and the consciousness, energy, and matter that fills it on all worlds and dimensions. The Self is alive and aware. It is the source of human life as well as the wellspring of bliss, joy, love, and pleasure, which animates it.

The singularity known as the Self is functionally the same as universal consciousness, or Brahman. Like Brahman, it exists outside linear-sequential time in what is called eternity or eternal time. Indeed, the Self is not limited by time-space as we experience it through the five senses or any phenomenal aspect of its creation. Thus, it can never die, nor is it subject to the rhythms of birth, life, and death. It never changes and is not bound by the limitations imposed on the phenomenal universe by evolution and involution. It exists everywhere and fills time-space on all dimensions in both the macrocosm and microcosm.

Considering that everything that was, is, and will be is contained within it, the Self wants nothing because it lacks nothing. It doesn't desire worship, nor does it have to be propitiated. Since everything is contained within it, the Self judges nothing because it would only be judging itself. Indeed, the phenomenal universe can be said to be a reflection of the Self and human beings metaphorically created in the image of the Self. "And God created man in his own image in the image of God; He created him; male and female . . ." (Genesis 1:27).

The Mandukya Upanishad calls the Self "Santam Sivam, Adwaitam" (Mand. UP. VII). The Self is peaceful, blessed, and nondual. The Self is tranquil, infinite, and complete. It is intelligent and blissful. The Self is the impersonal absolute. It contains within itself all that has emerged, and therefore has no second.

In Vedanta, Atman (the Self) has been described as Satchitananda—eternal existence, universal consciousness, and bliss, which is the radiant joy beyond causation.

In the *Bhagavad-Gita,* Krishna explains that Atman (the Self) can only be known when the knower, the field of knowing, and that which is known are experienced as one.

As a condition, the Self is eternal life with all its attributes, but none of the limitations normally associated with life on earth. Although the existence of Self can be inferred indirectly through the intellect, its existence can only be validated by direct experience. For the adept the only tools that can lead to such an experience are the higher mind (spirit, intellect, and soul), the lower mind (and their functions and aspects), and the human energy system. Unfortunately, in most cases these fields of energy and consciousness are so clouded by karmic baggage that the direct experience of the Self is almost impossible.

The Self Is You . . . Sort Of

Within the microcosm of each human being the Self emerges from the right side of the human heart into conscious awareness and expands from that point until it fills personal body space on all worlds and dimensions. From there, it radiates into the outer environment like the sun, "shining on saint and sinner alike." To get an idea of what living in union with the Self would be like we can use a metaphor.

For a moment imagine that you're in a theater, the sole spectator of a movie that you wrote, produced, directed, and in which you star. Now, imagine that after awhile you became so engrossed in the film and the character you were playing that you forgot who you were and began to identify with the part you were playing on the screen. Eventually, you might become so immersed in the thoughts, feelings, and sensations elicited by the events and characters in the movie that the movie might become more real than the *real* world.

Now, imagine that your attachment to the part you were playing and the events on the screen became complete. If the character you were playing were threatened you'd react with fear. If your character was rescued you'd be relieved. If you lost what you loved you would become despondent, if you regained it you'd become elated. In time, the very idea of breaking out of the illusion would be rejected as an act of self-destruction, so you would do nothing. You would remain attached to the events on the screen, living an illusion that you'd become convinced was real. Even if you had momentary doubts, the testimony of the individual mind and the ego and your attachments to the other actors would be convincing testimony that the dream was real. In truth, that is the human condition. Human beings identify so strongly with the character they're

playing as well as the sensations, feelings, and thoughts that are associated with it, that they've forgotten that the movie of their mind (which
they experience through their senses and process through the individual
mind and ego) isn't real. They have forgotten that they're not only the
creator of the movie, they're all the characters, including the character
they've been playing on the screen.

Now, imagine that after identifying with the character on the screen,
you once again remembered that the movie wasn't real and you no
longer chose to identify with your character and the thoughts, feelings,
and sensations that supported it. By withdrawing from the effect—the
movie—and returning to the cause—the Self—you would once again
remember who you really were. You would remember that you were in
fact the producer, director, and everything else that became the movie, as
well as the Self from which it all emerged. As soon as you'd freed yourself
from the illusion, maya—apparent reality—you would free yourself from
the effects of karmic attachment and the pain and suffering it caused you
while you mistakenly identified with the character on the screen.

Having accepted the truth and freed yourself, you wouldn't become
more spiritual in any real sense or become a better person. You would
simply remember who you were, and once again you would begin to
identify with what was real, while enjoying the movie of your mind. In
effect, that is the process you will be participating in as you overcome
karmic baggage. By giving up your attachment to the effect, the individual mind and ego, and returning to the cause, the Self, you will gradually
overcome karmic attachment, experience your a priori union with the
Self, and enjoy the bliss, intimacy, love, and pleasure that emerge from it.

Consciousness in the Natural World

As multiworld, multidimensional beings, human beings are composed of
consciousness, energy, and matter floating in a field of time-space. The
five basic building blocks listed previously emerged from the Self, universal consciousness, and continue to be supported by it.

In the natural world the manifestation of universal consciousness is more or less limited, so the Self cannot emerge in its fullness. In the mineral world consciousness, known as *cit* in Sanskrit, manifests as the lowest form of sentiency displayed by the reflexive response to stimuli. Among scientists this is known as atomic memory. The sentiency of plants is more developed, although it remains a dormant consciousness. The same type of limited sentiency is manifested in the class of micro-organisms that straddle the animal and vegetable kingdoms.

In the animal world consciousness becomes more centralized and complex as the animal increases in complexity, reaching its fullest development in humans who possess the psychic functions of intellect, cognition, perception, feeling, and will, and who can manifest the Self in its fullness through the vehicles of spirit, intellect, soul, lower mind, and body.

It should be noted, however, that the level of consciousness of a particular life form is dependent on the frequencies of unqualified energy (prana) that it can transmit and transmute through its subtle energy system (chakras, auras, and meridians). Animals are animated by a more limited range of frequencies than human beings, and a developed human being by a much larger range of frequencies than a more primitive one.

There are fluctuations in the consciousness of all living beings based on fluctuations in the range of energy frequencies (unqualified energy) radiating through their energy system, but the fluctuations cannot exceed the capabilities of the chakras and meridians to transmit and transmute them, and the auras to store them.

Individual Human Consciousness

It is through the higher and lower mind, their functions and aspects, as well as the energy system of a fully conscious human being, that universal consciousness, the Self, can emerge in its fullness. The higher mind (spirit, soul, and intellect) and lower mind emerge from the Self by way of the *tattvas*, the steps of evolution. The consciousness emerging through the higher and lower mind never seeks to understand, but rather observes until it knows. It doesn't judge, nor is its primary motive survival. In fact, because the experiences of the higher and lower mind and their functions and aspects are not filtered through the karmic baggage, which takes the form of the individual mind and ego, they are experienced directly, which means that the qualities of something observed are known through direct experience, insight, revelation, and/or intuition. Understanding is simply not a function of the higher and lower mind.

> Something mysteriously formed
> Born before heaven and earth.
> In the silence and the void,
> Standing alone and unchanging
> Ever present and in motion.
> Perhaps it is the mother of ten thousand things.
> I do not know its name.
> Call it the Tao.
> For the lack of a better word, I call it great.
>
> —Tao Te Ching, 25

Since emotions, feelings, and even sensations are functions of the human energy system, and the human energy system supports the higher and lower mind, they are a functional part of human consciousness. Thus, authentic emotions (anger, fear, pain, and joy) that emerge from the human energy system and are expressed through the communities of energy bodies are expressed spontaneously.

Authentic actions that express the will and intent of the higher and lower mind on whatever world and dimension they emerge are appropriate and efficient. They are not based on judgment, since the higher and lower mind are not attached to the individual mind and ego, so there is no gap between the intent of the higher and lower mind and the feeling and/or emotion that emerges and fuels subsequent action.

When the higher and lower mind motivate a human being to act, the energy that emerges is unqualified, which means the higher and lower mind do not influence what they act upon, except to vitalize it. They do not alter, control, manipulate, or change the qualities of anything in the external environment, even though they interact with it through the functions and aspects of mind. In fact, like the Self, anything that emerges from the higher and lower mind and their functions and aspects will enhance ones' experience of truth, freedom, and/or bliss.

Even though human consciousness has been associated with the cognitive aspects of the brain, it is not the brain, and can function independently of the physical-material body. Indeed, the higher and lower mind are part of an integrated system that is multiworld and multidimensional, which means it cannot be restricted by the limitations normally imposed by time-space on the physical brain and the physical-material body. Though they serve as vehicles for the Self, the higher and lower mind are still capable of moving into the external environment, in both the unqualified and qualified universe, and assuming the form of the objects of perception by using the functions and aspects of mind as their vehicle for cognition and assimilation.

"As water from a tank may flow through a channel into a plot of land and assume its shape (square, triangular, or any other form), so the radiant mind (higher and lower mind) goes out through the eye or any other sense organ to the place where an object is and becomes transformed into the shape of that object" (*Practice of Yoga*, Swami Sivananda, 113).

The vehicles of the higher and lower mind are the communities of energy bodies, which compose the spirit, intellect, soul, chakras bodies, and bodies of desire. The chakras, auras, and meridians, which are the organs of the human energy system, support the higher and lower mind energetically. The functions and aspects of mind make it possible for the communities of energy bodies to manifest intent and engage in activities, while remaining Self-aware and detached from the world of qualities.

The Bodies of Desire

Complementing the world of the higher mind is the world of the lower mind. The lower mind is composed of the communities of energetic vehicles called "bodies of desire." These energetic vehicles are the same size and shape as energy bodies and are composed of prana in the same three states: solid, liquid, and gaseous.

It is through the bodies of desire that one can experience, express, and resolve the primary desires necessary for life. These desires are a normal function of life on earth and shouldn't be confused with desires for specific things that create dependency and that emerge through the individual mind and ego.

Artha

The Vedas teach that there are four essential desires, which are functions of the bodies of desire. The first is *artha*. In Sanskrit, artha refers to the desire for material comfort or wealth. Artha is an essential desire, since it motivates human beings to be incarnated into a physical-material body and to act appropriately. Since it is an economic necessary to amass enough wealth to be free from the drudgery of continuous work, fulfilling this desire is a prerequisite for sustained spiritual growth and development.

Kama

Kama is the second desire. It denotes both pleasure and the desire for pleasure. It's one of the four essential desires that motivates a human being to be incarnated into a physical body and to act appropriately. In the *Bhagavad Gita*, desire is put at the center of living and is equated with the life force. Indeed, Vedanta never taught that pleasure should be repressed or disparaged as antispiritual. In fact, Vedanta teaches that Atman has two aspects. The first is consciousness, which contains within it everything that exists—therefore, it wants nothing, for it lacks nothing. This is *Paramatman*. Also emerging from Atman is the individual soul, *Jivamatman*. At the deepest levels of being, Jivamatman dictates an individual's desires and aspirations. It is Jivamatman that is the source of Dharma, the deepest desire of the heart.

Dharma

Dharma is the third desire that motivates human beings to be incarnated in a physical-material body and to act appropriately. Dharma literally means "that which holds together"—in essence, that which prevents

worldly relationships from dissolving into chaos. In the human community it is dharma that holds the social order together.

Dharma has two applications: shared dharma, which is common to all
mankind, and individual dharma, which is specific to each human being.
Shared dharma is righteousness or spiritual duty. Righteousness in this
context can be equated with appropriate activity. Appropriate activities
are those actions that promote the flow of prana, and that emerge from
the higher and lower mind and their functions and aspects. Individual
dharma is the specific path of appropriate activity, which leads a person
back into union with the Self.

Moksha

Moksha is the fourth desire that motivates human beings to be incarnated
in a physical-material body and to act appropriately. Moksha denotes
transcendence, which is spiritual freedom and liberation from karmic
attachment. Of the four desires, moksha is the highest. Advaita Vedanta
(the nondual path of Self-realization) teaches that jnana (knowledge),
which comes from direct experience, is the means to achieve moksha and
overcome ignorance.

The great twentieth-century Indian master Ramana Maharshi declared
that ignorance is nothing more than attachment to the "I" idea. Jainism,
as usual, is more detailed. It explains that moksha is the highest state of
separation and/or detachment. In moksha one is freed from all attachment to the external world of phenomena. Saivism equates moksha with
bliss, and Yoga likens it to the state of nirvakalpa-samadhi, the state of
unparalleled isolation and stillness.

The Functions of Mind

Since the Self remains aloof from its creation, to participate in the phenomenal universe it needs vehicles to manifest consciousness and prana.
In the higher mind the vehicles are the energy bodies, and in the lower
mind they are the bodies of desire.

All energy bodies and their corresponding energetic vehicles are composed of unqualified energy and subtle matter. To function synchronistically with other energy bodies as well as the functions and aspects of mind, each energy body must occupy the space on its dimension that corresponds to the space occupied by the physical-material body in the physical-material world.

The energy bodies and energetic vehicles (bodies of desire) of the higher and lower mind interact with the macrocosm through the three functions of mind, known as the *koshas, indyrias*, and *pranas*.

Koshas

The koshas are mental sheaths, and it is through the koshas that one becomes aware of themselves and the world around them. Although consciousness resides within the energy bodies, bodies of desire, and their corresponding energetic vehicles, consciousness can know nothing of itself. Therefore, it needs a mirror to experience its own reflection. On the different levels of awareness, in the higher and lower mind, the koshas perform this function. Koshas exist in time-space and are fields of activity, not abstract concepts or archetypes. There are twelve koshas, which correspond to the energy bodies, bodies of desire, and splenic bodies. Normally, each kosha remains within personal body space on the world and dimensions on which it is active, but a kosha can radiate beyond personal body space while it performs its functions. In fact, each kosha contacts and interacts with energy fields, objects, and beings in the external world, on the world and dimensions on which it is active. In this way the koshas function as an extension of human consciousness. Likewise, energy fields, objects, and beings radiate and/or project energy at the kosha active on their particular world and dimension. Hence, the degree of attachment or detachment to karmic baggage can be said to be closely related to the condition of the koshas and one's relationship to them.

Indyrias

On the levels of emotion, feeling, and sensation, the indyrias perform the same function as the koshas. There are two types of indyrias, jnana indyrias and karmic indyrias. Jnana indyrias are functions of soul that gather knowledge about the microcosm and macrocosm on the levels of activity associated with emotion, feeling, and sensation. Karma indyrias manifest knowledge through action after knowledge has been assimilated and integrated by the appropriate jnana indyria.

Once knowledge has been assimilated through the jnana indyrias, the karma indyrias permit one to interact with sentient beings, objects, and/ or energetic fields by externalizing sense awareness. The karma indyrias perform this function by taking on the qualities of whatever they interact with, but they can only do this when they are fully integrated into personal body space on the world and dimension on which they are active.

In fact, if either the jnana or karma indyrias on a particular dimension are not fully integrated, their functions can be disrupted and/or they can become attached to objects, energy fields, or beings, and their projections with which they've interacted.

In contrast, when the indyrias are fully integrated one will be able to function through them with conscious awareness and one's actions will be consistently appropriate.

Pranas

The energetic medium through which the functions of mind operate is known collectively as the pranas. There are two types of pranas, incoming and outgoing pranas. The incoming pranas provide an energetic medium for the continuous flow of information received and assimilated by the human energy field. This information is used by the higher and lower mind to discern the qualitative and quantitative features of the energy field surrounding them. The outgoing pranas provide the higher and lower mind with an energetic medium through which knowledge can manifest through action in the external environment. Each incoming and outgoing prana has an area of activity that corresponds to a specific portion of unqualified energy and/or qualified energy in the phenomenal universe.

When the incoming and outgoing pranas are active and functioning in a healthy way, actions on all levels will emerge through the higher and lower mind and their functions and aspects. In addition, the pranas will form a barrier to intrusions so that one can enjoy the peace that comes from achieving an internal state of equanimity.

The Aspects of Mind

The *manas, buddhi, chitta,* and *ahamkara* are known as the aspects of mind. Collectively, the aspects serve as a template that provides a structure for the synchronistic functions of the higher and lower mind, their functions, and the organs of the human energy system.

Manas

The manas grasps or takes hold of an object, being, and/or energy field in the external environment. In this way it is isolated so that it can be studied. This aspect, which is an essential element of personal identity, can be understood using the metaphor of looking as opposed to seeing. When looking there is no emphasis put on anything in particular, but in seeing, that which is seen is brought into a context where it can be compared and studied. The manas doesn't look, rather it sees by putting emphasis on something in its field of vision so that it can be separated from its environment.

Buddhi

The buddhi is the aspect of mind that analyzes and compares an object, being, and/or energy field that has been separated from its environment with what is already known. Although objects, beings, or energy fields may vary or change, the buddhi remains constant. In fact, it is the buddhi's consistency that allows it to put what it has studied into a specific context so that the chitta can confer a particular value on it.

Chitta

It is the chitta that confers a value on what has been isolated by manas and analyzed by buddhi. Value depends on the condition and character of the human being emerging through these aspects. When one is attached to the individual mind and ego, the value of something will be based on the desire-aversion reflex, and will be judged on whether it furthers physical or psychic well-being. When one has chosen the inner life and has begun to strengthen boundaries and remove karmic baggage, value will be accorded to something based on whether it promotes the flow of prana and/or enhances one's relationship to the Self.

Ahamkara

Ahamkara is the decision maker. It distills the information it receives from the other aspects of mind and uses it to create and/or support a person's view of themselves and their relationships. What it receives and accepts as valid and relevant not only adds to what one accepts as knowledge, it confirms experientially what one already knows about oneself.

When the information supports the individual mind and ego it confirms what the individual mind and ego have been proclaiming all along, that one is in fact an individual, and that one is motivated by survival and the need to achieve a state of psychic well-being. When the decision supports the Self it confirms one's inherent divinity and one's a priori union with the Self.

Chapter Three

*Let the entrance of thy healthful flames set the sluggish
heart alight; and the burning fire of thy sacred inspira-
tion enlighten me.*

—St. Anselm

Let's Talk a Little About Energy

Whenever we talk about the Self and the karmic baggage that limits one's
access to the bliss, joy, intimacy, and pleasure that emerge from it, a dis-
tinction must be made between qualified energy, which causes attachment to the external environment and the individual mind and ego, and
unqualified energy that has no qualities and which facilitates union with
the Self. We will make these distinctions first and then you will learn to
breath yogically, which will increase the flow of unqualified energy
through your energy system. After that you will learn a reliable technique
for activating the back of your heart chakra. The back of the chakra is activated first because it's masculine and more stable than the front of the
chakra, which is feminine.

Once you've activated the back of your heart chakra you will learn to
center yourself there so that your consciousness emerges from the higher and lower mind, rather than from the individual mind and ego.

Hermetics teaches that "The All is mind; the Universe is mental." This
means that, on the highest level, everything is unified into one singularity

called universal consciousness (Atman or the Self). However, as soon as time-space emerged through the tattvas (steps in evolution), and the phenomenal universe began to evolve from universal consciousness, unqualified energy expanded to fill all available space, which continued to expand along with it. This expansion (which we call evolution) and the relationship of universal consciousness (which is static) and unqualified energy (which is dynamic) is represented in Yoga and Tantra by the eternal dance of Shiva and Shakti (see figure 3-1).

Figure 3-1

It is the eternal dance of Shiva and Shakti, i.e. consciousness and energy. Energy in its various forms is known as shakti, prakriti, prana, aprana, and the kundalini-shakti, which serves as the foundation of both the physical and nonphysical universe.

Indeed, without the interaction of universal consciousness (Shiva) and dynamic energy (Shakti) there would be no phenomenal universe, no sentient beings with organs of perception to be aware of it, no spirit to come into union with it, no intellect to be conscious of it and no soul to interact with it.

After emerging from universal consciousness, Shakti, in

the form of dynamic, creative energy, or Prakriti (the primordial form of prana) began to function as the driving force of evolution, the movement toward diversity. In the future, Shakti will become the driving force for involution, the movement toward union with universal consciousness.

Prana in Sanskrit means "absolute energy" (the vital force). This vital force acts like a cosmic glue. It radiates from the universal consciousness—the Self—flowing into each world and dimension, filling all available space, connecting everything on all dimensions. Everything that exists emerges from and owes its existence to prana, which supports it and provides it with a medium through which it can move and express itself.

The Tattvas

Unqualified energy, although an essential element of consciousness, emerges as an apparently separate force by way of the tattvas. Although Yoga teaches that there are thirty-six tattvas (steps in evolution) that are responsible for the incredible diversity of the phenomenal universe, both on the subtle and physical-material planes—four will be of particular interest to us here.

The first tattva was the original world as it existed within the consciousness of Atman. From this, *Perusha* and *Prakriti* emerged. Perusha was the primordial consciousness, and Prakriti, the primordial source of power (unqualified energy) or prana. The next tattva, which results from their joining, is *Mahatattva*. It was at this stage that perfect balance in the primordial (nonphysical) universe was disrupted, and evolution as we know it and can conceive of it begins. As the Mahatattva began, Prakriti initiated the process of evolution, first on the higher and lower planes of consciousness, energy, and subtle matter, and then on the physical-material plane. It was from this primordial dynamic force that unqualified energy as it is known today (including the kundalini-shakti, prana in its different forms, and the aprana) emerged. It was also from this primordial force that joy emerged into the microcosm and through joy, intimacy, human love, and pleasure.

The Structure and Function of
Unqualified Energy

Unqualified energy cannot be measured or weighed by conventional means. It cannot be seen with the physical eye or visualized by any instruments that enhance human vision. It cannot be heard, felt, smelled, or tasted. Until now it has resisted detection via the instruments of science and the conscious awareness of the rational mind. Yet, in some ways, its existence has already been suggested by science, first in the mid-nineteenth century by George Riemann, who theorized that light was produced by the warping of the fifth dimensional space, and later by the superstring theory, which burst on the scene accidentally in 1968.

As the superstring theory suggests, everything in the physical universe owes its existence to six nonphysical dimensions that support the physical-material universe. Of course, for those people who are consciously aware of the functional aspects of human consciousness on the nonphysical dimensions, the existence of unqualified energy is an undisputed fact.

Since language is replete with modifiers used to describe the quality of something, and since unqualified energy has no qualities, it's a challenge to describe unqualified energy except indirectly by contrasting it with what it is not. Unqualified energy is not energy that has any sort of quality or feel to it, yet on both physical and nonphysical dimensions there exists an inner foundation of unqualified energy within a spectrum of frequencies corresponding to the density or mean frequency of qualified energy on the same dimension. Though qualities are absent, unqualified energy on different dimensions can be described as having different pitches, much like the differences in pitch observed when the same note, in different octaves, is played on a musical instrument. Viewed in this way, unqualified energy on higher worlds and dimensions would have a higher pitch or vibration than unqualified energy on lower worlds and dimensions, and anyone with discernment would recognize the different vibrations that are the signature of different pitches of unqualified energy.

Unqualified energy on the higher and lower dimensions can be transmuted from one state to another and can function in the three states that correspond to the states of energy and matter found in the physical-material world and the collective field of maya, solid, liquid, and gaseous. While functioning in the solid state on the subtle planes, unqualified energy exhibits some of the same properties as solids. It can exist in a host of different sizes and shapes, and show variations in strength and flexibility.

Unqualified energy that appears solid is the most stable. When it's in a solid state, unqualified energy serves as the foundation of the energy bodies, energetic vehicles, and the organs of the human energy system.

In a liquid state, unqualified energy will be less stable and will show wide variations in size and shape. The liquid state can be considered a transitory state that usually emerges through the aegis of the practitioner or healer when she or he creates tools and instruments of unqualified energy for use in healing and energy work.

Unqualified energy in the gaseous state is the least stable and can quickly change size or shape. It is unqualified energy in a gaseous state that fills the cavities of the energy bodies, energetic vehicles, and auric fields, enters the human energy system with each inhalation, emerges through the chakras and is transmitted through the meridians. In addition, unqualified energy in a gaseous state serves as the medium (on all worlds and dimensions) through which qualified energy moves. In this role it serves as the foundation of the phenomenal universe and the collective field of maya.

Because unqualified energy corresponds to universal consciousness — Shiva and Shakti are in eternal embrace—it is not subject to the principles of Hermetics, which means that regardless of the source of unqualified energy, it is not subject to the principles of mind, cause and effect, rhythm, polarity, correspondence, gender, and vibration (for more on Hermetics see chapter six).

Unqualified energy cannot be transmitted or transmuted by the individual mind and ego or any other functional aspect of the phenomenal

universe. This means that unqualified energy cannot be focused consciously or unconsciously by desire, fear, need, or any act of human will,
finite human consciousness, or ego.

Unqualified energy is at all times, in all situations, and all dimensions
independent of the ego and the individual mind. It radiates like the sun
unless focused by a source of unqualified energy and/or the consciousness (the Self, the higher and lower mind, and/or the functions and
aspects of mind).

Unqualified energy will never, under any circumstances, take the form
of waves, atmospheres, pools, cords, or karmic baggage, nor can it be
influenced directly by any physical or nonphysical being that lives and
functions exclusively in the qualified world of maya.

Though it may appear that unqualified energy is restricted during
times of stress, shock, and trauma to the one experiencing the effects, in
fact it is one's awareness or ability to *see* or experience unqualified energy
that has been affected by attachment to the individual mind and ego.

Though unqualified energy cannot be focused by the individual mind
and ego, it can be focused by the intent of the Self, through the higher
and lower mind (spirit, intellect, soul, and bodies of desire) and their
functions and aspects. As you will learn in the following chapters, unqualified energy focused by the intent of the higher and lower mind is the
most important tool you have for overcoming the effects of karmic baggage and the attachments and limitations it creates.

The Four Forms of Unqualified Energies

When unqualified energy emerges from the Self it takes the form of
prana, the aprana, the kundalini-shakti, and/or one of the incoming or
outgoing pranas.

Prana is the total of all energy in the universe, both in the microcosm
and macrocosm. It enters the human energy system with the breath on
each inhalation, and radiates through the chakras when they are active.

The aprana emerges from the apranic boundary. The apranic boundary
is located in the microcosm on all worlds and dimensions of the higher

and lower mind and surrounds personal body space at a distance of about eight inches (twenty centimeters). The aprana will move toward the surface of personal body space when the apranic boundary is free from the inordinate influence of karmic baggage.

The kundalini-shakti is a special form of unqualified energy that lies dormant at the first chakra (muladhara chakra), located in personal body space at a position that corresponds to the base of the spine. When it is aroused it begins to move upward through the shushumna-governor meridian (the main masculine meridian) that rises from the first chakra, and extends upward from the back of personal body space to the crown chakra, located at a position that corresponds to the top of the head. When the kundalini-shakti reaches the crown chakra it will either continue to move upward or it will spread out until the ida and pingala meridians, which flank the shushumna-governor meridian, merge with it (see figure 3-2).

Once the kundalini-shakti has reached the crown, one will recognize that they are a multiworld, multidimensional being and that their existence does not depend on being incarnated in a physical-material body.

The incoming and outgoing pranas emerge from the centers of human consciousness on all worlds of the higher and lower mind and extend human awareness and vitality beyond the limits of the human energy field.

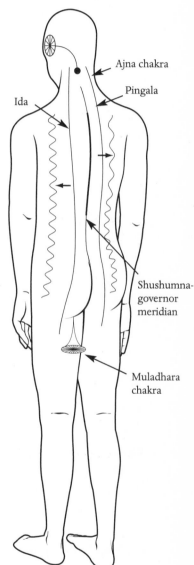

Figure 3-2 — The Shushumna, Ida, and Pingala meridians merge and spread across the back.

Prana and the Breath

The study of prana (pranayama) and its relationship to the breath has been an essential part of Yoga for millennia. The goal of pranayama is the separation of the breath from I, which boils down to wrenching control of the prana from the individual mind and ego. The ancient masters were well aware that prana in its various forms fills the universe on all dimensions, but they also knew that to sustain the life of a fully sentient human being a vast amount of prana is necessary. Thus a continuous unrestricted intake of prana was considered essential for health, well-being, and spiritual development.

The ancients also recognized that the individual mind and ego could disrupt the intake and distribution of prana and prevent it from revitalizing the communities of energy bodies and energetic vehicles, which compose the higher and lower mind and their functions and aspects. In order to counteract the function of the individual mind and ego they developed a system of exercises designed to wrest control of the breath and prana from the individual mind and ego. In this chapter I've included a technique called the "yogic breath," which is designed to increase your intake of prana and improve its distribution. By making it part of your regular practice you will bring more prana into your energy field and by accumulating it in pools you can use it at the appropriate time to overcome karmic baggage.

The Yogic Breath

The Yogic Breath is a synthesis of three basic breaths and is often called the "complete breath." The three breaths are the abdominal breath, mid-breath, and upper breath. In the abdominal breath the abdomen is expanded and stretched downward; in the mid-breath air and prana, having filled the chest cavity, expand to fill the rib cage and the shoulders; in the nasal breath air and prana fills the nasal passages and continues upward, filling the head. In the complete yogic breath not only will you bring more prana into your energy system, you will stimulate the chakras by bringing prana down through the abdomen and up to the top of the head.

Begin the yogic breath by sitting in a comfortable position with your back straight and your legs flat on the floor. You can use the lotus position if you like. Once you're comfortable, place your right hand on your abdomen, just below the solar plexus. This will help you feel the rhythm of your breath and will make it more fluid. Then close your eyes. Closing your eyes is not essential, but it will help you relax, making rhythmic breathing easier. In the yogic breath there should be no separation between inhalation and exhalation, and breathing should be conducted exclusively through the nose.

When you are comfortable, begin breathing in, first filling your lower lungs with air. With your hand on your abdomen you will feel the muscles of your diaphragm stretch as your stomach becomes slightly distended. Continue breathing inward, feeling the air fill the middle and upper part of your lungs. Your shoulders will lift and the muscles of the rib cage

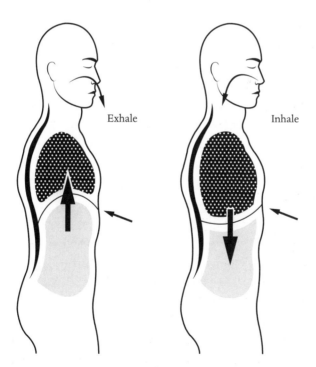

Exhale

Inhale

Figure 3-3 — The Yogic Breath. The arrows show
the direction of the breath.

will stretch as the lungs expand. During the mid-breath some people feel pain in the upper back between the shoulder blades. The pain is caused by the accumulation of karmic baggage, which has made the muscles contract and become stiff. Don't let a little discomfort discourage you— press on. If you continue, you will bring more prana into your energy system and your muscles will return to their normal state of elasticity.

After air and prana have filled your lungs, let it continue to rise, filling your nasal passages and head.

When you exhale, reverse the process—letting the nasal passages empty first and then the upper, middle, and finally the lower lungs. Your shoulders will naturally drop and the diaphragm will then return to its normal position. Without separation between inhalation and exhalation continue this exercise for about five minutes.

At first reserve special times during the day for practice. Later you can incorporate the yogic breath into your meditations and spiritual exercises. A note of caution: be sure that you are gentle with yourself. Now that you've learned the yogic breath don't become obsessive about it. If you do, you'll simply undermine yourself in other areas and instead of liberating your breath you will restrict it even more.

Aprana

The aprana is a special form of prana with a feminine polarity. It exists in all worlds and dimensions of the higher and lower mind and emerges from a position or boundary that surrounds personal body space, on each dimension, at a distance of approximately eight inches (twenty centimeters). The boundary or position from which the aprana emerges should not be confused with the surface of the auric fields. The apranic boundary is not a structure but rather a field boundary that is already present within the microcosm. When the aprana on each dimension is active, it tends to dislodge karmic baggage as it moves inward towards the surface of personal body space. The combination of the aprana with its feminine polarity emerging from outside personal body space and prana emerging from the chakras is so powerful that together they will dislodge karmic baggage and will wrest control of the vital area between the surface of personal body space and the apranic boundary from the control of the individual mind and ego.

The Chakras

The main function of the chakras is to keep the Self, universal consciousness, connected to the worlds and dimensions of the phenomenal universe. In this capacity the chakras serve as vortexes through which prana can enter the phenomenal universe. The chakras, in addition to serving as vortexes, transmit and transmute prana into different frequencies or pitches.

There are one hundred and forty-two chakras within the human energy system. Nine chakras are located within personal body space, the traditional seven chakras as well as the two splenic chakras, located between the second and third chakras. Sixty-three chakras are located above personal body space, directly above the crown chakra, and seventy chakras are located below personal body space, directly below the first chakra.

Prana emerges through all one hundred and forty-two chakras and is continuously being transmuted into the precise frequencies necessary to maintain the health of the human energy system and the communities of energy bodies that the energy system supports. You can begin to experience the prana radiating through the seven traditional chakras within personal body space by practicing the simple technique below.

Stimulating the Seven Traditional Chakras

Each of the seven traditional chakras regulates the transmission and transmutation of a portion of unqualified energy on the worlds of the higher and lower mind. The mean frequency of each chakra is called the chakra's resonance.

You can begin to feel the unique resonance of the seven traditional chakras within personal body space by using the the palm of your receptive (feminine) hand—your right hand if you're left-handed; your left hand if you're right-handed—to stimulate the front of the chakras (each palm contains a minor energy center through which prana radiates).

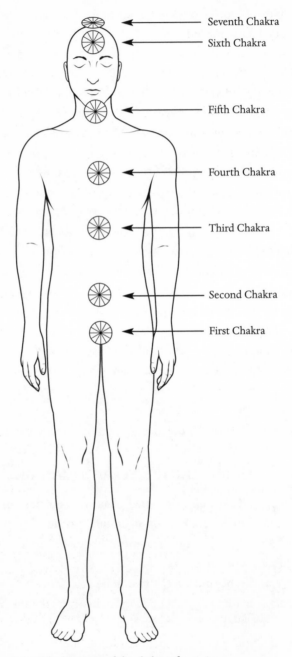

Figure 3-4 — The locations of the chakras; front view.

Once you've determined where the feminine pole of each chakra is located (first chakra at the base of the spine, second chakra four finger-widths below the navel, the third chakra at the solar plexus, the fourth chakra at the center of the breast bone, the fifth chakra at the throat, just below the adam's apple, the sixth chakra at the brow, directly between the eyes, and the seventh chakra at the crown of the head), begin to explore the region in the front of each chakra with the palm of your feminine hand (see figure 3-4). You will find that this technique works best if you keep the palm of your hand about six inches (fifteen centimeters) above the surface of personal body space, and you work down from the seventh chakra to the first.

As soon as you locate the female pole of a chakra with your palm the chakra will become active and you will experience a residual vibration. This vibration will continue even after you've removed your palm. You may also experience sensations that are unique to the chakra you've stimulated. The sensations you experience could be anything from a sense of security, if it is the first chakra, to contentment and/or comfort if it is the third chakra. A list of sensations, feelings, and emotions associated with the seven traditional chakras in personal body space follows:

First Chakra: security, self-confidence, body image, connection to the earth and its creatures.

Second Chakra: vitality, gender identity (masculinity or femininity), creativity, anger.

Third chakra: belonging, trust, intimacy, friendship, status, psychic well-being, fear.

Fourth Chakra: self-awareness, personal rights (this includes the right to control your physical body, to express and resolve your feelings, emotions, awareness and the right to follow your personal dharma), emotional pain.

Fifth Chakra: self-expression, enjoyment of personal space (which extends to the auric boundaries), integrity, joy.

Sixth Chakra: human awareness, memory, intuition, reasoning and
rational, deductive thought.

Seventh Chakra: transcendental consciousness.

The Kundalini-shakti

The word "kundalini" comes from the Sanskrit root *Kundala,* meaning
"coiled." The kundalini-shakti is often personified as the Devi (Goddess
Kundalini) or anthromorphosized as a coiled, sleeping snake. The kundalini emerges in two ways, as structural kundalini, and as the serpent
power, which lies dormant at the base of the spine.

Structural kundalini is an organizing function that permits energy
bodies and energetic vehicles to function synergistically with the organs
of the human energy system.

The coiled serpent energy at the base of the spine is the great store-
house of unqualified energy in the human energy system. Indeed, the
activation of this dormant energy is one of the most significant achieve-
ments in energy work.

When the serpent energy has been aroused and begins to rise through
the shushumna-governor meridian (the main masculine meridian), awareness will increase, unqualified energy will suffuse the energy system, and
consciousness will emerge exclusively through the higher and lower
mind.

Sensing Unqualified Energy

Most people are unaware of the presence of unqualified energy in their
lives, although vitality, unconditional joy, and creativity are signs of its
presence. There are instances, however, when the presence of unqualified
energy is impossible to deny (although it can be misinterpreted); these
include sexual intimacy, catharsis, deep meditation, and lucid dreaming.
These experiences are often accompanied by a profound sense of peace,
much like the "peace that passes all understanding," described by Jesus the
Nazarite, and/or the experience of intimacy and union experienced in

yogic or tantric meditation. Unfortunately, these experiences are rare, and most people become aware of unqualified energy only after it has interacted with the karmic baggage already present in their energy field.

When there is an inordinate amount of karmic baggage present in one's energy field, unqualified energy will be reflected off its surface and the friction or rubbing caused by the interaction will produce a burning sensation. When there is less qualified energy, or it is less dense, then the interaction of unqualified energy with qualified energy will produce a glowing sensation that can be quite pleasant. Experiences such as these tend to be short-lived or misunderstood, which explains why unqualified energy is rarely appreciated for what it is or given the priority it deserves.

Shifting Your Orientation

To overcome karmic baggage it is essential to be properly oriented within personal body space. To be properly oriented doesn't mean changing your physical position as much as shifting your awareness from the individual mind and ego to the higher and lower mind. By shifting your orientation you enter a reliable field of activity outside linear-sequential time that functionally transcends (or stands outside) the universe of qualified energy (maya) and is therefore immune to the influence or effects of karmic baggage.

There are three fields of activity where maya loses its influence and unqualified energy can be reliably accessed. The thumb-sized point to the right of the heart chakra, where unqualified energy emerges along with Atman is the first. Unqualified energy is the most difficult to access from Atman (the third heart) for two reasons: first, the point where Atman emerges is normally blanketed by layers of karmic sediment, and second, the prana that does emerge almost immediately diffuses through the human energy system.

Fortunately, unqualified energy can be accessed in two other ways. Prana enters the human energy system with each inhalation. By separating the breath from the "I" it is possible to detach awareness from the individual mind and ego. Once that has been achieved it is possible to center awareness in the pool of prana that enters with each inhalation. It must be done quickly, though, before the prana dissipates through the organs of the human energy system, the chakras, auras, and meridians.

As inexperienced students have found, mastering this technique can be difficult since it requires a certain amount of discernment (discernment is the ability to sense the pitch of unqualified energy and the qualities of qualified subfields). If discernment hasn't been developed, the pool of prana will diffuse through the energy system before it's possible to become centered in it.

The third technique, activating the back of the heart chakra, is the most attractive to inexperienced students new to energy work. In this technique one must simply activate the back of the heart chakra and remain centered in the unqualified energy emerging from it. Even without much experience, it is surprisingly easy to master this technique by following the instructions below.

Reorienting Yourself

Each chakra has two poles, a feminine pole in the front of the chakra and a masculine pole in the back. In this exercise you will activate the masculine pole of the heart chakra. The masculine pole has been selected because it's more stable than the feminine pole, which means it's less reactive to qualified subfields and projections.

To reorient yourself in personal body space you will begin with the "Standard method," which will be used throughout this book to relax and balance conscious and unconscious mental activity.

To begin, find a comfortable position with your back straight. When you're comfortable, begin breathing yogically. Continue for about five minutes, then slowly count backward from five to one. As you count backward, mentally repeat and visualize each number three times to yourself. Take your time and let your mind be as creative as it likes.

After you reach the number one, repeat this affirmation to yourself, "I'm now deeply relaxed and feeling much better than I did before." Continue to breath yogically and once again count backward, this time beginning with the number ten. Exhale as you mentally say ten. Then take another deep breath and, while exhaling, mentally say nine. Continue in this way until you've reached the number one. Then affirm, "Every time I come to this level of mind, I'm able to use more of my mind in more creative ways."

In many cases, physical tension stored within the musculature will prevent the free flow of prana through the human energy system, particularly the heart chakra. The Taoist concept of yin-yang explains that every action has an equal and opposite reaction, so in order to relax and release you must tighten and contract.

To release tension in the musculature you will begin by inhaling and contracting the muscles of your feet as much as possible. Hold your breath for three seconds. After three seconds release your breath and allow the muscles of your feet to relax. Inhale deeply again and repeat the process with your ankles and calves. Continue in the same way with your thighs, buttocks, pelvis, middle and upper abdomen, chest and shoulders, neck, arms, and hands. After you've isolated and relaxed all of these body parts, squeeze the muscles of your face and hold for three seconds. After three seconds, release and exhale. Next open your mouth, stick out your tongue, and stretch the muscles of your face as much as possible. Hold for three seconds, then release the muscles of your face and exhale.

To complete the standard method, contract your entire body (this time squeezing the muscles of your face) and hold your breath. After three seconds expel the breath through your nose and relax.

Now that you're relaxed and you've balanced conscious and unconscious mental activity, you can proceed to activate the back of the heart chakra. The heart chakra has been chosen because it's the center of human consciousness as well as a reliable source of unqualified energy.

The back of the heart chakra emerges from a position in personal body space that corresponds to the upper thoracic vertebrae directly behind the center of the sternum. We will use the intent to activate the back of the chakra rather than any ritual or less direct method, such as visualization, because in advanced energy work (such as releasing karmic sediment and recollecting and reintegrating energy bodies) it is necessary to work directly on the energy system. In fact, indirect methods will not produce the intended effects, since they emerge from the individual mind and ego.

It is also important to note that the intent is used instead of personal will and/or desire, because personal will and desire are usually trapped in the individual mind and ego. Until you become aware of your a priori union with the Self, they cannot be used to activate the organs of the human energy system.

When you're ready to activate the back of your heart chakra state, "It's my intent to activate the back of my heart chakra." State your intent in a normal voice, without doubt or effort. In a few moments you'll feel the back of the chakra begin to glow or vibrate as the level of prana emerging from it increases. By resisting the impulse to drift you'll discover that thoughts cease, or at least cease to affect you, and that prana radiates through your entire energy system.

Once the chakra has become active, take about five minutes to enjoy the shift in consciousness. After five minutes, count from one to five. When you reach the number five, open your eyes. You will feel wide awake, perfectly relaxed, and better than you did before.

Centering in the Back of the Heart Chakra

After you've activated the back of the heart chakra, the next step is to center yourself there. By centering yourself in the back of your heart chakra your awareness will emerge from the higher and lower mind rather than from the individual mind and ego.

To center yourself in the back of your heart chakra, find a comfortable position with your back straight. Then use the standard method to relax and balance conscious and unconscious mental activity. When you're ready to continue, state, "It is my intent to activate the back of my heart chakra." Then state, "It is my intent to center myself in the back of my heart chakra."

Once you're centered in the back of your heart chakra you'll become aware that thoughts cease or at least cease to disturb you. In addition, you'll experience a growing feeling of lightness that is accompanied by a heightened sense of well-being. You can enhance these effects by stating, "It is my intent to emerge from the back of my heart chakra." By emerging from the back of the heart chakra you'll become even more conscious of the shift that has taken place now that you're centered in the higher and lower mind.

Remain centered in the back of your heart chakra for fifteen minutes, and resist the urge to drift or to follow the movement of energetic waves or fields. Only karmic energy moves in waves or fields, and if you allow yourself to distracted by the movement of qualified energy your center of awareness will shift back to the individual mind and ego.

After fifteen minutes you can return to normal consciousness by counting from one to five. When you reach the number five, open your eyes. You will feel wide awake, perfectly relaxed, and better than you did before.

Chapter Four

*Even the Gods envy the saints, whose senses obey them
like well-trained horses and who are free from pride.
Patient like the earth, they stand like a threshold. They
are pure like a lake without mud, and free from the cycle
of birth and death.*

—Dhammapada, 7:94–5

Strengthening Your Boundaries

In order to overcome karmic baggage and the attachments it creates it is
essential to strengthen your boundaries on the worlds and dimensions of
the higher and lower mind, the world of the chakras and the splenic levels. Boundaries play a crucial role in overcoming karma by preventing
projections of qualified energy from entering personal space (the space
occupied by the energy bodies, energetic vehicles, and the human energy
system). In addition, strong boundaries are a prerequisite for advanced
energy work and for the experience of pleasure, intimacy, joy, and bliss
that emerges from the Self through the higher and lower mind.

Boundaries exist on all worlds and dimensions. In the microcosm there
are three types of boundaries that safeguard the human energy field and the
organs, energy bodies, and energetic vehicles contained within it. These
boundaries are not archetypes, metaphors, or psychological constructs.

They are structures, which exist in time-space. Hence, they perform essential activities in the human energy field.

All boundaries are composed of prana in a solid state, and function according to set principles (see Hermetics, chapter six). They can be influenced by the higher and lower mind and unqualified energy (prana), but they can't be directly influenced by qualified energy and/or the individual mind and ego. This means that projections of qualified energy cannot damage them, although their ability to function can be disrupted when there is an inordinate attachment to the individual mind and ego or there's been a violent intrusion of qualified energy into the microcosm.

The three groups of boundaries we will examine are the surface of personal body space, the apranic boundary, which surrounds the higher and lower mind (for more about the aprana go to chapter fourteen), and the surfaces of the auric fields.

Surface of Personal Body Space

Personal body space is the space on each world and dimension that corresponds to the space occupied by the physical-material body. On the worlds of the higher and lower mind (their functions and aspects, the world of the chakras, and the splenic levels) this space is occupied by an energy body or an energetic vehicle.

The surface of personal body space on a particular world and dimension stays strong and firm and will resist the intrusion of qualified energy as long as the energy body or corresponding energetic vehicle remains fixed in position (vertically integrated).

If one becomes attached to the individual mind and ego, karmic energy will begin to accumulate around personal body space. Once an inordinate amount of karmic baggage has accumulated or an energetic vehicle has been dimpled, tilted, or ejected from personal body space because of stress, shock, or trauma, it will become necessary to recollect and reintegrate the energy body and/or energetic vehicle and remove the karmic sediment that has displaced it.

The aprana, when it is active, will emerge from the apranic boundary and support the surface of personal body space by keeping the area surrounding it free from the inordinate buildup of karmic baggage.

Apranic Boundary

The Apranic Boundary is a field of activity that surrounds personal body space at a distance of eight inches (twenty centimeters) on the worlds and dimensions of the higher and lower mind. The aprana, a form of unqualified energy, emerges from the apranic boundary and has a feminine polarity, which means it moves toward personal body space. When it is active and its movement isn't obstructed, it will keep the surface of personal body space free of karmic sediment and will safeguard the integrity of the human energy field. Free of the burden of karmic sediment, energy bodies will remain fixed in position and the chakras—particularly the nine chakras within personal body space—will radiate prana freely through the human energy system and the surrounding auric fields.

The Surface of the Auric Fields

The surface boundaries surrounding the auric fields on the worlds and dimensions of the higher and lower mind, the world of the chakras, the splenic levels, and the functions and aspects of mind interpenetrate one another and extend outward from the surface of personal body space on their respective worlds and dimensions.

As extensions of the human energy field, the surfaces of the auric fields are the energy system's most effective defense against intrusions of dense, qualified energy from the external environment. To safeguard the human energy field against intrusions, which is the greatest cause of human suffering, these boundaries must remain strong and firm. Unfortunately, because of the inordinate accumulation of karmic energy within the human energy field, most people have had the surface of their auric fields significantly weakened.

To strengthen the auric boundaries one must begin by taking full responsibility for their personal well-being and spiritual evolution regardless of personal cost. Then, one must integrate their will (which has become fragmented by attachment to the independent mind and ego) with the will of the Self (Atman) at the center of their being.

In this chapter I've included a detailed description of the structure and function of the auric fields and, in particular, the boundaries surrounding them. In addition, I've included a list of three commitments. By choosing to make these commitments, and keeping them, you will integrate your will with the will of the Self and you will permanently strengthen your auric boundaries. In fact, by this simple action you will dramatically enhance the flow of prana through your energy field. This, in turn, will enhance your levels of pleasure, joy, personal power, and inner peace.

In later chapters you will learn to strengthen and protect the surface of personal body space and the apranic boundary, first by activating the aprana and then by recollecting and reintegrating your energy bodies and energetic vehicles.

The Auric Fields

The auric fields on each dimension serve as both reservoirs of unqualified energy (prana, aprana, and the kundalini-shakti) and boundaries that separate your internal environment, in each world and dimension, from the external environment.

For the human energy system to function within healthy parameters the auras on each dimension must be strong, firm, and free from the inordinate accumulation of karmic sediment. In addition, the internal cavities, which the surface boundaries surround and protect, must be kept filled with an adequate supply of unqualified energy.

From the surface of personal body space on each dimension the auric field extends outward in all directions, from about two inches (five centimeters) to more than twenty-six feet (eight meters). Since the auric fields are flexible structures, as a person develops spiritually, by removing karmic baggage, recollecting and reintegrating energy bodies and energetic vehicles, and activating the human energy system, the auras will grow larger and the boundaries surrounding them will expand and become more taut, like the surface of a full balloon. In a spiritually developed human being the auric fields can grow quite large and extend well beyond the normal limit of twenty-six feet (eight meters).

The Structure of the Auric Field

The auric field on each world and dimension is composed of an inner cavity and a thin surface boundary that surrounds it and gives it its characteristic egg shape (see figure 4-1). The inner cavity of the aura is bounded on the inside by the surface of personal body space and on the outside by the surface of the auric field. This sealed cavity is kept under pressure, which is regulated through the cooperative efforts of both surface boundaries, the first and seventh chakras, and the minor energy centers in the hands and feet.

The surfaces of the auras have an internal structure that is composed of a countless number of luminescent fibers that criss-cross each other in every imaginable direction. This makes surface boundaries porous, flexible enough to stretch along their entire surface, and extremely strong.

Although the auric boundary separates the internal environment from the external environment, it is possible for qualified energy to intrude through the surface of the aura into the auric field, particularly if the aura is weak. The intrusive energy can then accumulate as karmic sediment and become part of the karmic baggage that one carries from one lifetime to another. Since the inordinate buildup of karmic baggage can disrupt health and well-being, it is essential for the surface of the auric fields to remain healthy.

Function of the Auric Fields

The auric fields have several important functions that help maintain health, balance, and well-being in the human energy field.

In their most important function the auras, along with their corresponding energy bodies and energetic vehicles, serve as vehicles of awareness and self-expression. Without the auras neither the Self nor the higher and lower mind would be able to express themselves or participate fully within the phenomenal universe.

The auras also serve as reservoirs of unqualified energy that the communities of energy bodies and energetic vehicles can draw on in times of need. By extending the microcosm on each dimension beyond the boundaries of personal body space, the auric fields also provide additional space

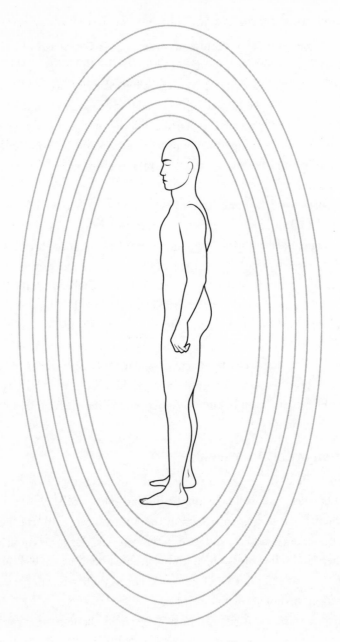

Figure 4-1 — The Auric Fields.

for emotions emerging from the chakras to be developed, expressed, and resolved.

Through a combination of structure and function, the auric boundaries protect the human energy field from intrusions of qualified energy. In addition, they serve as sensors, which enable one to register or sense the impact of qualified and unqualified energy on the human energy system. The auras perform this function by transferring impressions from the surface of the auras to the centers of consciousness, within personal body space, where they can be processed. Impressions are created when energy interacts with the auric boundary and causes a sympathetic resonance. The process can be likened to the way the string of one violin, when plucked, will cause a sympathetic resonance in another violin nearby. The complex relationship between the auric field and energy interacting with it makes it possible for one to sense the subtle atmospheres surrounding them and to discern the quality and quantity of energy (either qualified or unqualified) making an impression on the surface of their auric field.

In their final function the auric fields play a key role in releasing toxins from the human energy field. The auras perform this task on a continuous basis as globules of qualified energy emerging from the human energy system diffuse through the surface of the auras into the external environment.

What Weakens the Surface of the Auras

Although the auras are remarkably strong, most human beings have had their auric boundaries weakened by stress, shock, and trauma caused by the intrusion of dense, qualified energy into the human energy field. Initial weakness, rather than being seen as a symptom of a deeper problem and healed, is more often exacerbated by the introduction of nonphysical beings into the human energy field.

Unfortunately, many of the activities that introduce nonphysical beings into the human energy field have been embraced by the world's religions, orthodox health practitioners, and new age practitioners. Many of

them, in fact, have a long tradition and were even embraced by our an-
cestors who adhered to the nearly universal practice of shamanism.

The activities I'm speaking about are channeling and/or invoking nonphysical beings such as the gods and angels, elementals, spirit guides,
deceased human beings, ascended masters, nature spirits, or power animals for guidance, comfort, and/or sustenance.

There is a great diversity of life forms on the nonphysical dimensions,
but the one thing they have in common is their propensity to disrupt the
functions of the human energy system and weaken boundaries if and
when they are actively or passively permitted to intrude into the human
energy field.

With this in mind, we must take a moment to consider the widely held
belief, common in both east and west, that some nonphysical beings are
benevolent and have no self will, ego, or personal agenda. This belief that
has its origin among the ancient Hebrews—and is accepted by Judaism,
Christianity, and Islam—is not universally accepted. Hindu, Yogic, and
Tantric cosmology all accept the ancient Yogic principle of correspondence that states "as above so below; as below so above." They acknowledge that nonphysical beings, like their human counterparts, have an
individual mind and ego as well as a personal agenda that is self-serving
and oriented toward self-preservation. In fact, Hinduism teaches that
gods are human beings who ascend to these offices or posts because of
the good karma they've accumulated. After many incarnations, however,
these office holders inevitably use up their good karma and once again
must be incarnated on earth.

The only exception to this rule are *jivamuktis* (enlightened human
beings), *bodhisatvas* (masters born in union with Atman), and *avatars* (universal consciousness in human form) who have physical-material bodies
but remain centered in universal consciousness and detached from the
individual mind and ego.

The biblical metaphor of Lucifer and the fallen angels is also instruc-
tive when it comes to nonphysical beings (entities), free will, and the
influence of the individual mind and ego. Lucifer, who stood beside Jehovah's throne, as well as one third of the entities in heaven (the higher

dimensions) were unwilling to surrender their individual will to the will of universal consciousness (Atman). As a result, Lucifer and his cohorts metaphorically fell, cutting themselves off from universal consciousness. In spite of their fallen condition they still aspire to receive the benefits of union with Atman, without accepting the conditions, which were—and remain—detachment from the individual mind and ego, and surrender to universal consciousness. Yoga, as well as Tantra, Jainism, and Buddhism states quite clearly that without meeting these two conditions union with universal consciousness is impossible.

The solution these entities and all intrusive nonphysical beings have chosen to their personal conundrum is to find an independent source of bliss and prana, and to remain as close to it as possible. Their desire to be close to the source of bliss and prana from which they can feed explains why nonphysical beings choose to interact with human beings. It also explains why the greatest density of karmic baggage is found around the sources of prana, in the human energy field, the three hearts, the chakras, and the minor energy centers in the hands and feet.

Indeed, in order to overcome karmic baggage and reexperience union with universal consciousness it is essential to prevent qualified subfields (which are essentially nonphysical beings clothed in qualified energy) from entering or abiding in your energy field. The most effective way to do that is to deny nonphysical beings the right to enter your energy field by revoking their permission to enter or remain in your internal environment.

Strengthening the Boundaries

In addition to the aforementioned problems, nonphysical beings are responsible for the creation of a counterfeit mind, which is in opposition to the higher and lower mind, and which seeks to usurp its authority as well as its functions and aspects. This counterfeit mind is in fact the individual mind and ego, which is composed of nonphysical beings in the form of subfields of qualified energy—samskaras, vasanas, bumpy strings, and personas. It goes without saying that preventing further intrusions of nonphysical beings into your energy field by strengthening your boundaries is essential if you hope to permanently overcome the individual mind and ego and the attachments they create.

The most important step you can take to prevent further intrusions of qualified energy and nonphysical beings is to separate your will from the will of the entities and nonphysical beings that have integrated themselves into your personality—your individual mind and ego. The simplest and most effective way to do that is to use your intent and make a series of commitments to yourself to permanently sever all links to nonphysical beings, and to no longer communicate, invoke, and/or take comfort and solace in their presence.

The Commitments

Below you will find a series of commitments that will sever your links to nonphysical beings outside your energy field (those in your energy field will have to be released as karmic baggage), and will bring your will in accord with the will of the Self as it emerges through your higher and lower mind. In addition, these commitments will safeguard your energy field from any further intrusions of nonphysical beings by strengthening your boundaries on all worlds and dimensions, including the world of spirit, intellect, soul, lower mind, world of the chakras, and the levels of the splenic chakras.

If you know it's appropriate to make these commitments and you know you will keep them permanently, then simply read the commitments below, repeat them out loud, and affirm, "I agree to these three commitments."

The first commitment is: "If I have given permission or inadvertently given permission for any nonphysical beings to be in my world of my spirit, my world of my intellect, my world of my soul, my world of my chakras, my world of my lower mind, my level of my upper splenic chakra, and my level of my splenic chakra, I revoke that permission now and permanently in the future."

The second commitment is: "It is my desire and my will that all nonphysical beings depart from my world of my spirit, my world of

my intellect, my world of my soul, my world of my chakras, my world
of my lower mind, my level of my upper splenic chakra, and my level of
my splenic chakra now, and remain permanently outside them in the
future, I want you to leave now."

The third commitment is: "My world of my spirit, my world of my
intellect, my world of my soul, my world of my chakras, my world of
my lower mind, my level of my upper splenic chakra, and level of my
splenic chakra are my sacred space. It is my desire and my will that they
be occupied solely by myself and the light of God now and permanently
in the future."

If you know it's appropriate to make these commitments and you
know you will keep them for the rest of your life, affirm out loud, "I agree
to these three commitments."

By making these commitments (it's only necessary to make them
once) and keeping them, you will be taking responsibility for your inner
life and will be committing yourself to a life of personal integrity and
truth. In addition, you will be signifying your intent to put union with the
Self above the needs and desires of the mundane world that emerge
exclusively from your individual mind and ego.

Many people before you have made these commitments and have
experienced an immediate shift in their condition as prana—which had
been blocked and prevented from radiating freely by subfields of qualified energy and nonphysical beings—is set free. The expansion of prana
through your energy field will enhance your Self-awareness and personal
integrity. Authentic sensations, feelings, and emotions that were restricted by karmic baggage will have more room to emerge and to be resolved
through your energy bodies (energetic vehicles) and the auric fields surrounding them. Finally, qualified energy in the form of thoughts, attitudes, and beliefs (and the nonphysical beings within them) will be
prevented from continually intruding into personal body space, making it
easier for you to stay centered in the higher and lower mind and to access
the Self that emerges into conscious awareness from deep within personal body space.

While the shift is taking place it's not unusual for layers of karmic baggage to be dislodged and to be pushed away from personal body space. Don't interfere with the process by concentrating or fixing your attention on it. It will last only as long as necessary for your energy system to achieve a new balance.

Most people who've made these commitments have been amazed at how light and carefree they feel afterward. This should come as no surprise, since nonphysical beings feed off the prana (unqualified energy) that emerges from the Self and radiates through the human energy system. In the process, nonphysical beings add their will, finite awareness, emotions, feelings, sensations, and subtle matter to the karmic baggage (samskaras and vasanas) already present within the energy field of their host.

Although you may not have been aware of the cause and effect relationship between nonphysical beings within your energy field and your internal state of well-being, the fact is that nonphysical beings integrated into the individual mind and ego are the greatest cause of human suffering.

Chapter Five

*He who sees the Lord of all is ever the same in all that
is, immortal in the field of mortality—he sees the truth.*
—Bhagavad Gita, 13:27)

Interpenetrating Worlds

The Self emerges into the phenomenal universe by way of the tattvas, which are steps in the evolutionary process. As evolution proceeds, worlds are created; so too are dimensions within each world. In this chapter we will be looking at six of these worlds, the world of spirit, the world of intellect, the world of soul, the world of the lower mind (which includes the bodies of desire), the world of the chakras, and the world of maya.

Within each world there are one hundred and forty dimensions. In the microcosm—the internal environment of a human being—these worlds and dimensions and the communities of energy bodies within them function synchronistically with one another, as well as with the human energy system and the functions and aspects of mind.

The first three worlds, known respectively as the worlds of spirit, intellect, and soul, comprise the higher mind. Of these three, the world of spirit has the highest mean frequency. The world of intellect has a lower mean frequency, and the world of the soul has the lowest mean frequency. The fourth world is the world of the lower mind, which has a lower mean frequency than the worlds of the higher mind. The fifth world is the world of the chakras, which interpenetrates the higher and lower mind as well as their functions and aspects, and supports the communities of energy bodies within them. The final world is the world of maya, which is a conditional world, since it is composed of qualified energy and is not the same in the beginning, the middle, and the end.

The first five worlds are composed of consciousness, unqualified energy—prana—and subtle matter, also a form of prana. The world of maya is composed of finite consciousness (which emerges from qualified energy), qualified energy (which veils the consciousness of the Self through the three gunas, tamas, ragas, and sattva), and subtle matter in either a solid, liquid, or gaseous state (for more on the gunas see chapter six). The tenth-century sage Sri Shankara states that "From Mahat . . . (cosmic intelligence) . . . down to the gross body everything is the effect of Maya. These and Maya itself know thou to be the non-Self, and therefore unreal like the mirage in a desert" (*Viveda-Cudamani of Shankara*, 45).

A convenient way to picture the interpenetrating universe and the worlds and dimensions within it is to visualize it as five interpenetrating spheres (see figure 5-1). In the center of the spheres represented by a mathematical point is universal consciousness. Universal consciousness (the Self) has no dimensions, but supports both the physical and nonphysical universe with consciousness and unqualified energy. Radiating from that point are one hundred and forty equally spaced spokes that penetrate the spheres. These spokes represent the chakras, interdimensional vortexes of unqualified energy that extend outward from the Self as far as the world of the lower mind. The two splenic chakras emerge from Self but penetrate the etheric and physical-material world only (for more on the splenic chakras see chapter twelve).

The sphere closest to the Self represents the world of spirit, which was the first of these worlds to emerge from the Self, via the tattvas. The sphere is divided into one hundred and forty dimensions. Each dimension in the world of spirit is penetrated by a single chakra that goes on to penetrate the same dimension in the world of intellect, soul, lower mind, and their corresponding functions and aspects. The prana emerging from each chakra supports the communities of energy bodies and/or energetic vehicles on each world and dimension interpenetrated by the chakra.

Surrounding each sphere and closely resembling it in size, shape, and distance from the Self is the field of maya. The field of maya surrounds each sphere in the higher and lower mind, as well as the world of the chakras, the levels of the splenic chakras and their functions and aspects, and is divided into one hundred and forty dimensions.

The more dense the collective field of maya surrounding the dimensional fields in the world of spirit, the more difficult it will be for the chakras to support the communities of energy bodies contained within these fields, and the more difficult it will be for prana to flow through the chakras to the next world, the world of intellect.

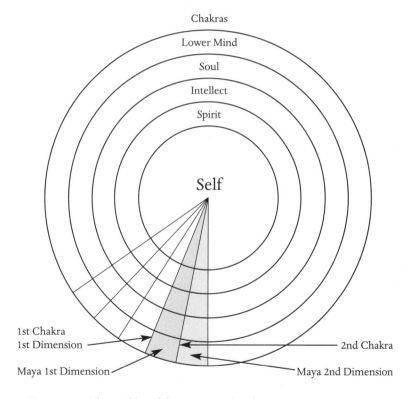

Figure 5-1 — The worlds and dimensions within the interpenetrating universe.

The world of intellect is represented in the figure by a second sphere divided into one hundred and forty dimensions. Like the world of spirit, the chakras penetrate and support the community of energy bodies on each dimension in the world of intellect.

Prana emerging from universal consciousness is continuously transmuted into lower pitches or frequencies by the chakras so that the energy bodies on the world of intellect can use it. Energy bodies on the world of intellect have a lower mean frequency than energy bodies in the world of spirit.

The more dense the field of maya surrounding the world of intellect, the more difficult it will be for the chakras to support the communities of energy bodies on each dimension, and the more difficult it will be for prana to be transmitted and transmuted for use by energy bodies on the world of soul.

Beyond the world of intellect is the world of soul, and beyond the world of soul is the world of the lower mind. Both of these worlds are represented in the figure by a sphere that is divided into one hundred and forty dimensions. Each dimension and the community of energy bodies and energetic vehicles within it is supported by a chakra, which penetrates it and supports the communities of energetic bodies and energetic vehicles contained within it.

The more dense the field of maya surrounding the world of soul and the world of the lower mind, the more difficult it will be for the chakras to support the communities of energy bodies and energetic vehicles on the dimensions of each world.

The World of Spirit

The world of spirit is composed of consciousness, unqualified energy (which vibrates in the spectrum of frequencies that correspond to spirit), and subtle matter. The world of spirit is often compared to the causal world—however, it is important to recognize that the Self (Atman) is in fact the cause—and both the physical and nonphysical universe, including the world of spirit, are the effect.

Since human beings are the universe in microcosm, each individual exists simultaneously on all one hundred and forty dimensions contained within the world of spirit, and each individual has a community of energy bodies on each dimension, which functions synchronistically with the communities of energy bodies on neighboring dimensions.

Within the world of spirit all energy bodies are the same size and shape as the physical-material body to which they correspond. Under normal circumstances the energy bodies are vertically integrated, which means they occupy personal body space on their particular dimension.

The communities of energy bodies that exist on the world of spirit interact with their external environment via the functions of mind, and emerge with an identity in the spiritual world via the aspects of mind.

The chakras that penetrate the world of spirit support the communities of energy bodies with prana and regulate polarity on the dimensions of the spiritual world by transmitting and transmuting unqualified energy as needed by individual energy bodies. In addition, the chakras and the auric fields work together with the centers of consciousness in the world of spirit to sense both unqualified and qualified energy in both the internal and external environment.

Spiritual consciousness as it emerges through the world of spirit expands human consciousness beyond the basic needs of personal survival. In fact, it is only after spiritual consciousness emerges into one's conscious awareness that the transcendental functions on the world of spirit can be fully integrated.

The World of Intellect

The world of intellect is the next world to emerge from the Self by way of the tattvas. Contained within the world of intellect are one hundred and forty dimensions, and on each dimension human beings have a community of energy bodies that function synchronistically with one another and the communities of energy bodies on neighboring worlds.

The communities of energy bodies that exist on the world of intellect interact with their external environment through the functions of mind and emerge with an identity through the aspects of mind.

All energy bodies in the world of intellect are the same size and shape as the physical-material body, and in a healthy human being they are vertically integrated.

Energy bodies in the world of intellect are supported energetically by the higher and lower chakras, which provide them with prana, transmute prana when necessary, regulate polarity, and along with the auric fields function as sensors.

The world of intellect vibrates in a spectrum of frequencies that correspond to the human intellect and finite awareness. As long as the communities of energy bodies on the world of intellect remain vertically integrated and continue to function healthfully, deductive and inductive reasoning will remain balanced, and intuition and insight will emerge into conscious awareness. Creativity will manifest in the world of intellect as originality. Thought will be kept at a minimum, and if it does emerge will be in the form of pictures and sound rather than ideation and worry, which are the basis of the internal dialogue. Since it is primarily through the intellect and soul that individuals within relationship interact, functioning healthfully on the world of intellect is essential for establishing and maintaining long-term intimate relationships.

The World of Soul

The world of soul is the next world to emerge from the Self by way of the tattvas. There are one hundred and forty dimensions in the world of soul, and on each dimension there exists a community of energy bodies that function synchronistically with energy bodies and energetic vehicles on neighboring worlds and dimensions.

Energy bodies in the world of soul are the same size and shape as the physical-material body, and in a healthy individual they are vertically integrated. They interact with their external environment via the functions of mind, and emerge with an identity via the aspects of mind. Energy bodies in the world of soul are supported energetically by the higher and lower chakras, which provide them with prana, transmute prana when necessary, regulate polarity, and, along with the auric fields, function as sensors.

The world of soul vibrates in the part of the energetic spectrum associated with emotions, feelings, and sensations. When the communities of energy bodies on the world of soul are functioning healthfully, one will be able to sense the emotions and feelings of both physical and nonphysical beings, and one will be able to feel, express, and resolve his or her own authentic emotions and feelings spontaneously.

Self-expression and assertiveness will be balanced by receptivity and empathy, and creativity will emerge as empathetic feelings and a visceral sense of relationship. Emotional conflict will be kept at a minimum; when it does emerge it will be recognized for what it is, a counterfeit function of the individual mind and ego. Since emotions, feelings, and sensations play an essential role in human communication, functioning more healthfully on the world of soul is essential for establishing and maintaining intimate, long-term relationships.

The World of the Lower Mind

The world of the lower mind is an extension of human consciousness with a lower mean frequency than the worlds of soul, intellect, and spirit. It remains, however, an essential part of human consciousness, and to ignore it is to deny the Self the right to emerge through the entire spectrum of human awareness.

There are one hundred and forty dimensions in the world of the lower mind. On each dimension human beings have a community of energetic vehicles called "bodies of desire." Structurally, the bodies of desire correspond to the energy bodies of the higher mind, and as vehicles of universal consciousness they function synchronistically with the communities of energy bodies on neighboring worlds and dimensions.

Bodies of desire interact with their external environment via the functions of mind and emerge with an identity in the world of the lower mind via the aspects of mind.

Chakras provide the bodies of desire with the prana. In addition, they regulate polarity, transmute unqualified energy, and, along with the auric fields, function as sensors.

All bodies of desire are the same size and shape as the physical-material body to which they correspond, and under normal circumstances they are vertically integrated, which means they occupy personal body space on their particular dimension.

The world of the lower mind contains consciousness, unqualified energy—which vibrates in the spectrum of frequencies that correspond to authentic human desire—and subtle matter. When functional elements of the lower mind emerge into conscious awareness one will be able to discern the difference between appropriate and inappropriate activity, and consistently choose to do what is appropriate.

The four desires that emerge from the lower mind when the bodies of desire are vertically integrated are artha, kama, dharma, and moksha. Artha refers to the desire for material comfort or wealth. Kama refers to the desire for pleasure. Dharma refers to the desire for impeccability (appropriate action), and moksha refers to the desire for spiritual freedom and liberation from karmic attachment.

The World of the Chakras

The world of the chakras interpenetrates and supports the worlds of the higher and lower mind, as well as the splenic levels and the functions and aspects of mind.

Individual chakras are commonly represented as a wheel or blossom connected to a shaft or stem (see figure 5-2). Although these representations depict the chakras' individual structure, chakras function within individual fields of unqualified energy and consciousness, which in structure correspond to the energy vehicles of the higher and lower mind. Like the energy bodies, these fields (each chakra is immersed in three of them) are the same size and shape as the physical-material body. Known as "chakra bodies," the three vehicles, on each dimension, must be vertically integrated for the chakras to function healthfully and remain free from the influence of maya and the subfields of qualified energy within it.

One hundred and forty chakras radiate from the Self and penetrate the worlds of the higher and lower mind and their functions and aspects. In addition, two splenic chakras emerge from the Self, but follow their own route, penetrating the two splenic levels and their functions and aspects.

The chakra bodies interact with energy bodies and energetic vehicles on neighboring worlds and dimensions and with subfields of qualified energy in the world of the chakras. Chakra bodies, like energy bodies and energetic vehicles in the higher and lower mind, can have their activities disrupted. Disruptions can occur when there has been an inordinate buildup of karmic baggage on one or more dimensions of the world of the chakras, or there has been a violent projection of qualified energy or the intrusion of nonphysical beings into the microcosm in the world of the chakras.

When the function of a chakra has been disrupted it's not enough to reactivate the individual chakra. One must also remove the karmic baggage and/or qualified subfield disrupting its activity on the dimension where the disruption has taken place, and reintegrate the chakra bodies if they've tilted or been ejected from personal body space.

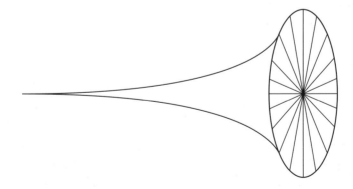

Figure 5-2 — An individual chakra resembles a wheel or blossom.

Worlds of Exercises

In the modern world most human beings are only conscious of a small part of the multiworld, multidimensional world that exists within them. As a result, they experience only a fraction of the pleasure, love, intimacy, and joy that can emerge through their higher and lower mind. Nevertheless, with knowledge and skill one can become more conscious and discern the specific resonance (mean frequency) of each world and dimension of the higher and lower mind, as well the different qualities of qualified subfields.

In the following series of exercises you will develop the skills necessary to locate and discern the resonance of specific worlds and dimensions within the worlds of the higher and lower mind. You will begin by learning to split your attention and to activate the front of your heart chakra. Once you learn to split your attention and to activate the front of your heart chakra you will look inward into the world spirit. By looking inward you will experience the resonance of the world of spirit on the fourth dimension, the level of the heart chakra.

In the exercise that follows you will activate the back of your heart chakra, center yourself there, and then look inward into the world of spirit. After that you will perform the same steps in the world of intellect, soul, and the lower mind.

Once you've completed the first series of exercises and you can discern the resonance of the heart chakra on each world of the higher and lower mind, you will look inward, on the level of the heart chakra (the fourth dimension) on more than one world. Then you will use what you've learned to look inward, on the level of the heart chakra, on all worlds of the higher and lower mind simultaneously.

After you've successfully completed the first series of exercises you will activate the seven traditional chakras in personal body space and look inward on all seven dimensions simultaneously on the worlds of the higher and lower mind. By looking inward on these first seven dimensions you will begin to get some idea of the breadth of your consciousness and the pleasure, love, intimacy, and joy that is available to you.

Splitting Your Attention and Activating the Front of the Heart Chakra

Before you can look inward on the level of the fourth chakra you must be able to split your attention and work with the second attention. In the exercises you've learned so far you've worked exclusively with the mental attention. In most of the techniques you will learn in this book, however, the mental attention will remain centered in the back of the heart chakra and the second attention will perform the prescribed energy work.

In this exercise you will activate and center yourself in the back of your heart chakra. Then you will split your attention and project your second attention to the front of the heart chakra by stating, "It is my intent to split my attention and to activate the front of my heart chakra."

To begin, find a comfortable position with your back straight. Then use the standard method to relax and balance conscious and unconscious mental activity. Continue by activating and centering yourself in the back of your heart chakra. Then split your attention and activate the front of the heart chakra by stating, "It is my intent to split my attention and to activate the front of my heart chakra."

Take about fifteen minutes to enjoy the unqualified energy emerging from the front of the heart chakra. Then count upward from one to five. When you reach the number five, open your eyes. You will feel wide awake, perfectly relaxed, and better than you did before.

Looking Inward on the World of Spirit

In this exercise you will activate and center yourself in the back of your heart chakra. Then you will split your attention, activate the front of your heart chakra, and look inward on the world of spirit.

As soon as you're ready to begin, find a comfortable position with your back straight. Then use the standard method to relax and balance conscious and unconscious mental activity.

When you're ready to continue, activate and center yourself in the back of your heart chakra. Then state, "It is my intent to split my attention and to activate the front of my heart chakra." Continue by stating, "On the level of the heart chakra it is my intent to look inward in the world of spirit." Take about fifteen minutes to enjoy the meditation. Then count from one to five. When you reach the number five, open your eyes. You will feel wide awake, perfectly relaxed, and better than you did before.

Looking Inward on the World of Intellect

In this exercise you will use the standard method to relax and balance conscious and unconscious mental activity. Then you will activate and center yourself in the back of your heart chakra. Once you're centered in the back of the heart chakra you will split your attention and activate the front of your heart chakra. Then you will look inward on the world of intellect by stating, "On the level of the heart chakra it is my intent to look inward on the world of intellect."

Take fifteen minutes to enjoy the meditation. Then count from one to five. When you reach the number five, open your eyes. You will feel wide awake, perfectly relaxed, and better than you did before.

After you've completed this exercise you can use the same method to experience the unique resonance of the heart chakra in the world of soul by stating, "On the level of the heart chakra it is my intent to look inward on the world of soul." You can continue by performing the same exercise in the world of the lower mind by stating, "On the level of the heart chakra it is my intent to look inward on the world of the lower mind." You can use the same method in the world of the chakras by stating, "On the level of the heart chakra it is my intent to look inward on the world of the chakras."

Looking Inward on All Worlds Simultaneously

In this exercise you will use the standard method to relax and balance conscious and unconscious mental activity. Then you will activate and center yourself in the back of your heart chakra. Once you're centered in the back of the heart chakra you will split your attention and activate the front of your heart chakra.

After you've activated the front of your heart chakra you will state, "On the level of the heart chakra it is my intent to look inward on the world of the lower mind." Then you will state, "On the level of the heart chakra it is my intent to look inward on the world of the soul." To continue you will state, "On the level of the heart chakra it's my intent to look inward in the world of intellect." Finally you will state, "On the level of the heart chakra it is my intent to look inward on the world of the spirit."

Take about fifteen minutes to enjoy the shift in consciousness you experience as you look inward simultaneously on the worlds of the higher and lower mind. Then count from one to five. When you reach the number five, open your eyes. You will feel wide awake, perfectly relaxed, and better than you did before.

Since this exercise can have a profound impact on your view of the multiworld, multidimensional universe, you may want to repeat it several times in order to enjoy the harmony created by the interaction of these energetic fields emerging simultaneously from the worlds of the higher and lower mind.

Activating the Seven Traditional Chakras

In the exercise below you will activate the seven traditional chakras within personal body space. In the series of exercises that follow you will active the seven traditional chakra, and then look inward on these dimensions in the worlds of the higher and lower mind.

Begin by finding a comfortable position with your back straight. Then use the standard method to relax and balance conscious and unconscious mental activity. When you're ready to continue, activate and center yourself in the back of your heart chakra. Then split your attention and activate the seven chakras in personal body space, beginning with the back of the first chakra and moving upward along the shushumna-governor meridian to the back of the seventh chakra (you can exclude the back of the heart chakra, which you've already activated). After you've activated the back of the seven traditional chakras, activate the front of the chakras, beginning with the seventh chakra and working downward to the first.

Once you've activated the back and front of the seven traditional chakras within personal body space, take about fifteen minutes to enjoy the changes you feel in your energy system. Then count from one to five. When you reach the number five, open your eyes. You will feel wide awake, perfectly relaxed, and better than you did before.

Spirit—Looking Inward on Seven Dimensions

In this exercise you will use what you've learned so far to look inward on the world of spirit on the levels of the seven traditional chakras.

When you are ready to begin find a comfortable position with your back straight. Then use the standard method to relax and balance conscious and unconscious mental activity. When you are ready to continue activate and center yourself in the back of your heart chakra. Then split your attention and activate the seven traditional chakras in personal body space beginning with the back of the first chakra and moving upward along the shushumna-governor meridian to the back of the seventh chakra (you can exclude the back of the heart chakra, which you've already activated). After you've activated the back of the seven traditional chakras activate the front of the chakras, beginning with the seventh chakra and working downward to the first.

Once the chakras are active you will look inward in the world of spirit on all seven dimensions simultaneously by stating, "It is my intent to look inward on the levels of the seven traditional chakras. In the world of spirit." By looking inward exclusively on the world of spirit you will have a direct experience of the world of spirit on the levels of the seven traditional chakras within personal body space.

Take about fifteen minutes to enjoy the meditation. Then count from one to five. When you reach the number five, open your eyes. You will feel wide awake, perfectly relaxed, and better than you did before.

Intellect—Looking Inward on Seven Dimensions

In this exercise you will use what you've learned so far to look inward on the world of intellect on the levels of the seven traditional chakras. The exercise will be identical to the one above, except that you will state, "It is my intent to look inward on the levels of the seven traditional chakras in the world of intellect." By looking inward exclusively on the world of intellect you will have a direct experience of the world of intellect on the levels of the seven traditional chakras.

To perform the exercise, follow the instructions above. Then take fifteen minutes to experience the seven traditional chakras in the world of intellect. After fifteen minutes, count from one to five. When you reach the number five, open your eyes. You will feel wide awake, perfectly relaxed, and better than you did before.

Soul—Looking Inward on Seven Dimensions

In this exercise you will use what you've learned so far to look inward in the world of soul on the levels of the seven traditional chakras.

The exercise will be identical to the one above, except that you will look inward on the world of soul by stating, "It is my intent to look inward on the levels of the seven traditional chakras in the world of soul."

To perform the exercise, follow the instructions above. Then take about fifteen minutes to experience the seven traditional chakras in the world of soul. After fifteen minutes, count from one to five. When you reach the number five, open your eyes. You will feel wide awake, perfectly relaxed, and better than you did before.

Lower Mind—Looking Inward on Seven Dimensions

In this exercise you will use what you've learned so far to look inward in the world of the lower mind on the levels of the seven traditional chakras.

The exercise will be identical to the one above, except that you will look inward on the world of the lower mind by stating, "It is my intent to look inward on the levels of the seven traditional chakras in the world of the lower mind."

To perform the exercise, follow the instructions above. Then take about fifteen minutes to enjoy the meditation. After fifteen minutes, count from one to five. When you reach the number five, open your eyes. You will feel wide awake, perfectly relaxed, and better than you did before.

Looking Inward on All Worlds Simultaneously

In this exercise you will combine what you've learned by looking inward in the worlds of the higher and lower mind simultaneously on the levels of the seven traditional chakras.

When you are ready to begin, find a comfortable position with your back straight. Then use the standard method to relax and balance conscious and unconscious mental activity. When you are ready to continue, activate and center yourself in the back of your heart chakra. Then split your attention and activate the seven chakras in personal body space, beginning with the back of the first chakra and moving upward along the shushumna-governor meridian to the back of the seventh chakra. You can exclude the back of the heart chakra which you've already activated. Once you've activated the back of the seven traditional chakras, activate the front of the chakras beginning with the seventh chakra and working downward to the first.

After you've activated the back and front of the seven traditional chakras within personal body space, you will look inward on the world of the spirit by stating, "It is my intent to look inward on the levels of the seven traditional chakras on the world of spirit." Then you will state, "It is my intent to look inward on the levels of the seven traditional chakras In the world of intellect." Continue by stating, "It is my intent to look inward on the levels of the seven traditional chakras on the world of soul," and finally state, "It is my intent to look inward on the levels of the seven traditional chakras in the world of the lower mind."

Take about fifteen minutes to enjoy the meditation. Then count from one to five. When you reach the number five, open your eyes. You will feel wide awake, perfectly relaxed, and better than you did before.

Part Two

Protecting Yourself

Chapter Six

Through this maya jivas . . . (embodied souls) . . .
experience seven stages of development as follows:
ignorance, veiling, multiplicity, indirect knowledge,
direct experience, freedom from misery, and supreme
bliss.

—Kaivalya Navaneeta, p 13

The Collective Field of Maya

Superimposed on the universal field of unqualified energy, in both the microcosm and macrocosm, is the collective field of qualified energy. In Sanskrit this collective field is known as *maya*. Maya can be defined as "the appearance of reality." Contained within the collective field of qualified energy are various subfields of qualified energy. These subfields interact with human beings on all worlds and dimensions—including the higher and lower mind, the world of the chakras, the levels of the splenic chakras, and the functions and aspects of mind. Indeed, because subfields of qualified energy can be found on all worlds and dimensions, in both the macrocosm and microcosm, dealing with them in an effective and timely manner is essential for overcoming karmic baggage and the attachment it creates.

Although divisions exist among diverse religious institutions and spiritual traditions, it is generally accepted that the qualified universe of maya, which exists on all worlds and dimensions, has existed and will continue to exist as long as there is a phenomenal universe. This is the

Vedic view, and is essentially the same view espoused by Hinduism, Yoga, Buddhism, and Jainism.

It was the great Vedic sage, Shankara, who fully integrated the concept of maya into Yogic cosmology and psychology. Shankara was born in a small village in Western Malabar, in southern India, in AD 788. Referring to maya, Shankara wrote "World appearance as it is experienced in the waking state may be likened to an imagined snake which proves, on closer inspection, to be nothing but a coil of rope. When the truth is known we are no longer deluded by the appearance of the snake; appearance vanishes into the reality of the rope and the world vanishes into Brahman."

According to Yoga, maya is said to have six parts: it has no beginning; it is terminated by jnana (knowledge); it veils the truth and/or consciousness and projects (radiating qualities). It cannot be defined, since it only has the appearance of being real; it is the nature of phenomenal existence (it evolves and involves but has no permanence), and it is located within each person (the microcosm), or in Brahman (universal consciousness).

As a function of its structure and its association with the dynamic aspect of universal consciousness, the collective field of maya and the qualified subfields within it must be considered animate or alive in the same way that everything from the most insentient stone to the highest form of sentient life is animated and alive to one degree or another. This principle, which we call the "animate universe," must be applied to everything in the world of maya, without exception. Indeed, because the principle of the animate universe holds true on all planes at all times—it holds true for qualified subfields, whatever their form and wherever they're found.

Although the collective field of maya, and the subfields of qualified energy within it, is considered only conditionally real, it contains all the constituent elements necessary for phenomenal existence, i.e., finite consciousness, qualified energy, and subtle as well as physical matter—all of which occupy space, evolve, and then involve within an expanding field of time-space, at least for the moment.

Indeed, all subfields of qualified energy within the collective field of maya have what you can think of as character or what I call a flavor. Its character is a function of the world and dimension on which the subfield is located, its particular resonance (mean frequency), density, and polarity as well as the number of CECs, Conscious Energy Concentrations (living entities) contained within it (for more on CECs, see chapter eight). As a function of their individual character, subfields of qualified energy and the CECs within them have will, awareness, and express themselves through a limited spectrum of emotional and etheric energy, (feelings and sensations).

Although not eternal like the Self or infinite like the higher and lower mind, the collective field of maya does continue to exist for billions of years. In fact, the physical-material universe owes its existence to the collective field of maya and is supported by it with particles of qualified energy which are continually transmuted into physical matter.

Indeed, the field of maya and individual subfields within it have a tremendous impact on the physical-material plane and the physical creatures within it, especially human beings. Qualified subfields—particularly those within the human energy field—influence physical health, and emotional and mental well-being and can inhibit one's awareness of one's internal and external environment through the aegis of the individual mind and ego.

Yoga teaches that maya can disrupt awareness in four ways: through, ". . . laya (torpidity), vikshepa (distraction), kashaya (attachment), and rasavada (egoistic enjoyment)" (*Essence of Vedanta*, 181). In addition to obscuring human awareness, maya and the subfields of qualified energy within it can set up a counterfeit reality in both the macrocosm and the microcosm.

Swami Shivananda explains how maya can create and support this counterfeit reality and how it can mimic the functions of the higher and lower mind. He calls this *adhyasa, or "superimposition." Adhyasa, he* states, ". . . is mistaking one thing for another through delusion. The mirage in the desert is a common phenomena experienced by many a traveler in deserts. The mirage presents not only the false presence of water but also buildings, meadows, and mansions . . . This kind of appearance has deceived not a few, who through ignorance of the unreality of the mirage, run after it . . . They then realize that what appeared to be a big reservoir of water and an oasis is only . . . the . . . sun's rays on the bed of hot sand, and not real water . . . In a similar manner, the ignorant . . . do not realize that this . . . world with countless creatures, mobile and immobile, living therein . . . is . . . apparently real only . . . .the Light of Absolute Consciousness reflected through Maya . . . " which is nothing less than . . . 'the Great Divine Illusion'" (*Essence of Vedanta*, 77).

Subfields in the Field of Maya

Subfields of qualified energy that exist within the collective field of maya take the form of atmospheres, pools, waves, and cords, and display the qualities of state (solid, liquid, and gaseous), size, shape, density, polarity, level of activity, surface texture, and, in some cases, color.

Normally qualified energy contained within subfields will be composed of energy within a narrow spectrum of frequencies and therefore will have distinctive qualities that differ from the qualified energy surrounding it—this explains why a person who has developed discernment is able to distinguish one qualified subfield from another.

In the external environment, subfields of qualified energy rarely combine. The case is somewhat different in the microcosm—the human energy field. Given enough time, subfields in the microcosm will combine to create second generation subfields, called "complex subfields," which are larger and more complex. Complex subfields include samskaras, vasanas, and bumpy strings (the main constituents of karmic baggage), personas, cords, controlling waves, and the ego. All subfields in the microcosm compete for their hosts' attention and have the ability to veil the effluence of the Self as it manifests through the higher and lower mind, their functions and aspects, and the human energy system.

The Jains pointed out more than a thousand years ago that subfields of qualified energy can obscure chit (knowledge) and ananda (bliss), though they cannot interfere with Sat (eternal life). The experience of Sat chit ananda is common to all beings who have achieved a state of Self-realization. In fact, the Jains recognized that the condition of one's energy field, one's access to knowledge, and intuition, as well as one's ability to observe and discern phenomena on the higher and lower dimensions, can be disturbed by an inordinate accumulation of qualified energy, in the form of karmic baggage, cords, energy blockages, personas, etc. Thus, for the Jains, or anyone else who has chosen to overcome karmic baggage, it becomes essential to overcome the attachment created by karmic baggage in order to become fully conscious on the worlds and dimensions of the higher and lower mind.

The Three Gunas

All subfields of qualified energy have a basic structure, which at the core includes at least one conscious energy concentration (CEC), living entities that have individual will, rudimentary consciousness, and qualified energy in a narrow spectrum of frequencies. Qualified energy surrounds the CEC and a boundary or surface membrane of subtle, qualified matter surrounds the reservoir. Subtle matter is actually qualified energy in a solid state. The surface membrane serves as a both a structural and functional boundary, which separates one subfield of qualified energy from another and all individual subfields from the collective field of maya.

In Yoga the *gunas* are used as a shorthand to describe the character of qualified energy. The Sanskrit word *guna* means "quality or attribute." The gunas describe the specific quality or flavor emerging from a qualified subfield in both the macrocosm and the microcosm. Since most qualified subfields aren't pure, but contain more than one CEC, the quality of a particular subfield, or its guna, can be thought of as the mean frequency or resonance of all CECs and qualified energy within the subfield.

There are three gunas, which are used to describe the qualities of qualified subfields: Sattva, Ragas, and Tamas. The *Kaivalya Navaneeta* states that, ". . . sattva, rajas, and tamas . . .(are) . . . pure white, red, and black respectively, or again, clear, turbid, and dark. Though equal, one of them will always predominate" (*Kaivalya Navaneeta*, Sri Ramanasramam, India, 7).

Tamasic Energy

Tamasic energy is the most dense and corresponds to energy (matter) in the physical-material world in a solid state. Its consistency ranges from hard and brittle to soft and cheesy. Tamasic energy is the most stable, and does not respond quickly to outside stimuli by moving, or changing size, shape, density, and level of activity. Tamasic energy that has intruded into the human energy field will cause the most distress and will have the most disruptive effect on human health. Once tamasic energy has entered the human energy field and is integrated, it is the most difficult to remove.

Ragistic Energy

Ragistic energy is less dense than tamasic energy. It corresponds to energy (matter) in the physical-material world in a liquid state. In form and consistency it ranges from thick and viscous to thin and watery. Ragistic energy is less stable than tamasic energy. Hence, it will respond more quickly to outside stimuli by moving, or changing size, shape, density, and level of activity. In most cases ragistic energy will be less difficult to release than tamasic energy and will have less impact on the human energy system and human health.

Sattvic energy

Sattvic energy is less dense than either tamasic or ragistic energy and is less disruptive to human health and well-being. It reacts quickly to outside stimuli, and is unstable, changing position often and changing size, shape, density, and level of activity easily. Because it is the least dense, it will be easier to release from the human energy field than either ragistic or tamasic energy.

We are told in the works of Laya Yoga that "The greater the presence or power of Sattva-guna, the greater the approach to the condition of Pure Consciousness. Similarly, the function of Tamas Guna is to suppress or veil consciousness. The function of Rajas Guna is to make active—that is, it works on Tamas to suppress Sattva, or on Sattva to suppress Tamas" (*Serpent Power*, 52).

The particular qualities and state (guna) of a qualified subfield will be determined by the number of CECs at its core and their state. Below is a detailed description of the qualities, in addition to state, present in qualified subfields in both the microcosm and the macrocosm.

Size: In both the microcosm and the macrocosm, the size of a qualified subfield will depend on the number of CECs at its core, the mass of qualified energy surrounding the CECs, its density, and its level of activity, which is determined by the subfield's level of polarity (see figure 6-1, bell curve) as well as the pressure exerted against it by other qualified subfields in its immediate environment. From figure 6-1 you can see that individual subfields can vary widely in size, with the greatest distribution falling in the middle of the bell curve, about the size of a grapefruit.

The size of a subfield is inversely proportional to its density, polarity and level of activity, which means that the larger the subfield, the less dense, less polarized, and less active it will be—this is a general rule and there will be exceptions.

The largest subfields, twelve inches (thirty centimeters) or more in diameter, will have a low density, weak polarity, and a low level of activity. Medium size subfields, six inches (fifteen centimeters) or more in diameter, will have an average density, medium polarity, and an average level of

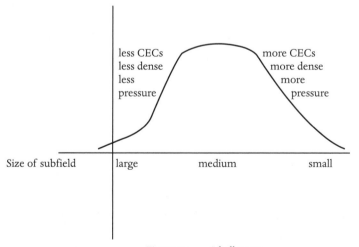

Figure 6-1 — A bell curve.

activity. Small subfields, smaller than six inches (fifteen centimeters) in diameter will be the most dense, most active, and most highly polarized.

In reference to state and guna, small subfields will tend to be solid and tamasic, medium subfields liquid and ragistic, and large subfields gaseous and sattvic.

Shape: Subfields of qualified energy can be found in a wide range of shapes. The shape of a subfield will be determined by its state, the number of CECs within it, its size, density, level of activity, and the pressure exerted against it by other qualified subfields in its immediate environment. The largest, least dense, least active subfields, which are free from outside influence, contain the least number of CECs. Hence, they will be gaseous (sattvic) and irregularly shaped.

Medium-sized subfields will be more dense and more active. These subfields contain more CECs and will be ragistic, slightly elongated, and may be influenced by other qualified subfields. The most dense, most active subfields, under the most pressure, will contain the most CECs and will be tamasic. These subfields will be highly polarized and will be small, solid, and almost always perfectly spherical or elongated and flattened. Within the macrocosm, subfields of qualified energy tend to have a greater range of shapes, since they are not subject to the same limitations as subfields within the microcosm.

Within the the human energy field, subfields of qualified energy can become more active and unstable (more dense and polarized) when additional CECs enter their immediate environment. Their instability will eventually cause them to migrate to one of the surface boundaries (the surface of personal body space or the surface of the auric field surrounding it) and lean up against it (see figure 6-2). If the surface texture of the subfield is sticky, which is usually a function of its density as well as the number of CECs contained within it (the more CECs and the more dense the subfield, the stickier it will be), it will either stick to the surface of the aura if it has a masculine polarity, and eventually polarize a portion of it, or it will stick to karmic sediment surrounding personal body space if it has a feminine polarity. In either case the subfield will quickly become flattened and elongated.

In the microcosm a subfield of qualified energy that is put under pressure or has migrated to a surface boundary can combine with other subfields that resonate in the same spectrum of frequencies. This process,

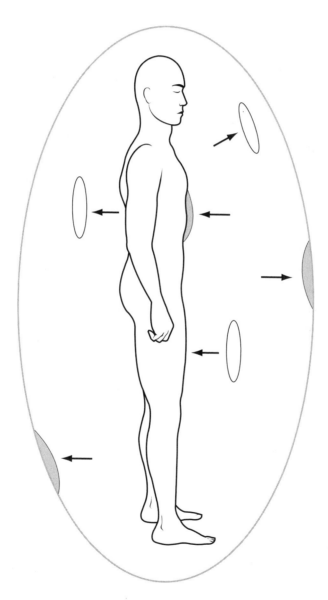

Figure 6-2 — Unstable subfields of qualified energy migrate to the surface boundaries.

known as enlargement, produces karmic sediment that is layered. Layered subfields that have been enlarged will redistribute the CECs throughout the individual layers. As a result layered subfields will have less variation in both shape and density.

Density: The density of a qualified subfield is dependent on the ratio of its size to mass. The greater the amount of qualified energy packed into the same space, the greater the subfield's density. The number of CECs contained within a subfield will also influence density. In fact, the more CECs in relationship to size, the more dense the subfield will be.

When any part of the human energy field becomes saturated with qualified subfields, space will diminish and the density of all subfields in the confined space will increase.

Subfields that have been layered will become increasingly dense (layering normally takes place in the area immediately surrounding personal body space) as more karmic sediment is deposited on top of them and they are put under increasing pressure.

Level of Activity: The level of activity displayed by a qualified subfield is directly related to the number of CECs within it, its level of polarity, and its density. The more CECs in a qualified subfield and the more polarized it has become, the more active it will be. In the external environment the ratio of size to mass is low, so the density and level of activity of subfields will be less than subfields within the internal environment. This variation can be easily explained: The size of a qualified subfield outside an enclosed space tends to expand—as a result its density decreases and it becomes less active.

In the microcosm, where the density of subfields is greater, individual subfields will have less room to expand. In fact, the more qualified subfields within one's energy field on a particular world and dimension, the greater will be their collective and individual level of activity. In contrast, once a subfield has been laid down as karmic baggage, its level of activity will decrease sharply—although its potential will remain the same—because it will be contained by the pressure exerted upon it by neighboring subfields.

It is important to recognize that attachment to the the individual mind and ego will increase the level of activity of all subfields, and the projection of qualified energy, as a controlling wave or cord, will increase the activity of the qualified subfield from which it emerges.

Polarity: The polarity of a qualified subfield will be determined by the number of CECs within it, its density level of activity, and its polar relationship to neighboring subfields. It follows that all qualitative subfields (and the CECs within them) are polarized, either masculine or feminine, to one degree or another. The more CECs of a particular gender in a subfield, the more polarized it will be.

Subfields of qualified energy that are masculine will display enhanced personal will and penetrating power (ability to penetrate the human energy field). Subfields that are feminine are less common. When they are present in small numbers, within the microcosm, they can compel their host to become more reactive and/or receptive to external subfields. When they are present in greater numbers they can manifest as an obsessive need or craving to have, own, and/or possess someone or something.

In some cases feminine subfields within the microcosm can create a charisma that will attract people to the subfield and to the person hosting it, making it possible for the host to influence people susceptible to being controlled or manipulated.

Surface Texture: The surface texture of a qualified subfield will be determined by the number of CECs within it, its density, and its level of polarity. The more CECs within a subfield, and the more dense and more polarized it is, the stickier its surface texture will be.

Tamasic subfields that are the most dense and polarized will have the stickiest surface texture. Ragistic subfields that are less dense and polarized will be less sticky, and sattvic subfields that are the least dense and the least polarized will have a smooth surface texture. The surface texture of an intrusive, qualified subfield—energy blockage, cord, controlling wave, or persona—will determine whether it will stick to independent qualified subfields and/or karmic baggage already laid down as sediment in the host's energy field.

Once a qualified subfield gets stuck, it can fold and combine with other subfields to create a complex subfield that is more dense and polarized. The complex subfield will then attract additional subfields from the macrocosm that can get stuck to qualified energy already within the host's energy field.

Color: Although qualified energy can be refracted into colors and viewed clairvoyantly, most subfields are clear and translucent. When a qualified subfield displays color, it is an indication that the subfield is inordinately dense and polarized and has a high degree of penetrating power. The most common colors displayed by subfields are black and white. Black subfields will be extremely dull and will appear to absorb light, while white subfields will appear dull, with a matte and chalky finish.

Subfields in the External Environment

In the external environment, subfields of qualified energy generally take the form of loose clouds or atmospheres, which can vary in size and shape. Although the number of CECs at the core of an external subfield may vary, it will generally be less than in qualified subfields trapped within the microcosm. Subfields in the macrocosm can vary in state, size, shape, polarity, density, level of activity, surface texture, and color. Variation in any of these qualities will depend on the number of CECs within the subfield, the mass of qualified energy contained within it, and the limiting factors imposed upon it by qualified subfields in its immediate environment.

External factors that influence the qualities of a subfield, within the macrocosm, include the proximity of one or more qualified subfields, the condition of the subfield's immediate environment (whether it is natural or man-made), and the energetic support given to the subfield by human projections.

External subfields are more commonly found in man-made environments than in natural environments. Subfields in man-made environments tend to be more dense and more highly polarized than those in natural environments. In addition, subfields in man-made environments tend to be less stable and more active, since they interact more often with human energy fields.

Qualified subfields in the external environment can linger in the same natural or man-made environment for years. From that vantage point they can disturb anyone with heightened sensitivity by interfering with their relationships or by becoming attached to them.

If an external subfield becomes highly polarized by coming into contact with another polarized energy field resonating at the same frequency, it can meander from one external environment to another or from an external environment into the internal environment of a living being.

External atmospheres can dissipate and reform as environmental conditions change. They can change state by degree, becoming more or less solid, liquid, or gaseous. In some cases subfields in the external environment can change states altogether as conditions around them change. Subfields can be partially absorbed by material in the environment if it is porous or negatively charged, and if a subfield is tamasic and its surface texture is sticky, it can get stuck to a physical surface already permeated by qualified energy.

Localized, man-made environments—particularly those that are self-contained, such as churches and concert halls—can be infested by atmospheres if and when groups of people with an inordinate amount of qualified energy in the same or similar frequencies regularly congregate within them and project qualified energy (either consciously or unconsciously) into the external environment.

Subfields located in the external environment can linger in the same place for years at a time, if left undisturbed. In such conditions the subfield may appear dormant, but no subfield is ever truly dormant. A subfield can become active and interact suddenly when a person who hosts qualified energy in the same frequency comes in contact with it.

Subfields in the Internal Environment

In the human energy field, subfields of qualified energy can be found as karmic sediment (samskaras, vasanas, and bumpy strings), energy blockages, waves, cords, and personas (as well as the human ego). If an energy body has been ejected from personal body space as a result of shock or trauma, subfields of qualified energy can intrude into personal body space as well as the central cavity of the ejected energy body (for more on shock and trauma (see chapter seventeen).

If a person has not strengthened their boundaries, fully activated their energy system, and recollected and reintegrated their energy bodies and corresponding energetic vehicles, subfields of qualified energy that have intruded into the microcosm can become integrated. Integrated subfields combine their functions to create complex subfields—in this case samskaras, vasanas, bumpy strings, and personas that function synchronistically as the individual mind and ego. Given the right conditions, the individual mind and ego can compete for dominance against the higher and lower mind and their functions and aspects.

Although the seeds of past life karma (samskaras) are carried from lifetime to lifetime, most subfields of qualified energy enter the human energy field as projections from other sentient beings in the form of cords, waves, personas, or energy blockages. This is an invasive process that begins in the womb and can continue throughout the successive stages of life as a function of vibration, polarity, and individual intent. Vibration will cause qualified energy to move, polar relationships between sentient beings will determine the direction of movement, and the intent of the people in relationships will determine the force of the energetic projection.

Once the receptive party in a polar relationship suffers an intrusion, the density, polarity, and surface texture of the intrusive energy will determine whether it becomes stuck and and then combines with other subfields to form larger, more complex subfields, which are held together by the subfields' shared polarity and mutual attraction.

The process cited above begins when subfields with the same or similar resonance combine to create complex subfields of qualified energy called "bumpy strings" (see figure 6-3, p. 99). Given enough time, bumpy strings will be compressed and laid down as sediment along the outer surface of personal body space. Once bumpy strings have been laid down as sediment they become "vasanas." Vasanas that are carried from one lifetime to another are known as "samskaras." Vasanas and samskaras that are integrated into the individual mind and ego and/or personified will become personas and will emerge into conscious awareness as a function of desire, fear, or personal will.

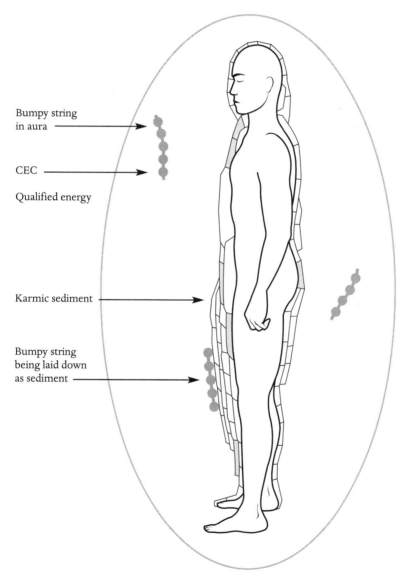

Bumpy string
in aura

CEC

Qualified energy

Karmic sediment

Bumpy string
being laid down
as sediment

Figure 6-3 — Bumpy string (qualified energy field).

Since we live in the Kali Yuga, the period in which the collective field of maya is most tamasic, it is impossible to be rid of the individual mind and ego. Nevertheless, it is possible to refine them and detach oneself from them so that they serve the Self rather than the collective will of the CECs contained within them. Subordinating the individual mind and ego to the will of the Self as it manifests through the higher and lower mind and their functions and aspects is an essential step in the process of overcoming karmic attachment.

Integrated or Independent Subfields

Subfields of qualified energy in the microcosm can be either integrated or independent. Those that have been integrated are subfields that have become part of the karmic baggage that is carried from lifetime to lifetime. Independent subfields float in the central cavity of the auric fields surrounding personal body space. They can migrate in and out of the microcosm or become integrated as a function of polarity, surface texture, or human choice and intent.

If a subfield has been integrated, it will become part of the host's karmic baggage and will create patterns of spiritual, mental, emotional, and/or physical behavior that can motivate a person to act or react by projecting fear or desire—or their variations: anxiety, terror, envy, lust, jealousy, etc.

Although independent subfields can be seen floating in the auric field on every world and dimension, including the functions and aspects of mind, independent subfields that remain in the microcosm long enough invariably become integrated by migrating to the nearest surface boundary where they are flattened against other subfields resonating at the same frequency.

Function of Qualified Energy

Although the collective field of maya has only the appearance of being real, it would be disingenuous to say that maya and the subfields of qualified energy within it don't exist, inasmuch as attachments to qualified subfields affect awareness, emotions, feelings, and even physical well-being.

In fact, subfields within the collective field of maya can cause a person to react, whether the person is conscious of it or not.

It is important to recognize, however, that reactivity is based as much—or more—on attachment to qualified subfields within the field of maya than the inherent power of the subfields themselves. The more attached one is to the collective field of maya and the qualified subfields within it (including the individual mind and ego), the more reactive one will be. In addition, it is important to note that in the Kali Yuga, the collective field of maya is more dense and polarized (tamasic) than in previous epochs, which means it interacts far more easily and more often with human beings, and more actively opposes the intent or will of the higher and lower mind.

Since the collective field of maya has become more complex in the Kali Yuga, by virtue of evolution, the subfields within it have become more active and polarized. Consequently, they can go through rapid qualitative changes as they react to changing conditions in their immediate environment. Indeed, changes in their immediate environment can trigger qualified subfields to merge and/or separate from one another. In some cases independent subfields can coalesce into one large, loose atmosphere, or break up into small, dense pools of qualified energy, as the CECs within them react independently to outside stimuli. This explains why the individual mind and ego—which is composed of qualified subfields—can change, appear ambivalent, and suffer from incessant conflict as the qualified subfields within them act and interact with each other and with qualified subfields in the external environment.

Hermetics

The interactions of qualified subfields within the collective field of maya are regulated by the principles of Hermetics. The Hermetic principles are as old as Yoga itself and, like Yoga, originated in the Kashmir Valley of India.

In the western world, legend has it that the principles were handed down to humankind by Thoth, the Egyptian god of wisdom, whom the

Greeks later called Hermes Trismegistrus. From the *Kybalian*, the most succinct compendium of Hermetic philosophy, we learn that there are seven principles: the principles of universal mind, correspondence, vibration, polarity, rhythm, cause and effect, and gender.

The Principle of Universal Mind

The first Hermetic principle, the principle of universal mind, teaches us that "The All is mind: the Universe is mental." From this principle we learn that the foundation of everything in the dualistic universe (collective field of maya) is universal consciousness, the Self. It follows, therefore, that consciousness, energy, and matter must be essentially the same, in the same way that water, ice, and steam are essentially the same. Indeed, from the analogy above we can deduce that consciousness emerging from the Self (the original cause) can be transmuted into unqualified energy, qualified energy, and/or matter, while remaining essentially the same. Applying this to the microcosm, it follows that regardless of how much karmic baggage one carries and how attached one has become to the external world of maya, the condition of one's energy field can be transmuted (fundamentally changed) because the foundation of everything including karmic baggage is universal consciousness. Indeed, by centering in the Self and functioning through the higher and lower mind and their functions and aspects, one can transmute their condition into one where bliss, power, and Self-knowledge overcome attachment to the world of maya and the qualified subfields within it.

The Principle of Correspondence

The second Hermetic principle, the principle of correspondence, teaches us that "As above, so below; as below, so above." From this principle we learn that the same principles regulate the transmission and transmutation of qualified energy at all times, on all phenomenal worlds and dimensions, including the physical-material world.

It naturally follows, therefore, that all nonphysical beings must abide by the same principles as creatures on earth. Since all physical beings are motivated by their own personal agendas and an instinct to survive, and all physical beings have an individual mind and ego, it follows that all nonphysical beings, regardless of where they exist, must have an individual mind and ego and must be motivated by their own personal agendas and instinct to survive. The only exceptions to this rule are enlightened men and women, bodhisatvas and avatara. Though these beings exist on the physical-material plane, they have two things in common that make them different. They have transcended attachment to the individual mind and ego, and they are consciously aware of their union with the Self.

From the principle of correspondence we also learn that all subfields of qualified energy (including qualified subfields and CECs) can be released using the same methods based on the same fundamental principles. This means that the techniques that you will learn and practice in this book will be effective on all worlds and dimensions of the phenomenal universe.

The Principle of Vibration

The third Hermetic principle, the principle of vibration, teaches us that "Nothing rests; everything moves; everything vibrates." From this principle we learn that the differences between one subfield of qualified energy and another can be accounted for by differences in their individual frequencies or resonance. It also explains that everything that vibrates, including subfields of qualified energy, must have a characteristic rate of vibration (resonance) that is its unique mark. Since each qualified subfield has is own specific resonance, which can mimic or counterfeit one or more functions of the higher and lower mind and their functions and aspects, it follows that a qualified subfield that has become integrated in the individual mind and ego can usurp the activities of the higher and lower mind and their functions and aspects.

In addition, the principle of vibration accounts for discernment, which is the ability to distinguish the resonance of a qualified subfield by scanning it for variations in state, density, polarity, and level of activity—all of which are a function of the subfield's resonance or mean frequency.

The principle of vibration also explains how the mental attention, intent, and prana (which are essential elements of the higher and lower mind) in their various forms can be used to diagnose and release a subfield of qualified energy (karmic baggage), regardless of the subfield's mean frequency or location.

The Principle of Polarity

The principle of polarity teaches us that "Everything is dual; everything has poles; everything has its pair of opposites; like and unlike are the same. Opposites are identical in nature, but different in degree; extremes meet." This principle explains that all qualified subfields, regardless of where they are located, manifest qualities within a larger spectrum of qualified energy, and that, given the right environmental influences, the qualities of a subfield can shift from one end of the spectrum to another. In fact, a qualified subfield can shift from one state to another, become larger or smaller, more or less dense, more or less active, and more or less polarized, as well as more or less masculine or feminine.

The principle of polarity also explains, and in some cases predicts, the effects and consequences of appropriate and inappropriate activity in the microcosm and the macrocosm. Appropriate activity emerges from the higher and lower mind and their functions and aspects, and will keep one centered in unqualified energy so that one is no longer subject to the principle of polarity. Inappropriate activity emerges from the individual mind and ego, and compels one to react to qualified subfields in both the microcosm and the macrocosm by becoming more or less polarized, more or less active, and more or less dense, and so forth.

In addition, the principle of polarity teaches that universal consciousness (the Self) and human beings (which emerge from the Self) exist within the same energetic spectrum and are therefore essentially the same. As the analogy points out, individual poles—in this case human beings and the Self—differ from each other only in degree. Both the Self and each human being, regardless of their spiritual development, partake of the same essential essence or nature, which is consciousness and prana.

". . . He (the Self) is the eye of eyes, the ear of ears, the speech of speech, the mind of mind, the life among the living, the wise one knows that all are His and in vain are all vanities" (*Kenopanisad*, 17).

The Principle of Rhythm

The fifth Hermetic principle, the principle of rhythm, teaches us that "Everything flows out and in; everything has its tides; all things rise and fall; the pendulum swing manifests in everything; the measure of the swing to the right is the measure of the swing to the left; rhythm compensates." From the principle of rhythm we learn that within the dualistic universe energy continuously ebbs and flows, which means the balance between the extremes is constantly in flux. This explains why one day you're happy but the next day you're not, why one day you feel full of vitality and the next day you don't. In the qualified world of maya there is a natural rhythm to everything and this rhythm constantly changes by degree as it evolves through linear-sequential time.

The fifth hermetic principle also explains why intimacy and bliss can never be manifest in the qualified world of maya via the activities of the individual mind and ego. To achieve a state of intimacy and bliss it is necessary, at least temporarily, to transcend the principle of rhythm. This means transcending the rhythmic changes that take place in the qualified world of maya, and the attachment to the individual mind and ego that counterfeit the manifestations of consciousness and prana, which are unchanging, and that emerge through the higher and lower mind and their functions and aspects.

The Principle of Cause and Effect

The sixth Hermetic principle teaches us that "Every cause has its effect; every effect has its cause; everything happens according to the law; chance is but a name for law not recognized; there are many planes of causation, but nothing escapes the law."

The principle of cause and effect explains what healers and metaphysicians have known for centuries—that treating the symptoms will not heal the disease. It also explains that to find the cause of disease, a healer must trace the chain of cause and effect back to its roots, which can be found on the dimensions of energy and consciousness.

Cause and effect is the fundamental principle behind energy work: if there are tangible symptoms such as pain, emotional suffering, relationship problems, and/or physical disease, the healer must trace these symptoms back through the chain of cause and effect to their root and then remove the karmic baggage and/or qualified subfield that has disrupted the synchronistic function of the human energy system and the vertical integration of the energy bodies and their corresponding energetic vehicles.

In addition, the principle of cause and effect explains that there is no magic on the physical-material dimension or on the worlds and dimensions of the higher and lower mind. This means that nothing happens by accident. There are no victims or villains. Each person is ultimately responsible for their condition, since all events and activities in the dualistic world are caused by the interaction of qualified subfields.

The Principle of Gender

The seventh Hermetic principle teaches us that "Gender is in everything; everything has its masculine and feminine principles; gender manifests on all planes."

Since life is predicated on the principle of gender, each individual creature, and, therefore, each person is born gender specific, either male or female. This gender orientation is a powerful influence. To a large degree it determines how a person will respond physically and energetically to the external world (the macrocosm), and how the world will respond to them. In fact, gender orientation and the polarity it creates between masculine and feminine forces is the preeminent cause of attraction and repulsion between human beings in relationship.

In addition, gender orientation affects the balance of polarity in the human energy field. If an individual is centered in their individual mind and ego, they will try to balance their specific gender orientation by seeking relationship with someone or something—either a person, creature, object, or concept—from the external environment. The more extreme their gender orientation and the polarity it creates, the more extreme the solution a person must achieve through relationship in order to attain balance. Inordinately masculine beings will seek an inordinately feminine solution, which is often an extremely receptive partner. An inordinately feminine person will seek an inordinately masculine solution, often an extremely assertive partner.

Gender balance remains a lifelong issue for most people. In fact, it is a problem without a permanent solution, since the polarity of karmic baggage is constantly changing as qualified subfields are added to or subtracted from the human energy field, and rhythmic shifts in polarity occur. Indeed, given enough time, each human being will discover that only by transcending the individual mind and ego and the collective field of maya will they achieve a permanent solution to the problem of gender and balance.

Chapter Seven

. . . the sole necessity for Self-Realization is purity of mind. The only impurity of the mind is thought. To make it thought-free is to keep it pure.

—Tripura Rahasya, 124

The Kali Yuga

Although there has never been a time when the collective field of maya and the subfields of qualified energy within it did not exist, the quantity, quality, and level of activity, as well as the intrusive force exerted by subfields, can vary. Variation in the quality and quantity of qualified energy and the force it exerts (penetrating power) as it intrudes into human affairs has been the subject of religious myth and literature for untold generations.

It is interesting to note that for the greater part of human history, the collective field of maya has been, and continues to be, out of balance with a higher proportion of evil than good, dark than light, or, as Tantrics and Yogis prefer to say, a higher proportion of tamasic energy than less dense ragistic and sattvic energy. In regard to this period (the Kali Yuga), the new testament declares "For nation will rise up against nation, and kingdom against kingdom, and in various places there will be famines and earthquakes . . . And at that time many will fall away and will deliver up one another and hate one another and because lawlessness increased,

most people's love will grow cold" (Matthew 24:7, 24:10, 24:12). In the
Shiva Puranas, an ancient Hindu text, we read "At the advent of the terri-
ble age of Kali men have become devoid of merits. They are engaged in
evil ways of life. They have turned their faces from truthful avocations . . .
They view the physical body as the soul, deluded as they are; they are
atheists of mere brutish sense; they hate their parents . . . they are slaves
to lust" (*Shiva Puranas,* 1:12, 1:14).

An increase in the quantity and density of qualified subfields, particularly those carried as karmic sediment, can make it increasingly difficult
for one to act appropriately and follow one's individual dharma. In fact,
by disrupting boundaries and inhibiting access to the pleasure, joy, intimacy, and/or bliss, dense, highly polarized qualified energy can disrupt
human affairs and relationships, and create an environment that promotes fear and suffering .

The quantity and quality of qualified energy—whether it is tamasic,
ragistic, or sattvic—can vary from one epoch to another (one yuga to
another), but it is important to note that the more dense and highly
polarized the subfields of qualified energy that intrude into human
affairs, the darker the affairs of humanity become.

Hindu mythology teaches that humankind has lived through three
yugas already: the Satya, Treta, and Dvapara. In the Satya yuga, also
known as the golden age of humankind, the collective field of maya was
primarily sattvic, which was reflected in the human condition. Human
beings lived long lives, centered in the higher and lower mind, and experienced, with virtually no interruption, the pleasure, love, intimacy, and
joy that emerged from the Self, but in each succeeding yuga the collective
field of maya become more dense. Pleasure, love, intimacy, and joy
diminished and people found it increasingly difficult to remain centered
in the higher and lower mind. In the Treta Yuga known as the silver age,
spiritual awareness decreased by 25 percent. By the Dvapara Yuga it had
decreased by 50 percent, and in the Kali Yuga, it had decreased by 75 percent. This decline in spiritual awareness is easily explained by the buildup
of dense qualified energy in the collective field of maya and the individual mind and ego.

In the present yuga the increase in dense qualified energy has been so dramatic that even enlightened beings, though completely detached from the individual mind and ego, have been unable to shed the ego completely. The great Indian master Ramakrishna declared "In the Kaliyuga it is difficult to have the feeling, 'I am not the body, I am not the mind . . . I am beyond pleasure and pain. I am above disease and grief, old age and death'" (*Gospel of Ramakrishna*, 172).

The effects of the Kali Yuga have become even more pronounced in the west since the seventeenth century. Since then, thinking and the pursuit of knowledge has been dominated by Cartesian thought. The crux of Descartes' method was called radical doubt. His method was analytic, based exclusively on the concepts formulated by the individual mind and ego that arranged phenomena in logical order so that they could be analyzed. "There is nothing included in the concept of body," he wrote, "that belongs to the mind and nothing in the mind that belongs to the body" (Descartes *cogito*).

The Cartesian perspective that elevated the functions of the individual mind and ego above those of the higher and lower mind and their functions and aspects has been largely responsible for the development of the scientific method, which as we know has meant a world-wide technological explosion over the past two centuries.

Nevertheless, we can now see that it has been the mode of perception (sensory perception, understanding, and the judgment of the individual mind and ego) championed by Descartes that has had a catastrophic effect on people living in modern technological cultures, inasmuch as it has taught them to be aware of themselves as isolated egos existing within physical bodies, but in some critical way separated from them. As a consequence of this unnatural juxtaposition, entire generations of people, particularly in the west, have grown up alienated from themselves and the hierarchy of worlds and dimensions on which they exist and function.

Karma is Your Roadmap

For the vast majority of people it is identification with the individual mind and ego, which have grown increasingly tamasic in the Kali Yuga, that has attached them to the collective field of maya and obstructed their access to their higher and lower mind. In the process of overcoming karma it is essential to center oneself in the higher and lower mind, and to discern the unique resonance of each world and dimension within it. It is also essential to discern the qualities of qualified subfields that combine to create the individual mind and ego so that it becomes possible to distinguish one subfield from another, and qualified subfields from the fields of unqualified energy that compose the higher and lower mind and their functions and aspects.

By mastering the skills presented here, known collectively as "scanning," you will be developing the mental attention as an effective tool, and by combining the mental attention with the intent of the higher and lower mind and then adding the appropriate prana, you will be able to discern variations in pitch between the worlds and dimensions of the higher and lower mind, as well as the unique qualities of qualified subfields that compose the individual mind and ego.

It is important to remember that when you use the mental attention as a tool for discernment, you won't be fixing your mind on the object of your attention while closing yourself off to everything else, which is the technique you use in concentration. Instead, you will be centering yourself in the higher and lower mind by centering yourself in unqualified energy. Then you will enjoy the object of your attention while letting everything else move through your field of awareness without becoming distracted or attached to it.

To center yourself in the higher mind and to use the mental attention as a tool for discernment, you must first activate the back of the heart chakra and then center yourself there. You mastered these skills in chapter three, and you may want to review them before you proceed.

In this chapter you will develop your discernment by building on those skills, but before you proceed take note: it is important to keep your attention singular, so that you're not paying attention from the higher and lower mind while you are watching what you're doing with the individual mind and ego. This is a common mistake called "splitting the ego," and it should be scrupulously avoided while you perfect your ability to scan energy fields in the higher and lower mind and the collective field of maya.

The Mental Attention

The mental attention functions simultaneously on all worlds and dimensions in both the microcosm and the macrocosm. It can be transmuted from state to state and can be split into as many parts as necessary. With the addition of prana it can be formed into different shapes, moved in any direction, or held fixed at one point, with or without conscious effort or attention.

The mental attention is linked to the functions and aspects of mind and the centers of consciousness within the human energy field that enables it to locate, observe, and discern the unique resonance and/or quality of whatever enters its field of awareness.

With the intent as a guide, the mental attention can isolate what it observes from its environment so that it can be examined. When used to scan an organ of the human energy system (auric boundary, auric cavity, surface of an energy body, etc.), it can discern both the organ's location and condition. In the case of a qualified subfield it can be used to discern location, state, size, shape, density, polarity, level of activity, surface texture, and color.

The Intent

The intent serves the same function in the higher and lower mind as a software program does in a computer. Software programs function by instructing a computer to perform a particular task or series of tasks. The intent functions in the same way by programming the higher and lower mind to perform a particular task or a series of tasks. In the case of scanning, the intent will program the higher and lower mind to become aware on a particular world and dimension and to scan a particular field, organ, or subfield of qualified energy to the exclusion of everything else.

The intent is composed of three elements: class, type, and location.

Class: Class designates the class of work to be performed during the procedure. In this case the class of work to be performed will be a scan. Other classifications of work that can be performed include releasing (qualified subfields), recollecting (energy bodies), reintegrating (energy bodies), and activating (chakras and minor energy centers).

Type: Type designates the type of structure or object to be scanned, released, activated, recollected, and/or reintegrated. Included in this category are samskaras, vasanas, bumpy strings, cords, controlling waves, atmospheres, personas, independent blockages, the surface of personal body space, the surface of an energy body, the surface of the aura, the internal cavity of an aura, the internal cavity of an energy body, or corresponding energetic vehicle, etc.

Location: Location designates the specific local, world, dimension, or field of activity, and/or organ of the human energy system, energy body, or corresponding energetic vehicle where the work will take place—personal body space, aura, energy body, etc.

If your class is scan, type is bumpy string, and the location of the bumpy string is the world of soul, the level of the fourth chakra, your intent would be "It's my intent to scan for bumpy strings, in the auric field, in the world of soul, on the level of the fourth chakra."

Setting the intent is a two-part process. Before you begin you designate your intent, and after you've centered yourself in the back of your heart chakra you set your intent. Some people have found it useful to write down their intent when they designate it, and when it's time to set it, read it aloud.

Combining the Intent with the Mental Attention

In the exercises below you will combine your intent with the mental attention first by designating your intent and then by setting it. In each exercise you will find a comfortable position with your back straight, designate your intent, and use the standard method to relax. Then you will activate the back of your heart chakra, center yourself there, and after splitting your attention and activating the front of the heart chakra, you will set your intent. After your intent has been set you will remain centered in the back of your heart chakra for ten minutes. When ten minutes have passed, you will count from one to five and bring yourself out of the meditation.

Exercise 1: In this exercise you will prepare to scan the surface of personal body space in the world or the lower mind, level of the heart chakra: Designate your intent, relax, and center yourself in the higher mind. Then set your intent and remain centered in the back of your heart chakra for ten minutes. After ten minutes count from one to five and bring yourself out of the meditation.

Exercise 2: In this exercise you will prepare to scan the surface of personal body space in the world of spirit, on the level of the first chakra.

Exercise 3: In this exercise you will prepare to look inward (into personal body space) in the world of soul, on the level of the sixth chakra.

Exercise 4: In this exercise you will prepare to look inward (into personal body space) in the world of the intellect, on the level of the seventh chakra.

Exercise 5: In this exercise you will prepare to scan the auric field in the world of the lower mind, on the level of the second chakra.

The Second Attention with Emphasis

Another essential step in the process of scanning is shifting emphasis to the second attention. Once you've designated your intent, and activated and centered yourself in the back of your heart chakra, it will be necessary to split your attention in order to perform a scan, or engage in any useful work. You already learned to split your attention when you activated the seven traditional chakras in personal body space (see chapter five). In this chapter you're going to build on that skill by shifting your emphasis from the first attention, the back of your heart chakra, to the second attention that can be projected anywhere that useful work such as scanning can be performed.

When your attention was undivided and kept solely on the back of the heart chakra, emphasis wasn't an issue because your attention and your emphasis emerged from the same point. Once you split your attention, however, the issue of emphasis becomes an important one because it is only from the point of emphasis that useful work can be performed. This means that when your emphasis emerges from the back of your heart chakra, you can project prana from the back of the heart chakra and focus the mental attention from the back of the heart chakra, but as long as the emphasis remains centered in the back of the heart chakra no work such as scanning can be performed anywhere else.

Once you've split your attention, however, and your emphasis emerges from the second attention, work can be performed anywhere where the second attention has been projected. In fact, whenever emphasis emerges from the second attention, the second attention becomes an extension of the higher and lower mind, in the same way that in microscopic surgery the camera and surgical tools controlled by the joy stick and manipulated by the surgeon become an extension of the doctor's eyes and hands.

Indeed, once emphasis emerges from the second attention a skilled practitioner can scan (in combination with other skills) the organs of the human energy system and the energy bodies and energetic vehicles of the higher and lower mind to determine their location and condition. Likewise, one can scan subfields of qualified energy to determine their qualities and by tracing their resonance to their source determine their point of origin.

Shifting Emphasis

To shift your emphasis to your second attention, you must first activate and center yourself in the back of your heart chakra. Then you can split your attention, project your second attention to another location, and bring your emphasis to it.

In the exercise below you will activate and center yourself in the back of your heart chakra. Then you will split your attention and project your second attention into the world of soul, level of the fourth chakra, to a position on the surface of personal body space that corresponds to your solar plexus. Once you've split your attention you will shift your emphasis from your first attention (at the back of your heart chakra) to your second attention. After five minutes, you will return your emphasis to the back of the heart chakra and remain centered there. Then you will release the second attention, and after counting from one to five, you will bring yourself out of the meditation.

Since you won't be doing any work you need not designate your intent. Instead, you will assert the appropriate intent as you proceed from one part of the exercise to another.

To begin, find a comfortable position with your back straight. Then use the standard method to relax and balance conscious and unconscious mental activity. To continue, state "It is my intent to activate the back of my heart chakra." Then say "It is my intent to center myself in the back of my heart chakra." Once you're centered in the the back of your heart chakra, state "It is my intent to split my attention and project my second attention into the world of soul, level of the fourth chakra, to a position on the surface of personal body space that corresponds to my solar plexus." Then state "It is my intent to shift my emphasis to my second attention." Take five minutes to experience the shift of emphasis. Then shift your emphasis to the back of the heart chakra and release the second attention by stating, "It is my intent to shift my emphasis to the back of my heart chakra and to release my second attention." Then count from one to five. When you reach the number five, open your eyes. You will feel wide awake, perfectly relaxed, and better than you did before.

You can develop your skill by practicing the two exercises below.

Exercise 1: Center yourself in the back of your heart chakra, split your attention, and project your second attention to the surface of personal body space in the world of intellect, level of the fourth chakra, to a position that corresponds to your chin. Then shift your emphasis from your first attention to your second attention. Take five minutes to experience the shift of emphasis. Then bring your emphasis to the back of your heart chakra, release your second attention, and count from one to five. When you reach the number five, open your eyes. You will feel wide awake, perfectly relaxed, and better than you did before.

Exercise 2: Center yourself in the back of your heart chakra. Then split your attention and project your second attention to the surface of your auric field in the world of spirit, level of the fifth chakra, to a position that corresponds to your abdomen. Then shift your emphasis from your first to your second attention. Take five minutes to experience the shift of emphasis. Then bring your emphasis to the back of your heart chakra, release your second attention, and count from one to five to bring yourself out of the meditation.

The Power of Prana

In the process of scanning it will be necessary to combine the mental attention and intent with prana—otherwise the mental attention will remain fixed in position (consciousness is by nature static). Although there are several sources of prana—the incoming and outgoing pranas, the kundalini-shakti, the aprana, and the chakras—to observe a field of energy by scanning it, particularly qualified subfields, it is most efficient to use the prana entering the human energy field on each inhalation.

With the help of the intent and mental attention, the prana entering on each inhalation can be directed to any position where the second attention has been projected. What's more, because of its inherent flexibility the inhaled prana can be used to move the mental attention smoothly and precisely from one position to another.

By providing power, prana permits you to perform several important tasks while scanning. It allows you to move the mental attention smoothly in any direction. It allows you to shape the mental attention into a tool that you can use to discern the qualities or the particular pitch emerging from the energy field or organ being scanned. It provides you with the power to move your mental attention and any scanning tool you construct through dense atmospheres or push aside obstructions of qualified energy if necessary. Finally, it creates a pool of unqualified energy surrounding the mental attention that will prevent qualified energy from interfering with your scan.

Combining the Mental Attention with Prana

Although the mental attention can be moved from one fixed position to another by repeatedly releasing it and then projecting it to a new location, this kind of jumpy movement is not suitable for scanning because it's not fluid. It is prana that gives the mental attention the fluidity it needs to move smoothly from one point to another. Like a locomotive that can either push or pull a train, prana can be used to push or pull the mental attention smoothly and precisely from one position to another.

Once the mental attention has been split, the practitioner will breathe into the point where the second attention has been projected. The prana that enters with each inhalation will then push or pull the mental attention through the human energy field or the desired external energy field—up and down, in and out, or from side to side. In fact, as one becomes more skilled, the incoming prana can be used to guide the mental attention in any direction one chooses.

Moving the Mental Attention

In the exercise below you will combine the mental attention and intent with prana and move it from one position to another in the world of intellect, level of the third chakra, starting at a point on the surface of personal body space corresponding to the right elbow. There will be no designated intent in this exercise. Instead, you will assert your intent as you proceed from one part of the exercise to another.

To begin, find a comfortable position with your back straight. Then use the standard method to relax and balance conscious and unconscious mental activity. When you are ready, activate and center yourself in the back of your heart chakra. Then split your attention and activate the front of your heart chakra. Once it is active, look inward on the world of the intellect, level of the heart chakra.

Continue by splitting your attention and projecting your second attention to a point on the surface of personal body space corresponding to the right elbow, in the world of intellect, level of the third chakra. Once you've completed these steps simply breathe into your second attention, and every time you inhale prana will be directed to your second attention.

As soon as you've combined prana with your mental attention, the area corresponding to your right elbow will vibrate and become warm. Take a moment to enjoy the shift, then bring your emphasis to your second attention in your right elbow by stating "It is my intent to shift my emphasis to my second attention." Then state "It is my intent to move my second attention upward to my right shoulder." You can control the speed of your second attention by pulling the breath upward more slowly or more quickly.

Once your second attention has reached your right shoulder, use prana emerging during your exhalation to push your mental attention back to the right elbow. When you're finished, switch to the left arm and repeat the process.

When you've completed the process shift your emphasis to the back of your heart chakra and release your second attention. Then take ten minutes to enjoy the meditation. After ten minutes count from one to five. When you reach the number five, open your eyes. You will feel wide awake, perfectly relaxed, and better than you did before.

You can develop your skill by practicing the same technique in the worlds and dimensions listed below.

- Project your second attention into the world of the lower mind, level of the second chakra, and push the mental attention from your right palm to your right elbow.

- Project your second attention into the world of spirit, level of the fifth chakra, and pull the mental attention from your left palm to your left elbow.

- Project your second attention into the world of intellect, level of the seventh chakra, and pull the mental attention from the sole of your right foot to your right knee.

- Project your second attention into the world of soul, level of the third chakra, and push the mental attention from your chin to the top of your forehead.

- Project your second attention into the world of the lower mind, level of the first chakra, and push the mental attention from the left side of your waist, across the back, to the right side of your waist.

Creating a Scanning Tool

In order to successfully conduct a scan in either the microcosm or the macrocosm, it will be necessary to create a scanning tool. You can create a scanning tool using a combination of the intent and the mental attention.

A scanning tool must be simple, flexible, easy to move, and simple to construct. The most efficient tool will be thin, narrow, and longer than it is wide. It will have a smooth surface with a narrow blunt edge that tapers at each end (see figure 7-1). Once you have these characteristics in mind and you know where the scanning tool will be used, you can state, "It is my intent to create a scanning tool." Instantly, as a function of the intent and the higher and lower mind, a scanning tool will appear at the location you designated, with the exact characteristics you require to successfully perform the scan.

Once you've completed your scan, you can release your scanning tool by stating "It is my intent to release my scanning tool."

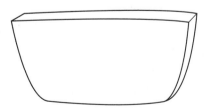

Figure 7-1 — A scanning tool.

In each exercise where a scan will be conducted, a scanning tool will be created after the second attention has been projected to the designated area. Once you've created a scanning tool, it will take the place of the second attention and will be combined with the appropriate prana and your emphasis to perform the scan. After you've created a scanning tool it won't be necessary to create it again unless you wish to change its characteristics. Each time you wish to conduct a scan you will only have to state "It is my intent to conduct a scan (on a particular world and dimension)," and your scanning tool will appear in the appropriate location.

Scanning in the World of Spirit

In the following exercise you will scan the surface of personal body space in the world of spirit on the level of the fourth chakra. The scan will be conducted in the front of personal body space in the area between the first and fifth chakras. You will expand your mental attention into a broad, thin scanning tool and will make up and down overlapping motions, starting at a position that corresponds to your left shoulder. As you move from left to right you will become aware of any dimpling or general weakness which has distorted the surface of your energy bodies in personal body space on this level. You will also notice, even though it was not included in your intent, any qualified energy such as intrusions, cords and/or controlling waves that have intruded through the surface of personal body space or interfered with its function.

To begin find a comfortable position with your back straight. Your designated intent for this exercise will be: "It's my intent to scan the surface of personal body space in the world of spirit, level of the fourth chakra." When you're ready to continue use the standard method to relax and balance conscious and unconscious mental activity. Then activate and center yourself in the back of your heart chakra. Take a moment to enjoy the shift you experience. Then split your attention and activate the front of your heart chakra. As soon as the front of the chakra is active set your intent and assert, "It's my intent to look inward on the world of spirit, level of the fourth chakra." Continue by stating, "It is my intent to split my attention and to project my second attention to the world of the spirit, level of the fourth chakra, at a point corresponding to my left shoulder." Bring your emphasis to your second attention by asserting, "It's my intent to project my emphasis to my second attention." Then create a scanning tool by stating "It is my intent to create a scanning tool." As soon as the scanning tool appears, begin making up and down overlapping motions along the surface of personal body space from your shoulder to your waist. Once you've completed your scan mentally record your findings, then release your scanning tool. Return your emphasis to the back of your heart chakra and release your second attention.

Then count from one to five. When you reach the number five, open your eyes. You will feel wide awake, perfectly relaxed, and better than you did before.

Scanning the Auric Field

In the following exercise you will scan a portion of your auric field in the world of soul, level of the fourth chakra. The auric field on this level will extend about eighteen inches (forty-eight centimeters) from the surface of personal body space. When it is functioning healthfully it will be egg-shaped, smooth, and taut along its entire surface. If there has been an inordinate build-up of karmic baggage and/or the intrusion of cords, controlling waves, or foreign energy bodies, you will find that the surface of the aura has become dimpled and its shape distorted.

In your scan you will be looking for any distortion along the surface of the aura, including dimpling and changes in texture. Changes in texture include bumpiness, stickiness and/or a lack of resilience. You will also be scanning for karmic sediment and/or cords that may be intruding or leaning up against the surface of the aura from the inside of the field.

When you're ready to begin find a comfortable position with your back straight. Your designated intent for this exercise will be: "It is my intent to scan the outer surface of the auric field, in the world of the soul, level of the fourth chakra."

Use the standard method to relax and balance conscious and unconscious mental activity. Then activate and center yourself in the back of your heart chakra. Take a moment to enjoy the shift in consciousness. Then split your attention, activate the front of your heart chakra, and set your intent. Once you've set your intent look inward in the world of soul, level of the fourth chakra. Then split your attention once again and project your second attention into the world of soul, level of the fourth chakra, to a point on the outside surface of your auric field by your left shoulder. Shift your emphasis to your second attention and create or activate your scanning tool. Then begin making up and down overlapping strokes from left to right along the outer surface of auric field from your shoulder down to your waist. As you proceed mentally record your findings.

When you've completed your scan release your scanning tool. Return your emphasis to the back of your heart chakra and release your second attention. Then count from one to five. When you reach the number five, open your eyes. You will feel wide awake, perfectly relaxed, and better than you did before.

Scanning for Qualified Subfields

In the exercise below you will scan for independent energy blockages in the world of the lower mind, level of the third chakra.

Take note: when scanning qualified subfields (samskaras, vasanas, bumpy strings, independent blockages, cords and controlling waves), particularly those destined to be released, it is advisable to state the guna as part of your intent. By including the guna in your intent you will isolate subfields with specific qualities from other subfields in their immediate environment.

In this scan your designated intent will be, "It is my intent to scan for tamasic, independent blockages in the world of the lower mind, level of the third chakra, in the auric field facing me."

Use the standard method to relax and balance conscious and unconscious mental activity. Then activate and center yourself in the back of your heart chakra. Take a moment to enjoy the shift in consciousness.

Then split your attention, activate the front of your heart chakra, and set your intent. Continue by stating "It is my intent to look inward on the world of the lower mind, level of the third chakra, tamasic." Then say "It is my intent to split my attention and project my second attention to the world of the lower mind, level of the third chakra, tamasic, in the auric field by my left shoulder." Shift your emphasis to your second attention and create or activate your scanning tool. Then begin making up and down overlapping strokes from left to right within your auric field from your shoulder down to your waist.

Independent energy blockages will be easy to locate since they float freely in the auric fields on all worlds and dimensions. When you locate an independent energy blockage scan it for state, size, shape, density, polarity, level of activity, and surface texture.

Once you've completed your scan and recorded your findings, release your scanning tool and return your emphasis to the back of your heart chakra. Then release your second attention and count from one to five. When you reach the number five, open your eyes. You will feel wide awake, perfectly relaxed, and better than you did before.

You can develop your skills by practicing the same technique in the worlds and dimensions listed below.

1. Scan for independent blockages in the world of soul, level of the third chakra, tamasic.

2. Scan the surface of your aura in the world of spirit, level of the sixth chakra.

3. Scan the surface of personal body space in the world of soul, level of the first chakra.

4. Scan for independent blockages in the world of intellect, level of the seventh chakra, tamasic.

5. Scan the surface of your aura in the world of the lower mind, level of the first chakra.

Your own Self is your master; who else could be? With yourself well controlled, you gain a master very hard to find.

—Dhammapada, 12:160

Conscious Energy Concentrations

At the core of all qualified subfields in both the macrocosm and the microcosm are conscious energy concentrations, referred to as CECs. CECs are nonphysical beings, entities that exist in the collective field of maya and in all subfields of qualified energy. In the external environment they can be found in atmospheres, pools, and waves. In the human energy field they can be found in karmic sediment (samskaras and vasanas), bumpy strings, personas, energy blockages, cords, controlling waves, and independent blockages. In addition, large numbers are concentrated in the ego and within intrusions—intrusions are qualified subfields that intrude into personal body space after an energetic vehicle has been ejected. In extreme cases CECs can be found within energy bodies and energetic vehicles that have been ejected from personal body space, and have been contaminated by subfields of qualified energy.

CECs emerged into the phenomenal universe eons ago by way of the tattvas, along with the collective field of maya. They can be found in every world and dimension, including the world of spirit, intellect, soul, lower mind, the world of the chakras, the splenic levels, and the functions and aspects of mind.

At the present time (the Kali Yuga), CECs numbers far exceed the number of living creatures that exist in the physical-material universe.

Shamans in traditional cultures, aware that the universe was animate and trained to be more discerning than people living in advanced technological cultures, called CECs names such as spirits, elementals, nymphs, sprites, fairies, entities, spirit guides, angels, demons, etc., and classified them based on their disposition toward human beings.

For shamans and indigenous people in traditional cultures, there was a spirit in the mountain, a spirit in the stream, a spirit of love, a spirit of hate, etc., all of which were alive and interacted with each other as well as with human beings via the human energy field and the functions and aspects of mind. In one way or another traditional people incorporated these spirits or CECs into their religion, and strove to accommodate them through sacrifice, ritual, and petitionary prayer.

In Christian circles, particularly in the patriarchal cultures of Europe and the Middle East, CECs were viewed quite differently. Like traditional people, early Christians recognized that CECs could penetrate the human energy field and could then influence a human being's character and subsequent behavior. In response, Christians, like the Hebrews before them, held firmly to a dualistic cosmology with two hierarchies of non-physical beings that competed with one another for dominance. The first hierarchy was under a personal God called Jehovah (*Ishvara* in Sanskrit), the second was under the control of an oppressive male deity, called Satan, who opposed Jehovah and strove to dominate mankind. Though they acknowledged that CECs could trap a human being in the phenomenal universe, both Hebrew and Christian clerics failed to realize that good and evil were two sides of the same coin and that CECs in both hierarchies could prevent a person from accessing the pleasure, intimacy, joy, and bliss that emerge from the Self, the original *cause* who, unlike both Jehovah or Satan, existed outside the world of duality.

In contrast, eastern religions, such as Hinduism, Jainism, Buddhism, and Tantra viewed all CECs as manifestations of the same female principle, regardless of their disposition toward humankind. These religions recognized through direct experience that CECs emerged from the collective field of maya and were an essential part of the ecology of the phenomenal universe. They also acknowledged that CECs, like all life forms—with the exception of avatars, bodhisatvas, and enlightened masters—have an individual mind, ego, and the will to fulfill their individual needs.

Yoga, which is a system of personal development rather than a religion, never saw CECs as essentially good or evil. Instead, the masters of Yoga treated CECs as vittri or chitti, field modifications and mind stuff, which were a product of maya and the individual mind and ego. Rather than investing them with the qualities of living creatures, as shamans and clerics had done, they viewed CECs as concentrations of energy with particular qualities that were either tamasic, ragistic, or sattvic.

Whether you choose to demonize CECs, sanctify them, or view them yogically as vittri and chitta, the fact remains that at the core of every qualified subfield is one or more CEC, and although the cognitive ability of CECs, as well as their ability to act and express themselves, is severely limited in comparison to the wide spectrum enjoyed by human beings, CECs do have individual will, a form of finite consciousness, rudimentary emotions and feelings, and the ability to express these qualities through time-space on the world and dimension on which they exist.

Although CECs emerge from the collective field of maya, diverse spiritual traditions agree that CECs are at the root of many of humanity's most intransigent problems. Foremost in the long list of crimes charged against CECs is the original and ongoing act of separating mankind from universal consciousness. Although on their own CECs cannot separate a human being from the Self, one must identify with the CECs in their energy field for that to happen. They can penetrate the human energy field, restrict the flow of prana, and effectively veil the effluence of the Self.

CECs intrude into the human energy field, not out of malice, but in an effort to experience the radiance (prana) that emerges from the Self, without submitting to the Self through self-sacrifice and surrender. Like moths, they are attracted to the light (emerging from the Self), yet they refuse to submit their individual will to the source of the light.

In spite of their apparent crimes against humanity it is important to recognize that CECs are an essential part of the ecology of the phenomenal universe. As each world and dimension emerged via the tattvas, so did the myriad of nonphysical beings that inhabit the collective field of maya.

CECs and Subtle Forms of Life

All living beings that exist in the the collective field of maya are composed of the three elements necessary for life: consciousness, energy, and subtle matter. Indeed, it has never been a prerequisite for life to be clothed in a physical-material body in order to exist and display all the qualities of a living being.

On all worlds and dimensions within the collective field of maya, nonphysical life exists in profusion. On these planes life must abide by the same principles as life on the physical-material plane. Indeed, since life on the higher and lower planes is composed of qualified energy in various combinations, like their physical-material counterparts, CECs must be either predominantly sattvic, ragistic, or tamasic.

Nonphysical beings (CECs) that are primarily sattvic are the least dense and active, and have the least impact on human health, personality, and behavior. When they are integrated into the human energy field and the individual mind and ego, they can do little to obscure the effluence of the Self as it emerges through the higher and lower mind and their functions and aspects.

Nonphysical beings that are ragistic are more dense, more active, and have a greater impact on human health, personality, and behavior. When they are integrated into the individual mind and ego they obscure the effluence of the Self and disrupt the flow of prana radiating through the human energy system by creating a push and pull with objects, qualified subfields, and creatures in their environment. As a result they externalize their host's awareness and make their host more reactive to external stimuli.

Nonphysical beings that are primarily tamasic are the most dense and polarized and have the greatest impact on human health, personality, and behavior. Since they exist in a solid state they are the most polarized, have the most penetrating power, and can block the effluence of the Self most thoroughly.

When tamasic CECs are projected from one sentient being to another, they can intrude deeply and violently into the human energy field where they can disrupt the flow of prana and the functions of the higher and lower mind. Indeed, tamasic CECs are responsible for the most serious forms of spiritual, mental, emotional, and physical disfunction and disease.

All CECs, whether they are sattvic, ragistic, or tamasic have finite awareness and a limited spectrum of emotional and etheric energy, feelings that they can project or use to counterfeit the activities and functions of the higher and lower mind. Like all living creatures they function in time-space and react when stimulated. They can act individually, or form communities and act in concert with other CECs. Although much of their activity can have a negative effect on human beings, like creatures on the physical-material plane, they act in accordance with their nature, which is a function of their specific level of consciousness and the spectrum of energy that they are able to transmit and transmute.

Structure and Function of CECs

CECs on all dimensions have a consistent structure that consists of a nucleus, a central cavity, and a surface boundary that surrounds it. The nucleus is normally quite small. Surrounding the nucleus is a pool of qualified energy that can vary in size and shape depending on its mass and density. Encircling the pool of qualified energy is a thin membrane composed of luminescent fibers that crisscross each other in every conceivable direction, much like felt. The surface membrane is mostly open space, which makes it extremely flexible and strong. Because of its porosity, the surface boundary provides space through which both qualified and unqualified energy can diffuse. This last property makes it possible to release CECs from the human energy field using techniques that you will learn later in this book.

In terms of structure, tamasic CECs will be the smallest, most highly polarized, most active, and will have the stickiest surface texture. Ragistic CECs will be larger, less polarized, less active, and have a smoother surface texture. Sattvic CECs will be the largest, least polarized, most active, and will have the smoothest surface texture. However, this is a general rule and may not be true in all cases.

The force or penetrating power of a CEC (its ability to penetrate the human energy field) is determined by its density, polarity, and level of activity. The more dense, more polarized, and more active the CEC, the more penetrating power it will have.

CECs on different worlds and dimensions, within the collective field of maya, resonate at different frequencies, and therefore exhibit different qualities. CECs in the field of maya surrounding the world of the lower mind will exhibit a myriad of desires, needs, cravings, and obsessions that can overwhelm the four authentic desires. CECs in the field of maya surrounding the world of soul will exhibit a wide range of sensations, feelings, and emotions that routinely counterfeit authentic human sensations, feelings, and emotions. CECs in the field of maya surrounding the world of intellect will exhibit awareness, ideation, belief, judgment, and prejudice, and have a predisposition to try to understand what can only be known through intuition, insight, and direct experience. CECs in the world of maya surrounding the world of spirit will exhibit glowing sensations, burning sensations, an intense sense of mission, and a litany of spurious revelations, which make one feel special or unique in some way.

Since CECs at the core of qualified subfields have a measure of personal will, subfields of qualified energy rarely vacate the human energy field unless they're released by a skilled practitioner. The reason behind their reticence is easy to understand. Without an internal source of unqualified energy or access to divine consciousness, CECs have a strong incentive to remain as close to an external source of prana as possible. The human energy system is a never ending source of prana that CECs can use to sustain themselves.

Their lack of resources also explains why CECs tend to work their way deeper into their host's energy field—closer to the chakras, minor energy centers, and the third heart, Atman. It also explains why their host will experience so much internal conflict when an inordinate amount of karmic baggage has been deposited in their energy field. In effect, the human being who has become their unwitting host is trying to control the movement of the CECs in an attempt to keep them from intruding more deeply into his or her energy field.

Complex Subfields

Given enough time, independent, qualified subfields can combine with other qualified subfields with a similar resonance to form "complex sub-fields" such as bumpy strings, vasanas, samskaras, cords, controlling waves, and personas.

Complex subfields can vary in size and shape depending on the num-ber of CECs in the subfield and the amount of qualified energy sur-rounding them. Samskaras and vasanas are thin and layered because they are under pressure and stacked on top of one another like sediment. In general, they occupy very little space. Bumpy strings are not under as much pressure and will generally occupy more space. Changes in pres-sure can cause shifts in the state of bumpy strings, depending on whether they remain free-floating or have begun to flatten into karmic sediment. Cords and controlling waves can extend over long distances and remain remarkably stable for long periods. Personas can repeatedly emerge into or out of their host's conscious awareness.

If complex subfields and the CECs within them are integrated they will become part of the host's karmic sediment and will eventually man-ifest their qualities through the host's individual mind and ego. This process is well established in most peoples' lives, and is considered quite normal in most cultures.

So What's Normal . . . Anyway?

In post-modern technological societies there are several human attributes that are universally accepted as normal, even though they emerge from the individual mind and ego and the CECs within them. Belief is one of them. Although it appears to be a normal human attribute, belief emerges exclusively from the individual mind and ego. The higher and lower mind are incapable of believing. In fact, the enlightened master remains detached from the individual mind and ego, and believes nothing. By remaining centered in the Self and emerging through the higher and lower mind and their functions and aspects, the master observes until she or he knows, and if he or she doesn't know continues to observe.

Understanding is another function of the individual mind and ego, and the CECs within it. The master recognizes that understanding is an illusion because nothing stops changing long enough to be understood. In fact, understanding is nothing more than a clever stratagem used by the individual mind and ego to prevent the higher and lower mind from having a direct experience of the inner qualities of what it is observing, which is the only way true knowledge can be acquired.

Hope is another device used by the individual mind and ego and the CECs within them to maintain their preeminent position. The primary motivation of the individual mind and ego is survival. And this motivation generates hope for the future. Once someone has had a direct experience of their innate divinity, however, hope becomes superfluous. What is there to hope for when one recognizes that their natural condition is eternal life (sat), all knowledge (chit); and bliss (ananda)?

Power of CECs

CECs, particularly those that combine their functions in complex subfields, seem to have extraordinary powers to manipulate, coerce, threaten, tempt, and seduce unwary human beings. However, those who have observed their activities have learned that their power is more apparent than real. In fact, the power that CECs have to veil the effluence of the

Self by disrupting the function of the human energy system comes by default. In the book of Romans, the apostle declares, ". . . Neither death nor life, nor angels, nor principalities, nor things present, nor things to come, nor powers, nor height, nor depth, nor any other created thing, shall be able to separate us from the love of God . . ." (Romans 8:38–9).

The truth is that CECs have power to disrupt the human energy field only as long as a human being remains ignorant of the nature of the higher and lower mind, and the power of unqualified energy at their disposal. Indeed, as long as one remains ignorant and chooses to identify with the individual mind and ego, qualified subfields, particularly complex subfields, and the CECs within them will have power to control and manipulate their actions. And so we come to the crux. In fields of qualified energy—particularly the individual mind and ego—CECs can exert tremendous power, but in the fields of unqualified energy the power of CECs is severely limited, and where unqualified energy is combined with the mental attention and intent CECs must sooner or later give way to the hegemony of the higher and lower mind.

Chapter Nine

As soon as all impurities have been removed by the practice of spiritual disciplines . . . a man's spiritual vision opens to the light-giving knowledge of Atman.

—Pantanjali, 28

Complex Subfields

In the Kali Yuga people have become so identified with their karmic baggage that they have unwittingly sublimated the will of the Self, as it emerges through the higher and lower mind, to the CECs in their individual mind and ego. As a result, whenever they express a thought, emotion, or feeling that emerges from karmic baggage, qualified energy and CECs are projected as a wave, cord, or energy blockage to the object or person they have in mind. These projections, whether they are conscious or not, are the major cause of human suffering for both the perpetrator and his or her target.

People project qualified energy for a host of reasons, but all projections are caused by a combination of CECs and attachment to the individual mind and ego, which is composed of complex qualified subfields that have usurped control of an essential function or aspect of the higher and lower mind. Indeed, in all cases where there have been projections, the human perpetrator will mistakenly believe that fulfilling his or her needs is essential for well-being.

The complex subfields we will look at in this chapter are bumpy strings, vasanas, samskaras, energy blockages, cords, and controlling waves. Although complex subfields can be found in the macrocosm, particularly in man-made environments, it is much more common to find them in the microcosm, where conditions favor their development.

In the macrocosm, complex subfields are found in both man-made and natural environments, although they tend to congregate where living beings are found in large numbers. In man-made environments, where subfields are more dense, they can be absorbed by both subtle and physical material.

There are several types of complex subfields from which projections emerge. In the following pages we will study them and then you will scan them to discern their individual qualities.

Controlling Waves

Controlling waves are complex qualified subfields that are polarized and highly active. They contain at least two CECs and are projected from the functions of mind, which assert awareness and interact with energetic fields, both qualified and unqualified, in the external environment.

When controlling waves emerge from a person's energy field they will be wedge-shaped, with the narrow end facing the target and most of the CECs at the leading edge. Once the wave enters the target's energy field it will quickly expand to fill a large portion of the internal environment on the world and dimension on which it is active.

Although a controlling wave can be projected consciously, it is more common for the perpetrator to be only partially aware of the qualified energy and CECs she or he is projecting.

The perpetrator's motivation for projecting is usually complex. She or he may want to influence the target but may not know that the desire or need to change, control, manipulate, connect, belong to, or harm their target is enough to cause a projection. In addition, the perpetrator may not be aware that a projection of qualified energy—which they often perceive only as a thought, emotion, or feeling—can disrupt their target's energy system as well as their target's ability to manifest or express themselves freely in the phenomenal universe.

In the case of a controlling wave, the aim of the projection will be to influence the functions or aspects of the higher and lower mind that manifest the target's intent and identity. When the perpetrator has unfulfilled expectations, the controlling wave will be projected at the front of the target's energy field. When there is disappointment and perceived loss, or when the target has rejected the perpetrator, the wave will be projected at the back of the target's energy field.

Controlling waves that are projected at the front of the target's energy field will remain in place as long as the perpetrator has expectations that his or her desires or needs will be fulfilled. Controlling waves projected at the back of the target's energy field will remain in place as long as the perpetrator has hope of regaining what he or she perceives has been lost.

Controlling waves tend to put pressure on the bumpy strings, vasanas, samskaras, and personas already present in the target's energy field on the level from which the wave is projected. The increased pressure caused by controlling waves is the most common source of stress and stress-related symptoms.

In fact, controlling waves are at least partially responsible for a number of psychosomatic diseases, including migraines, anxiety, depression, colitis, lower back pain, sinusitus, and psoriasis. When controlling waves put pressure on particularly dense karmic sediment, the host can experience acute pain, which can appear to originate in the physical-material body. The pain, which begins as a reaction to the intrusion, can become chronic when karmic baggage pushed into personal body space is held under pressure by the controlling wave.

Controlling waves can attach the target to the perpetrator for years, or dissipate as soon as the perpetrator loses interest. In most cases, however, the wave will remain intact as long as it serves the perpetrator's purpose, which can be as simple as holding onto the target, even if the desire or need for relationship isn't reciprocated. Purpose need not be rooted in conscious intent—unconscious intent is sufficient. This means that a controlling wave can remain in the target's energy field without the conscious support of the perpetrator.

Cords

Cords are complex subfields that contain at least two CECs and are projected from one sentient being to another. They are normally highly polarized and extremely active. Structurally and functionally, they differ from controlling waves in several important ways.

Cords are generally more dense than controlling waves, and their structure doesn't change after they've been projected. In fact, cords closely resemble thin tubes that have a consistent diameter along their entire length. Rather than being projected from the functions and/or aspects of mind, they are projected directly from karmic sediment surrounding the worlds and dimensions of the higher and lower mind.

Cords can be either active or dormant. When they are initially projected they will be active. An active cord will allow the perpetrator to project qualified energy through the hollow center. In most cases the transfer of qualified energy though the cord will cause a significant disruption in the target's energy field.

Cords are a manifestation of dependency, need, or desire that can border on obsession. Unlike a controlling wave that is projected to control an aspect of the target's personality, a cord manifests the perpetrator's desire or need to hold onto or have contact with their target.

Cords remain active as long as the perpetrator holds onto the false impression that they need or desire something, even if it is just a contact from their target. Once they abandon that idea, the cord will become dormant and qualified energy will no longer flow through it. However, even if a cord has become functionally dormant, it will remain structurally intact, keeping the target connected to the perpetrator—in some cases for years after the initial projection.

Cords accompany both overt and covert sexual abuse. In either case there will be two penetrations, a physical penetration that is accompanied by the violent penetration of qualified energy in the form of a cord, which is the primary instrument of control. The presence of a cord explains the pervasive fear a victim of sexual abuse will have for the perpetrator.

Bumpy Strings

Bumpy strings are complex subfields composed of independent subfields, primarily independent energy blockages, with a similar resonance. They contain at least two CECs and can be found on all worlds and dimensions of the higher and lower mind and their functions and aspects. Bumpy strings normally reside in the auric fields, although they are sometimes found in an energy body or energetic vehicle if it has tilted or been ejected from personal body space.

Bumpy strings are not stable for long periods. They are transitional structures that exist for a time and are then transformed into vasanas once they are laid down as karmic sediment. Because bumpy strings are a transitional structure, they tend to show greater variation in density, polarity, and level of activity than either vasanas or samskaras.

The structure of a bumpy string can vary depending on the quantity and quality of the CECs within it, the state of qualified energy surrounding the CECs, and the pressure exerted on the CECs by other qualified subfields in their immediate environment.

As its name suggests, a bumpy string looks like a flattened string with a series of knots or bumps tied along its length. The knots are the CECs. Variations along the length of a bumpy string tend to be minor, since differences in the mean frequency of CECs within it tend to be quite small. CECs whose qualities vary too widely wouldn't normally combine to form a bumpy string.

Bumpy strings tend to be long and thin, but they can also form spirals or coils that are highly active. When there are a large number of bumpy strings in close proximity within the microcosm, they can become intertwined and will resemble long strands or coils that move erratically as the host or someone in their energetic environment consciously or unconsciously activates them with their mental attention.

Vasanas

Vasanas are complex subfields located in the microcosm surrounding personal body space. Individual vasanas contain at least two CECs and, along with samskaras, form the bulk of karmic sediment on each world and dimension of the higher and lower mind, the splenic levels, and the functions and aspects of mind.

The seeds of karma are carried from one lifetime to another in the form of samskaras, while vasanas are more recent additions laid down during the present lifetime and/or the nine-month period between conception and birth.

The more karmic sediment one carries in the form of samskaras and vasanas, the further from the surface of personal body space vasanas will extend. When there has been an inordinate accumulation of karmic sediment on a particular dimension, vasanas will merge with the ego and their interaction will enhance the ego's influence.

Several types of complex subfields can become transformed into vasanas. These include bumpy strings, independent blockages, dormant cords, and controlling waves.

Once a complex subfield has been laid down as karmic sediment, its host will be forced to make a choice. This choice may be made under duress, it may be made incrementally, in some cases the choice may be largely unconscious, but sooner or later the host will either integrate the subfield and its qualities into their personality or the host will reject them. If the subfield is integrated, it will become a vasana, and the qualities that emerge from it will become an integral part of the individual mind and ego. If the subfield is rejected, it will remain in the microcosm until it is released or the process of integration begins once again.

Vasanas can be laid down as karmic sediment anywhere around the surface of personal body space. Most are pressed thin by pressure from above. Though they may be layered and subject to the effects of pressure, vasanas don't lose any of the following qualities: state, polarity, density, level of activity, surface texture, and color. These qualities will emerge undiminished if vasanas emerge spontaneously as personas or if they are in the process of being released. Although vasanas are not as intrusive and disruptive as samskaras, they do have an effect on the individual mind and ego proportionate to their density, polarity, and level of activity.

Along with samskaras, vasanas are the primary source of impressions that emerge from the individual mind and ego. In most cases vasanas support samskaras, particularly those that compose one's dominant persona. However, it is possible for vasanas to create subordinate personas that are in opposition to one's dominant persona. Although this may create conflict, as cultural markers, vasanas either support the dominant cultural paradigm or they motivate a person to reject it by adopting an alternative paradigm with alternative values and goals.

Samskaras

Samskaras are complex subfields that are carried from one lifetime to another. Swami Shivananda tells us "Every man is born with his Samskaras. The mind is not a blank sheet of paper. It contains the impressions of thoughts and actions of . . . previous births" (*Practice of Yoga*, 198).

Samskaras contain at least two CECs and are thin and elongated, since they are kept under constant pressure by other samskaras, vasanas, and bumpy strings. The quantity and quality of samskaras carried by a person will depend on how many lifetimes they've lived, how they've lived, and how attached they've become to the individual mind and ego.

Since samskaras comprise the oldest layers of karmic sediment, they form the foundation of the individual mind and ego. Indeed, the quality and quantity of samskaras a person carries in their energy field and their relationship to them will determine their personality type and will serve as a template for spiritual orientation, belief, ideation, emotional expression, preference, taste, and behavior. Since these impressions form an essential part of personal identity, most people will not only identify with their samskaras, they will actively defend them when their samskaras are threatened.

Activities such as channeling and/or communication with celestial or demonic beings in past incarnations will be represented in this incarnation as layers of dense samskaras surrounding personal body space.

These layers will make it increasingly difficult to go inward and will increase the possibility of conflict between one's dominant and subordinate personas.

In the exercises that follow you will locate and scan bumpy strings, vasanas, and samskaras for size, shape, state, density, polarity, level of activity, surface texture, and color. By practicing these exercises, you will develop the skill necessary to distinguish complex subfields from fields of unqualified energy, and different types of complex subfields from one another.

Scanning for Bumpy Strings

In this exercise you will scan your energy field for bumpy strings. Your designated intent will be "It is my intent to scan for bumpy strings in the world of soul, level of the fourth chakra, in the auric field facing me."

When you're ready to begin, find a comfortable position with your back straight. Then use the standard method to relax and balance conscious and unconscious mental activity. Continue by activating and centering yourself in the back of your heart chakra. Then set your intent, split your attention, and activate the front of your heart chakra. Once the front of your heart chakra has become active, look inward on the world of soul on the level of the fourth chakra. Then split your attention once again and project your second attention into the world of soul, level of the heart chakra, to a position about eight inches (twenty centimeters) in front of your heart chakra. To continue, shift your emphasis to the second attention and use your intent to activate your scanning tool. Then scan the area between the surface of personal body space and the apranic boundary from the fifth to the first chakra. Since bumpy strings are common, it's likely that you'll find one quickly. If not, then scan the remaining area between personal body space and the apranic boundary.

When you locate a bumpy string, scan its entire length and record information on its state, size, shape, density, polarity level of activity, and surface texture. If information about its awareness, attitude, and personality emerges, record it as well. When you're satisfied with your scan and the information you've gathered, shift your emphasis to the back of your heart chakra and release your second attention.

Then count from one to five. When you reach the number five, open your eyes. You will feel wide awake, perfectly relaxed, and better than you did before.

Scanning for Vasanas

In this exercise you will scan for vasanas in the world of the intellect, level of the third chakra, in the auric field facing you. Your designated intent will be "In the world of intellect, level of the third chakra, it is my intent to scan for vasanas in the auric field facing me."

Begin by finding a comfortable position with your back straight. Then use the standard method to relax and balance conscious and unconscious mental activity. When you're ready to continue, activate and center yourself in the back of your heart chakra. Then set your intent, split your attention, and activate the front of your heart chakra. Once the front of your heart chakra has become active, look inward on the world of intellect on the level of the third chakra. Then split your attention once again and project your second attention into the world of intellect, level of the third chakra, to a position eight inches (twenty centimeters) in front of your heart chakra. Bring your emphasis to your second attention, activate your scanning tool, and scan for vasanas, using the same technique you used to scan for bumpy strings.

When you are satisfied with your scan and the information you've gathered, shift your emphasis to the back of your heart chakra and release your second attention.

Then count from one to five. When you reach the number five, open your eyes. You will feel wide awake, perfectly relaxed, and better than you did before.

Scanning for Samskaras

In this exercise you will scan for samskaras in the world of the lower mind, level of the second chakra, in the auric field facing you. Your designated intent will be "In the world of the lower mind, level of the second chakra, it is my intent to scan for vasanas in the auric field facing me."

Since the border between vasanas and samskaras is often vague, you should scan for samskaras just outside the surface of personal body space.

Once you've found a comfortable position with your back straight, use the standard method to relax and balance conscious and unconscious mental activity. Then activate and center yourself in the back of your heart chakra. Continue by using the same technique you used to scan for vasanas and bumpy strings.

When you are satisfied with your scan and the information you've gathered, shift your emphasis to the back of your heart chakra and release your second attention.

Then count from one to five. When you reach the number five, open your eyes. You will feel wide awake, perfectly relaxed, and better than you did before.

Chapter Ten

*To regard the noneternal as eternal, the impure as pure,
the painful as pleasant and the non-Atman—this is
ignorance.*

*To identify consciousness with that which merely re-
flects consciousness—this is egoism.*

—Pantanjali's *Yoga Suras,* 78

Individual Mind and Ego

Each human being has come into this life with layers of qualified energy
in their energy field from past lives and from experiences in the womb.
The seeds from past lives, in the form of samskaras, form the foundation
of the individual mind and ego. The layers that are deposited in this present life, which are laid down on top of samskars, are called vasanas.
Other qualified subfields such as bumpy strings, independent energy
blockages, personas, controlling waves, and cords, which have intruded
or have been projected into one's energy field support (and in some cases
oppose), the individual mind and ego. This array of karmic baggage,
which includes the dominant persona, ego, and subordinate personas, is
collectively and individually capable of asserting energy in the form of
thoughts, emotions, feelings, and sensations. Indeed, as a collective field of
activity, they are capable of functioning as a surrogate mind—the individ-

ual mind and ego—which can counterfeit the activities of the higher and lower mind and appropriate the functions and aspects of mind to advance their agenda.

If It's Not Real, What Is It?

The individual mind and ego is not a structural part of the human energy field or a functional part of higher mind or lower mind. In fact, it has no definite structure that defines it—rather it is an evolving community of CECs, qualified subfields, and qualified energy.

From the study of Yoga we learn that by the time a child is seven years old, the process by which the higher and lower mind is subordinated to the individual mind and ego is almost complete. Indeed, if the density, polarity, and level of activity of the individual mind and ego become great enough, and one becomes attached to the personas emerging from them, the individual mind and ego can overwhelm the will of the Self emerging through the higher and lower mind, and prevent the functions and aspects of mind from expressing intent and asserting identity. Once the individual mind and ego have usurped the activities of the higher and lower mind, they will begin to function independently by asserting the collective will and identity of the CECs within them.

The ego, which is an independent community of qualified subfields, complements the individual mind. It filters the experiences of the phenomenal world and focuses the will of the individual mind as it emerges from the human energy field. To perform these functions, it appropriates control of the functions and aspects of mind as well as memory and deductive reasoning.

The strength of the individual mind and ego on each world and dimension will be determined by the collective strength and will of the CECs contained within them and the level of attachment their host has to them.

The individual mind and ego reach their apex of power in a particular world and dimension when one or more energy bodies or energetic vehicles have been ejected from personal body space and CECs—in the form of intrusions—have usurped their functions and aspects.

Development of the Individual Mind

The individual mind and ego develop independently on each world and dimension. Unlike the higher and lower mind and their functions and aspects, however, neither the individual mind nor ego are stable entities, since they continually expand and contract as qualified subfields are added or removed, and attachment to them increases or decreases.

Although the process of accumulating karma remains dormant between lifetimes, even in the period between conception and birth karmic baggage can be added to the unborn child in the form of vasanas, bumpy strings, and personas. Indeed, because this process is a continuous one, there isn't a moment when the individual mind and ego are formed or created—rather, they evolve as a person evolves and individuates from one lifetime to another.

Although additional karma can accumulate shortly after conception, it is only after birth, as a child evolves physically and psychically, that the individual mind and ego, after a period of dormancy, once again begin to develop. There are four distinct stages of development, which coincide with a child's physical growth and sexual development.

In the first stage, which begins at birth and lasts about six years, a child is protected to a large degree against the intrusion of qualified energy because the "I" (ego identity) is not fully developed and the externalization of awareness has not reached its full development.

As the child grows, however, there is a shift of attention toward the external world that coincides with the development of the "I" and greater identification with the individual mind and ego. What is inside and outside becomes clearly defined, and the ability to analyze, conceptualize, and view the world abstractly is developed to a greater degree. During the second stage many children become more aware of the legacy of past action, and the limitations imposed on them and their free range of activities (both internal and external) by karma, particularly samskaras. At the same time they begin to experience a more fixed personality and rigid orientation toward themselves and the external world.

It is during this period, as a function of ego development and attachment to people, objects, and energy fields, that a child becomes increasingly prone to intrusions of dense qualified energy, particularly from adults who exercise authority over them.

The third stage of development begins at puberty and extends through early adolescence. In this stage, hormones come into play, and the primary arena of growth and development is the physical-material body. Secondary sexual characteristics develop and there is an increase in sexual sensitivity, along with an increase in genital awareness.

It is at this stage—at least for the majority of children—that the individual mind and ego eclipse the functions of the higher and lower mind, and the "I", the focal point of the individual mind and ego, becomes dominant. As identification with the "I" becomes stronger, gender identification becomes more focused. Patterns of energy that distinguish men from women become more pronounced, with boys asserting energy forward from the second chakra and accepting or receiving energy by the heart chakra. In contrast, girls will assert energy from the heart chakra and will accept or receive energy by the second chakra. These patterns of polarity will (for most children) become the blueprint for future intimate relationships. In some cases, however, this stage will be marked by confusion in gender identification (personal identity), caused primarily by an accumulation of karmic baggage in the human energy system.

The fourth stage of development normally begins between the ages of fifteen and sixteen for both boys and girls. By this stage identification with the "I" is usually complete, along with the externalization of conscious awareness and the development of a fixed personality. The flow of subtle energy becomes more or less restricted as control is imposed on the adolescent from the outside.

The development of a fixed ego and personality brings with it an end to the undifferentiated sense of Self that was a hallmark of childhood. This loss has far-reaching consequences, since access to the Self and to the pleasure, intimacy, joy, and bliss that emerge from it will determine how freely sexual energy will radiate through the human energy system, and how much inner joy one will experience as one moves through the later stages of life.

Intuition, which had played a more important role in the earlier stages of development, can be effectively suppressed by the individual mind and ego by this stage, and authority can be transferred from the Self, as it emerges through higher and lower mind, to some outside institution, agency, or individual. With the disruption of Self-awareness and trust, in the fourth stage of development alienation from the body and its pleasure centers becomes complete. This inevitably leads to a loss of conscious awareness and a restriction in one's ability to express oneself through the vehicles of spirit, intellect, soul, and authentic desire.

Structure of the Individual Mind

The individual mind is composed of several types of complex subfields and is by nature decentralized, with elements surrounding all worlds and dimensions of the higher and lower mind and their corresponding functions and aspects. Samskaras, which serve as the foundation, are carried from lifetime to lifetime, while vasanas, bumpy strings, cords, controlling waves, independent blockages, and sometimes even foreign energy bodies are added during each incarnation.

The structural and functional center of the individual mind on each dimension is the area between the surface of personal body space and the apranic boundary. On those dimensions where intrusions of karmic energy have replaced energy bodies and/or energetic vehicles, however, the structural and functional center will shift inward to personal body space.

Although fields of qualified energy, in the individual mind, can function as individual centers of activity on each world and dimension, it is more common for them to coordinate their activities in a loose federation that evolves in fits and starts as different qualified subfields temporarily cooperate or come into conflict, or their host becomes more or less attached to them. The dominant part of the federation, in terms of size and influence, will be samskaras. After samskaras, in descending order of importance, are foreign energy bodies, vasanas, bumpy strings, attached complex blockages (cords and controlling waves), and independent blockages. Although qualified subfields contribute to the overall density, polarity, and level of activity of the individual mind, it is the CECs at their center that are the essential functional units.

Attached complex subfields, which include cords, controlling waves, and foreign energy bodies or energetic vehicles pose an additional set of problems for the host and perpetrator, since they connect the protagonists together energetically and disrupt the synchronistic function of their energy fields.

Foreign energy bodies or energetic vehicles can be particularly disruptive, since they add the perpetrator's will, finite awareness, emotions, and feelings to the host's individual mind and ego. The effects of an intrusive energy body or vehicle on the host's energy field will be even more pronounced if it penetrates personal body space. If penetration takes place, the intrusive energy body or vehicle will oppose the reintegration of the host's ejected energy body or vehicle. In addition, the intrusive energy body or vehicle will appropriate the functions and aspects of mind and will create a counterfeit mind on the dimension in question, which will invariably overwhelm the host's dominant persona.

The individual mind is a part of the collective field of maya and has no functional relationship to the human energy system and/or the higher and lower mind. Instead, it serves the collective will of the CECs contained within it.

In some cases when a qualified subfield seems particularly distasteful—because its resonance and the activities associated with it are incompatible with one's dominant personal—one can compensate by pushing the subfield out of conscious awareness through denial.

A qualified subfield that has been denied can never be completely hidden, however. Sooner or later it will reemerge into conscious awareness and become active again. In fact, the reemergence of a denied subfield, with all its obsessive and compulsive characteristics, explains many forms of anti-Self and antisocial behavior that suddenly and without any apparent cause bursts forth.

The Ego

The human ego is a multiworld, multidimensional field of qualified energy that owes its existence to qualified subfields and CECs that have intruded into the microcosm. Elements of the ego exist within the human energy field on all worlds and dimensions of the higher and lower mind, the world of the chakras, the splenic levels and their functions and aspects, at a distance of about four inches (ten centimeters) in front and in back of the heart chakra. In an embryonic form, the ego is present at birth, but it has little impact on the consciousness of a newborn, since it takes an average of seven years for the ego to mature, and even longer for attachment to it to become complete.

The ego serves as the focal point of the individual mind by emerging along with the functions and aspects of mind, and infiltrating them as they emerge into the macrocosm. Infiltration can also take place when an intrusive energy body or energy vehicle links itself to the ego and projects extensions into the functions and aspects of mind.

It is important to note that the ego is not a structural or functional part of the human energy system or the higher and lower mind. This means that it can't process unqualified energy in any form. Consequently, it can't be used as a vehicle to express authentic human awareness, emotions, feelings, or sensations, all of which emerge from the human energy system and/or the higher and lower mind and their functions and aspects. The ego can only focus and filter qualified energy that has intruded into the microcosm or has been projected from the individual mind and ego into the external environment. Hence, as a therapeutic tool its value is severely limited, since it can't be used by the higher and lower mind as a diagnostic tool to locate and discern the qualities of qualified subfields, or to remove karmic baggage once it has been located.

Since the ego can obstruct the activities of the human energy system and the higher and lower mind and its functions and aspects, it is essential to become fully conscious so that the ego can be subordinated to the will of the Self as it emerges through the higher and lower mind. One must remember the goal of energy work is not to destroy the ego, but to learn how it functions, purify it, and become detached from it so that the Self can emerge into conscious awareness through the higher and lower mind and their functions and aspects.

Structure of the Ego

The ego's structural and functional center on each world and dimension is approximately four inches (eight centimeters) in front and in back of the heart chakra. Qualified subfields that comprise the ego on each dimension have been pressed together by their mutual attraction and shared polarity. This gives the ego the look of a misshapen ball. Each qualified subfield within the ego on a particular dimension contains one or more CECs, and each CEC contains and projects a different set of qualities through extensions into both the microcosm and the macrocosm.

Extensions are structures that connect the ego to qualified subfields, objects, and living beings in both the microcosm and macrocosm. These cord-like structures are continually changing, sometimes growing stronger or weaker, even changing size, polarity, and state as conditions in the environment surrounding the ego change. Structurally, the ego and its extensions on each dimension resemble a nerve cell that has a body and dendrites radiating from it. The dendrites connect the neuron to other cells. Similarly, extensions emerging from the ego connect the ego to other sentient beings, qualified subfields, and objects.

None of the structural elements that combine to form the ego on a particular dimension have a uniform shape, structure, and/or resonance. They do, however, experience qualitative shifts as the ego evolves and involves and/or reacts to external stimuli. In fact, the ego can grow larger or smaller, more or less dense, more or less active, and more or less polarized as one evolves or involves back into union with the Self.

Function of the Ego

The ego has no functional relationship to the human energy system, the higher and lower mind, or their functions and aspects. Instead, it focuses the will of the individual mind and filters information from the external environment as it is received by the functions and aspects of mind and the centers of consciousness within the human energy system.

The power and influence of the ego will depend on several factors, including the quality and quantity of CECs contained within it, how attached the host has become to it and its extensions, and how attached the host has become to external subfields to which the ego has attached them.

When qualified energy within the ego is predominantly sattvic, the power of the ego will be relatively weak. When qualified energy within the ego is predominantly ragistic, it will be stronger, and when qualified energy within the ego is predominantly tamasic, it will be strongest.

In a human being who has achieved union with the Self, the ego will be predominantly sattvic, but one must remember that, in the Kali Yuga, living without the individual mind and ego is impossible, even for enlightened masters and those born in union with the Self. Indeed, the essential difference between a master and the average person is that the master has refined his or her ego and become detached from it, while the average person has not.

Scanning the Ego

In the exercise below, you will scan the ego, facing you, in the world of soul, level of the fourth chakra. Your designated intent will be "In the world of soul, it is my intent to scan my ego, facing me, on the level of the fourth chakra."

Begin by finding a comfortable position with your back straight. Then use the standard method to relax and balance conscious and unconscious mental activity. Continue by activating and centering yourself in the back of your heart chakra. Once the front of your heart chakra is active, look inward in the world of soul on the level of your heart chakra. Then split your attention once again and project your second attention four inches (ten centimeters) in front of your heart chakra. Bring your emphasis to the second attention. Then activate your scanning tool and begin your scan. Once you've located your ego, scan its body. Then follow its extensions and record your findings. When you're satisfied with your scan and the information you've collected on the size, shape, state, density, level of activity, surface texture, and the network of extensions emerging from your ego, release your scanning tool, return your emphasis to the back of your heart chakra and release your second attention.

Then count from one to five. When you reach the number five, open your eyes. You will feel wide awake, perfectly relaxed, and better than you did before.

You can develop your skill and learn more about the condition of your ego by practicing the exercises listed below.

1. Scan the front of your ego on the world of the lower mind, level of the second chakra.

2. Scan the back of your ego on the world of spirit, level of the seventh chakra.

3. Scan the front of your ego on the splenic level.

4. Scan the back of your ego on the upper splenic level.

5. Scan the front and back of your ego on the world of intellect, level of the third chakra.

Part Three

Expanding Yourself

Chapter Eleven

The Supreme Reality stands revealed in the conscious-
ness of those who have conquered themselves. They live
in peace, alike in cold and heat, pleasure and pain,
praise and blame.

—Bhagavad Gita, 6:7

Structure of the Human Energy System

To successfully overcome the effects of karmic baggage, it is necessary to have a working knowledge of the structure and function of the human energy system. With that knowledge and the skill you develop by mastering the exercises in the following chapters, you'll be able to activate the splenic chakras, the eighth and ninth chakras in personal body space, as well as the chakras above and below personal body space. You'll also be able to increase the flow of prana through the system of meridians (nadis), and you'll be able to activate and integrate the energy of the minor energy centers in your hands and feet with the other organs of the human energy system.

The human energy system is composed of five groups of organs that function synergistically with one another and the communities of energy bodies in the higher and lower mind (see figure 11-1, p. 160). The five groups are the chakras, auras, meridians, minor energy centers in the hands and feet, and the kandas. The human energy system, as a structural and functional unit, can be thought of as a power plant and grid of substations and power lines that transmute the consciousness of the Self

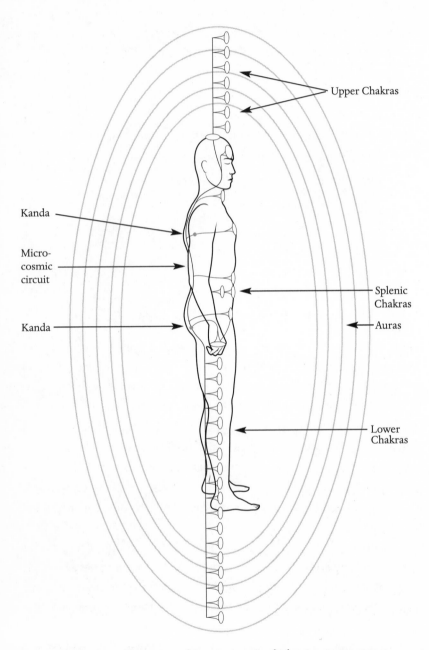

Figure 11-1 — Five groups of organs comprise the human energy system.

(Atman) into unqualified energy (prana), unqualified energy from one frequency into another, and unqualified energy into subtle matter.

The energy system as a unit coordinates its systemic activities in the microcosm. This means that while some organs function on one or more worlds and dimensions, others function simultaneously on all of them. In fact, the human energy system links the worlds and the dimensions within the microcosm together so that a human being can function as a structural and functional whole.

There are one hundred and forty-two chakras in the human energy system that we will examine, seventy higher chakras, seventy lower chakras, and the two splenic chakras that regulate unqualified energy within the physical-material body and the etheric double. The etheric double is a functional part of the physical-material body.

The first seven (higher) chakras are located in personal body space, and the remaining sixty-three are located above personal body space, directly above the crown chakra. Complementing the higher chakras are seventy lower chakras located below personal body space, directly below the muladhara chakra, at a point that corresponds to the base of the spine. The splenic chakras—the eighth and ninth chakras within personal body space—are located between the second and third chakras (see figure 11-2, at right).

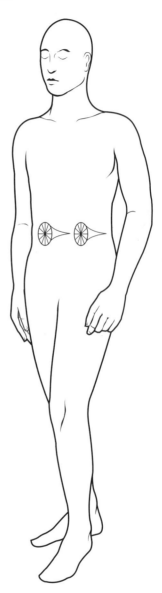

Figure 11-2 — The splenic (8th and 9th) chakras.

Connecting the chakras to one another are channels known as meridians, or nadis. The meridians are very numerous, although there is dis-
agreement on just how many there are. One ancient text tells us that
there are seventy-two thousand nadis (meridians) emerging from the
kandas. Other texts tell us there are over three hundred and fifty thousand. The disagreements in the ancient texts shouldn't concern us too
much because among the thousands of meridians that carry prana
throughout the human energy system there are ten major meridians that
are of particular interest. These include the shushumna-governor and
conceptual meridians, as well as the ancillary meridians that connect the
higher and lower chakras to the communities of energy bodies and energetic vehicles in the higher and lower mind.

The kandas are hubs from which the major meridians emerge. One
kanda is located at the base of the spine and the other is located about
two inches (five centimeters) forward from the back of the heart chakra.
Though the kandas (which function like mathematical points) occupy no
space, they do perform an important organizational function by facilitating the transmission and transmutation of prana throughout the human
energy system.

The auric fields are reservoirs of unqualified energy that surround
personal body space on each world and dimension. They extend the
human energy field beyond personal body space as far as twenty-six feet
(eight meters), and they form a boundary between the human energy
field (the microcosm) and the external environment (the macrocosm).

The last unit of the human energy system is the system of minor
energy centers, which are located at positions in personal body space that
correspond to the hands and feet. The minor energy centers are points
where major meridians converge. Their main functions are to facilitate
the movement of prana through the chakras and meridians and to maintain the pressure within the human energy system at healthy levels.

The Chakras

There are one hundred and forty-two chakras that support the higher and lower mind and the splenic levels in the human energy system: seventy higher chakras, seventy lower chakras, and two splenic chakras. Nine chakras are located in personal body space, the seven traditional chakras and the two splenic chakras, sixty-three chakras are located above personal body space directly above the crown chakra, and seventy chakras are located below personal body space, directly below the first chakra.

The word "chakra" comes from Sanskrit and means "wheel."

When viewed with the mental attention the chakras appear as brightly colored disks, each spinning rapidly at the end of what looks like a long axle or stalk. The wheel portion is about three inches in diameter (eight centimeters) and perpetually moves or spins around a central axis. Emerging from the center of the disk are what appear to be spokes. The chakras on the highest and lowest dimensions have the most spokes.

Prana moving up the main masculine meridian (the shushumna-governor) passes through the male pole of each chakra. Prana moving down the main feminine meridian (the conceptual) in the front of personal body space passes through the female pole of each chakra.

The chakras have been described as miniature suns, each spinning and radiating a different quality of color in the visual spectrum of light. Although prana is colorless, the refraction of light gives the disk portion of the chakra its distinct hue, which is bright and clear when the chakra is functioning healthfully.

As each chakra rotates, the disk portion, which has a feminine polarity, glows with a faint light. The intensity of the light will increase along with the diameter of the disk as the chakra becomes more active, and more unqualified energy radiates through it.

The sixty-three chakras above personal body space are stacked directly above the crown chakra, at intervals of about three inches (eight centimeters). The seventy chakras below personal body space are stacked at the same intervals directly below the first chakra. The distance between the male and female poles of the chakras above and below body space is about two and a half inches (six centimeters).

The system of chakras has been designed to transmit and transmute prana. When energy bodies and energetic vehicles in the higher and lower mind are vertically integrated and there is little or no interference from karmic baggage, the system will perform its job perfectly and unqualified energy will flow through the human energy field without disruption, but take note, the chakras are not designed to transmit or transmute qualified energy, in any form—and qualified energy should never be introduced into the chakras or the system of meridians connecting them.

Collective Functions of the Chakras

In their most important function, the chakras serve as energetic gateways and/or vortexes that link the Self to the worlds and dimensions of the higher and lower mind, their functions and aspects, and the splenic levels. In addition, the chakras transmute the consciousness of the Self into prana, and in conjunction with the meridians distribute it through the communities of energy bodies and their corresponding energetic vehicles

In their third function, the chakras serve as transformers, performing this function by transmuting unqualified energy from one pitch or frequency to another. The transmutation of unqualified energy takes place automatically whenever an energy body (energetic vehicle) and/or an auric field is in an energy-deficient condition. When energy is needed by either an energy body (energetic vehicle) or an auric field, prana will be transmitted to the chakra that supports it, and the chakra will transmute the energy into the appropriate pitch (frequency) needed.

In their fourth function, the chakras regulate and balance the forces of polarity and gender by permitting unqualified energy to move through the human energy system in four general directions: up the back, down the front, forward from the back to the front, and backward from the front to the back. Maintaining a healthy balance between the forces of polarity and gender will keep pressure within the energy system within healthy parameters, which in turn will enhance the full expression of feelings, emotions, and finite human consciousness.

In their final function, the chakras serve as sensors or organs of perception. Along with the surface of the auras, and, in some cases, the functions and aspects of mind and the unqualified energy contained within the auric fields, the chakras allow one to discriminate between different frequencies of unqualified and/or qualified energy that make an impact on the human energy field.

How chakras sense energy in the external environment is explained below. Unqualified energy and/or qualified energy in the form of waves, pools, and subfields vibrate at a particular resonance or pitch. When this qualified (or unqualified) energy makes contact with the surface of the aura and/or functions and aspects of mind that can extend beyond the surface of an auric field, it will cause the energy within the field to vibrate. The vibration will then be carried inward to the chakra attuned to its specific frequency or pitch. The chakra will register this vibration, and the information will be carried to the centers of consciousness in the higher and lower mind where it will be assimilated.

The Chakras Within Personal Body Space

From Yoga we learn that the first seven (higher) chakras and the two splenic chakras are located within personal body space, with the masculine pole of the first seven chakras immersed in the shushumna-governor meridian and the feminine pole immersed in the conceptual meridian. The two splenic chakras remain outside the system of higher and lower chakras and separate from the meridians that connect them to each other. They are directly connected to the Self and are located between the second and third chakras.

The first seven chakras are responsible for regulating life on the dimensions dedicated to feeling, emotion, finite human consciousness, relationship, and psychic well-being. The splenic chakras—the eighth and ninth chakras within personal body space—are responsible for regulating physical well-being and integrating the physical-material body and the etheric double with the energy system and the communities of energy bodies on the dimensions of the higher and lower mind.

Below is a description of the structure and function of the chakras within personal body space, beginning with the first chakra.

The Muladhara Chakra

The first chakra in personal body space is called muladhara. In Sanskrit *mula* means "root," *adhara* means "to support."

The muladhara chakra originates from within the shushumna-governor meridian at the base of the spine, directly behind the sexual organs at a point corresponding to the perineum in the physical-material body. From that point the stalk curves downward in a semi-circle and the disk emerges within the conceptual meridian, six inches (fifteen centimeters) below the perineum, at a point midway between the thighs.

The muladhara chakra is responsible for regulating the transmission and transmutation of unqualified energy in the lower section of personal body space, including the legs and feet and the lower part of the torso—from the perineum to a point four inches (ten centimeters) above it.

When the first chakra is functioning properly, one will feel secure and comfortable in the physical-material world. Pleasure will emerge spontaneously, and one won't feel compelled to justify their existence or their right to be who they are. In addition, one will recognize that they are responsible for their own well-being and won't feel the need to lean on others for support.

On the other hand, the disruption of the first chakra by karmic sediment and/or energetic blockages will make life on earth a trial as prana radiating through the first chakra is blocked and pleasure is restricted. When there is an inordinate amount of karmic baggage disrupting the function of the first chakra there will be a concurrent fear of death, which will emerge as an internal struggle for personal survival.

It is from the muladhara chakra that the kundalini-shakti emerges, and it is the kundalini-shakti that is the most powerful source of prana in the human energy system. When the kundalini-shakti is blocked, the entire energy system will suffer. Not only will the transmission and transmutation of prana be inhibited, pleasure will be restricted, boundaries will be weakened, and the synchronistic function of the energy bodies and the organs of the human energy system will be disrupted.

The Svadhistana Chakra

The second chakra has its point of origin in the shushumna-governor meridian about three and a half inches (eight centimeters) above the first chakra. In Sanskrit *svad* means "that which belongs to itself," and *dhisthana* means "its actual place." From the male pole immersed in the shushumna-governor meridian the chakra extends forward to a point in the conceptual meridian two and a half inches (six centimeters) below the navel.

The second chakra regulates energy in the horizontal portion of personal body space from the navel to a position four inches (ten centimeters) below the chakra. When the chakra is functioning healthfully, pleasure will emerge as the natural response to human interaction and appropriate activity.

The second chakra is responsible for sexual function and gender identity, as well as creativity and vitality. When the chakra is active, one will be able to manifest their creativity through the higher and lower mind and manifest it in the physical-material world.

Anger, the authentic human emotion with the lowest mean frequency, is regulated by the second chakra. When the flow of energy through the chakra is restricted because of fear or physical and energetic contraction, anger will emerge.

When the functions of the second chakra have been disrupted vitality will diminish. In some cases this will lead to depression, which can become chronic if the chakra is burdened by an inordinate amount of karmic sediment. The disruption of the second chakra can also lead to sexual dysfunction in both men and women. This, in turn, can cause sudden outbursts of anger or a pattern of passive-aggressive activity.

When the chakra is functioning healthfully, the kundalini-shakti will remain active and the aroused kundalini will move upward through shushumna-governor meridian to the second chakra and beyond. The aroused kundalini will elevate human consciousness beyond the base needs of survival, reproduction, and the compelling drives of physiology and instinct.

The Manipura Chakra

The third chakra has its origin within the shushumna-governor meridian, directly behind the solar plexus. It is called *manipura*, which means "city of jewels."

From its point of origin in personal body space, it extends forward to a point that corresponds to the bottom of the breastbone. From there it opens directly into the conceptual meridian.

The manipura chakra is concerned primarily with people, places, and things, as well as one's association to ideals, institutions, community, and family. The sense of belonging, friendship, trust, contentment, and commitment, as well as the ability to remain calm during times of duress, are all regulated by the third chakra. So, too, are status, psychic well-being, emotional intimacy, and comfort.

When the chakra is functioning healthfully one will feel content and there will be no compulsion to compromise personal integrity in order to participate or belong. Relationships will be based on appropriateness, not on dependency, need, control, or manipulation. When participation is appropriate, it will be a natural response to environmental conditions. Hence, it will be fluid and playful. Those who have greater status will not diminish those with less status, and respect will be given to authority when it is earned, and withdrawn when it has been abused.

The third chakra regulates the emotion of fear; when the chakra is blocked fear will emerge in response.

The Anahata Chakra

The fourth chakra is the heart chakra. It emerges from the shushumna-governor meridian at a point that corresponds to the eighth cervical vertebra. It is called *anshata* in Sanskrit, which means "unbeaten." From its point of origin it extends forward to the center of the breastbone on the surface of personal body space. The fourth chakra regulates the horizontal section of personal body space from a point two inches (five centimeters) above the solar plexus to a point one inch (two and a half centimeters) below the upper end of the breast bone.

Since the heart chakra is the center of intuitive consciousness, it is from the heart chakra that the inner meanings of things can be grasped.

One's personal rights are also upheld by the heart chakra. In the spiritual world the heart chakra upholds the right to engage in spiritual practice and share spiritual experience when appropriate, even when there is internal (from the individual mind and ego) and external (from people, institutions, and culture) opposition. The heart chakra also upholds the right to choose one's individual spiritual path and to acknowledge publicly—when appropriate—that ultimate authority in spiritual matters resides in the Self, not in tradition or the collective beliefs of a people or their cultural and religious institutions.

In the world of intellect the heart chakra upholds the right to trust personal intuition, insight, and the functions of finite human consciousness, no matter how these functions choose to manifest intellectually, creatively, verbally, through metaphor, the written word, or the arts.

In the world of soul the heart chakra upholds the right to feel, express, and resolve emotions, or to curtail their outward expression when circumstances demand. Indeed, all four authentic emotions that emerge from the chakras—anger, fear, pain, and joy—have the right to be expressed and resolved. No outside authority has the right to make one feel ashamed or guilty for their spontaneous and appropriate expression.

In the world of the lower mind the heart chakra upholds the right to experience, feel, and act on authentic desires including artha, kama, dharma, and moksha (for more on authentic desires see chapter seventeen).

It is also important to point out that one's center has its foundation on the level of the heart. For the developing person it will be the human heart, for the developed person it will be the heart chakra, and for the transcendent person it will be Atman (the Self) that emerges from the right side of the heart chakra.

The emotion regulated by the heart chakra is pain. If the heart chakra is blocked and its function has been disrupted, pain will emerge. If the chakra remains blocked and one has become attached to the individual mind and ego the disruption can lead to feelings of hopelessness and/or despair.

The Visuddha Chakra

The fifth chakra emerges from a point in the shushumna-governor meridian that corresponds to the third cervical vertebra, just below the medulla oblongata. From there it extends forward to a point that corresponds to the throat. In Sanskrit it is called *visuddha,* which means "pure." The fifth chakra regulates the horizontal area of personal body space, which extends from the base of the nose to the base of the throat.

The visuddha chakra can be described as pure because it transmutes prana into unconditional joy as it moves upward through the shushumna-governor meridian. In this way, it purifies the emotions that are created when energy emerging from the second through fourth chakras has been blocked or restricted.

In addition, the fifth chakra regulates self-expression—this includes verbal expression and the expression of feelings, emotions, ideas, creativity, and spirituality. The fifth chakra's ability to function healthfully will also determine how much space a person takes up and how easily they can emerge and express themselves through their energy system and the functions and aspects of mind.

When the activities of the chakra have been disrupted, one may compensate for their inability to express themselves through the human energy system and the functions and aspects of mind by becoming attached to qualified subfields and emerging through the individual mind and ego.

The emotion regulated by the fifth chakra is joy. Joy emerges when prana moving up the shushumna-governor meridian becomes restricted and moves forward through the fifth chakra rather than upward through the meridian to the higher chakras where it would be transmuted into consciousness.

The Ajna Chakra

The sixth chakra emerges from a point in the shushumna-governor meridian directly above the upper palate. From its point of origin it extends up and forward to a point on the brow, directly between the eyes. In Sanskrit it is called *ajna*, which means "command."

The ajna chakra regulates the portion of personal body space that extends from the base of the nose to a point one inch (two and a half centimeters) above the brow. Will is an important function of the sixth chakra, as is human intent. The ability to visualize, imagine, and conceptualize emerge from the sixth chakra. Deductive reasoning, rational problem-solving, intuition, and extrasensory abilities such as discernment (the ability to sense energy fields), precognition, clairvoyance, clairaudience, and clairsentience are regulated by the sixth chakra as well.

The sixth chakra has an important influence on memory. When the chakra is functioning healthfully one will remember events by reexperiencing the energetic fields associated with them, including those that emerge as sensations, feelings, and emotions. For adults, the memory of energetic fields associated with past events can provide much-needed continuity with childhood. Unfortunately, one's memory of energetic fields can be disrupted by the accumulation of karmic baggage on the worlds and dimensions supported by the sixth chakra.

There is no emotion associated with the ajna center. However, when the functions of the chakra have been disrupted, one's ability to express intent, emerge with mental clarity, and solve problems through insight and rational problem-solving will be disrupted.

The Sahasrara Chakra

The seventh chakra emerges from the shushumna-governor meridian at a point three quarters of an inch (three centimeters) above the sixth chakra. From its point of origin within personal body space it extends directly upward to a point at the top of the head. In Sanskrit it is called *sahasrara*, which means "thousand-petaled lotus."

Some ancient Yogic texts suggest that the seventh chakra is located above personal body space and that its resonance transcends finite human awareness. Other texts make contradictory claims. What we do know for sure is that the seventh chakra serves as a bridge between the chakras within personal body space and the chakras above it. In fact, it is only after the seventh chakra has become active that one will be able to function with conscious awareness on the higher dimensions—those above personal body space—and it is only after one has raised the kundalini to the crown chakra that one will recognize that consciousness transcends the limitations imposed on it by the physical-material body and the organs of the human energy system.

The seventh chakra plays a key role in regulating pressure within personal body space. It performs this function in conjunction with the first chakra and the minor energy centers in the hands and feet.

There is no emotion associated with the the seventh chakra. Nevertheless, when the seventh chakra has become active there will be a sense of completion and / or satisfaction, which coincides with the recognition that limitations imposed by the individual mind and ego and the collective field of maya are to be overcome and not accepted with resignation.

The Splenic Chakras

For millennium there has been confusion about the location and function of the second chakra. Some Yogic and Tantric texts have declared that the second chakra was the splenic chakra, while others have declared that the second chakra was just below the navel, the traditional position of the second chakra. Additional texts have even suggested that the the splenic chakra was the third chakra and the solar plexus chakra didn't exist. Fortunately, we now know that the traditional seven chakras in personal body space are in their correct position and that there are two additional chakras, the splenic chakra and the upper splenic chakra.

The splenic chakra is located by the spleen on the left side of personal body space and the upper splenic chakra is located directly across from it. The second chakra, which regulates sexual energy, and the solar plexus chakra, which regulates all forms of belonging, work in conjunction with the remaining five traditional chakras in personal body space. The splenic chakras, on the other hand, function independently. Both the splenic chakra and the upper splenic chakra have the same structure as the traditional chakras, though they are connected directly to the Self and remain outside the system of one hundred and forty chakras that support the higher and lower mind.

The prana emerging through the splenic chakras support the activities of the splenic bodies, the physical-material body—which in Yoga is considered an energy body—and the etheric double. Indeed, the two splenic chakras must be functioning healthfully for spiritual life to be grounded in the physical-material body and etheric double, and for the normal demands and responsibilities of life on the physical-material plane to be integrated with the functions of the higher and lower mind. In fact, it is prana emerging from the splenic chakras that connects one to the earth and the creatures of the earth with whom one shares the planet.

For the splenic chakras to function healthfully and synchronistically with the energy bodies and energetic vehicles of the higher and lower mind, the splenic bodies (which the splenic chakras support) must be firmly anchored in personal body space. When the splenic bodies are vertically integrated and the splenic chakras are functioning healthfully, one will be fortified against the coercive and seductive activities of the individual mind and ego that condemn the normal activities of the physical-material world—such as eating, working, and participating in intimate relationships—and seek to substitute a counterfeit spirituality that interferes with or rejects them.

Activating the Splenic Chakras

In the preceding chapters you activated the seven traditional chakras in personal body space. In the two exercises that follow, you will activate the eighth and ninth chakras in personal body space (the splenic and upper splenic chakras) and experience their unique resonance. Your designated intent in the first exercise will be "It is my intent to activate my splenic chakra and look inward on the splenic level."

To begin, find a comfortable position with your back straight. Then use the standard method to relax and balance conscious and unconscious mental activity. Continue by activating and centering yourself in the back of your heart chakra. Then split your attention and activate the front of your heart chakra. Once the front of your heart chakra has become active, set your intent. Then state "It is my intent to split my attention and to activate the back of my splenic chakra." Take a few moments to experience the shift. Then state "It is my intent to split my attention and to activate the front of my splenic chakra." Once the front of the chakra has become active, state "On the level of the splenic chakra it is my intent to look inward."

Take fifteen minutes to enjoy the meditation. Then release your second attention and count from one to five. When you reach the number five, open your eyes. You will be wide awake, perfectly relaxed, and feel better than you did before.

In the next exercise you will activate the upper splenic chakra and look inward on the upper splenic level. Your designated intent for this exercise will be "It is my intent to activate my upper splenic chakra and look inward on the upper splenic level." Continue by following the instructions in the exercise above.

It is important to note that although people use various techniques to ground themselves, unless the splenic and upper splenic chakras have become active, there will be no true grounding and the foundation necessary for more advanced energy work will not have been properly laid.

Companion Chakras

Companion chakras, within personal body space, are two chakras with complementary functions that coordinate their activities. Their relationship affects the well-being of both chakras and the energy bodies and/or energetic vehicles they support.

When one chakra in companionship has had its function disrupted symptoms will appear in both chakras. If the disruption is severe enough to make the afflicted chakra go numb, then its companion will develop acute symptoms that will be more noticeable and easier to diagnose. Acute symptoms can manifest as pain, pressure, and/or the restriction of what appear to be physical functions, including breathing, digestion, sexual function, and evacuation.

Becoming aware of the complementary functions of both chakras in relationship is essential because symptoms in one chakra—such as tension in the musculature, discomfort, and/or pain, etc.—may mask a deeper problem in its companion.

When the functions of a chakra have been disrupted because of stress, shock, or trauma and the chakra has become numb, the condition may go unnoticed if the host is unable to discern subtle shifts in their non-physical environment. Its companion may not suffer the same shock or trauma, but it will develop symptoms nonetheless because of its relationship to the afflicted chakra. Though far from pleasant, the symptoms in the companion chakra provide a valuable diagnostic tool.

The pairs of chakras that form partnerships are the first and third chakras, the second and fifth chakras, the fourth and sixth chakras, and finally, a special triangular partnership that exists between the first and seventh chakras and the minor energy centers in the hands and feet.

The First Pair

The first pair of chakras in partnership consist of the first and third chakras. Their partnership is based on the complementary roles they play in stability, security, and the joy of existence. The first chakra regulates the frequencies of energy associated with security in personal body space, which can be thought of as one's inalienable right to exist. It also regulates the frequencies of energy devoted to *joie de vivre*, enjoyed by all creatures, and which is a manifestation of a healthy relationship to the physical-material world and the worlds of the higher and lower mind.

The third chakra regulates the frequencies of energy related to belonging, including status and security within a relationship. When the third chakra is functioning healthfully, one will feel stable and secure within a relationship and will enjoy the fruits of shared empathy, intimacy, and mutual trust.

On the splenic levels security will emerge as the right to live on the physical plane without having to justify one's existence. On the world of the lower mind it will manifest as the right to satisfy appropriate desires without shame or guilt. On the world of soul it will manifest as the expression of one's soul urge in all appropriate circumstances. On the world of intellect it will manifest as the right to exhibit human awareness and to express it creatively within an institutional framework. In the world of spirit it will manifest as the right to experience union, manifest knowledge, and live without attachment to the collective field of maya.

The Second Pair

The second pair of chakras in partnership consists of the second and fifth chakras. Their partnership is based on the complementary roles they play in regulating self-expression and joy, including both conditional joy, which is based on achieving a multiworld, multidimensional state of well-being, and unconditional joy, whose manifestation requires no external catalyst.

The second chakra regulates the frequencies of energy responsible for Self-expression on the most fundamental level: sexual expression, the expression of vitality, and the expression of creativity, which humans share with all sentient beings. In addition, it regulates the frequencies of energy responsible for pleasure that has a clear object—sexual pleasure, pleasure from a job well done, and pleasure that comes from the approval of one's peers.

The fifth chakra regulates verbal and nonverbal expression through body language. It also regulates the frequencies of energy responsible for unconditional joy. Unconditional joy exists in all people, and emerges into conscious awareness once the fifth chakra has become active. Unconditional joy can be expressed by the human energy system and the organs of the physical-material body. On the splenic level, it can be expressed through the musculature of the face and through the organs of speech. On the dimensions of the higher and lower mind, it can be expressed as intimacy or empathy, which can emerge into the external environment through the functions and aspects of mind.

The Third Pair

The third pair of chakras in partnership consists of the fourth and sixth chakras. Their partnership is based on the complementary roles they play in recognizing and securing basic human rights. On the splenic levels, the fourth chakra upholds the right to to experience, express, and fulfill the needs of the physical-material body and etheric double. On the world of soul, the fourth chakra upholds the right to experience, express, and resolve feelings and emotions. On the world of intellect it upholds the right to experience and express the intent of the higher and lower mind through finite human awareness. In the world of spirit it upholds the right to experience and express the intent of transcendental consciousness.

The sixth chakra plays a direct role in safeguarding human rights through its influence on will. Will can emerge in two ways. It can emerge through appropriate activity and the expression of the four authentic desires that emerge from the bodies of desire, or it can emerge through the combined will of the CECs within the individual mind and ego. If the sixth chakra is functioning healthfully and synchronistically with its partner, the fourth chakra, then appropriate activity will safeguard personal rights. If it is not functioning healthfully, then the will of the Self and human rights that emerge through appropriate activity and authentic desire will be overwhelmed by the weight of karmic baggage and the collective will of the CECs within it.

Since the collective will of the individual mind and ego is to penetrate personal body space, by abandoning appropriate activity a person will surrender their intrinsic rights, and by default they will fall under the domination of the individual mind and ego. This form of surrender, sometimes disguised as openness, will disrupt the human energy system by allowing karmic baggage to accumulate. Worse still, it will permit the individual mind and ego to usurp the functions and activities of the higher and lower mind.

Indeed, once the functions of the fourth chakra are overwhelmed by the will of the individual mind and ego, the need to believe and understand will supplant the right to acquire and express knowledge through the continuous act of becoming. The sixth chakra plays an important role in the process of becoming through its relationship to appropriate activity and dharma as well as its ability, in association with the heart chakra, to discern energy fields. In fact, Yoga is quite clear that without discernment there is no samadhi, and without samadhi there can be no direct experience or union with the Self.

First and Seventh Chakras and Minor Energy Centers

The functional partnership between the first and seventh chakras and the minor energy centers in the hands and feet is based on the role they play in regulating pressure in the human energy system. Like the circulatory system in the the physical-material body, the organs of the human energy system function under pressure in a closed system. The pressure facilitates the movement of unqualified energy through the chakras, auras, and meridians, and maintains a healthy balance of polarity and gender.

The pressure within the seven traditional chakras and the meridians in personal body space—which can be thought of as the control center of the human energy system—will affect pressure in the larger system of meridians, chakras, and auras, as well as the energy bodies in the higher and lower mind.

The first and seventh chakra also function as bridges that connect the chakras within personal body space with those above and below it. The chakras above and below personal body space deal with issues of transcendence, while those within personal body space deal with physical and psychic survival. The first and seventh chakras play an essential role in integrating these seemingly unrelated human activities .

First Pair Meditation

The first pair meditation is designed to enhance your awareness of the complementary activities and resonance of the first chakra pair. Your designated intent will be "It is my intent to activate the first chakra pair and look inward in the world of soul on the levels of the first and third chakras."

Begin by finding a comfortable position with your back straight. Then use the standard method to relax and balance conscious and unconscious mental activity. Continue by activating and and centering yourself in the back of your heart chakra. Then split your attention and activate the front of your heart chakra. Once the front of your heart chakra has become active, set your intent. Then state "It is my intent to split my attention and to activate the back of my first chakra." Once the back of the chakra is active, state "It is my intent to split my attention and activate the front of my first chakra."

Take a moment to experience the activity of your first chakra. Then state "It is my intent to split my attention and to activate the back of my third chakra." Continue by saying "It is my intent to split my attention and to activate the front of my third chakra." Once both chakras are active, state "It is my intent to look inward, in the world of soul on the levels of the first and third chakras."

Take about fifteen minutes to enjoy the meditation. Then count from one to five. When you reach the number five, open your eyes. You will feel wide awake, perfectly relaxed, and better than you did before.

Second Pair Meditation

In the second pair meditation you will activate the second and fourth chakras and look inward in the world of soul. Your designated intent will be "It is my intent to activate my second chakra pair and to look inward in the world of soul on the levels of the second and fourth chakras."

As soon as you're ready to begin, find a comfortable position with your back straight. When you are comfortable, use the standard method to relax and balance conscious and unconscious mental activity. Then activate and center yourself in the back of your heart chakra. Once you're centered, split your attention, activate the front of your heart chakra, and set your intent. Then state "It is my intent to split my attention and to activate the back of my second chakra." Continue by saying "It is my intent to split my attention and to activate the front of my second chakra." Since the front and back of your heart chakra are already active, you can proceed to look inward in the world of soul on the levels of the second and fourth chakras by stating "It is my intent to look inward in the world of soul on the levels of the second and fourth chakras."

Take about fifteen minutes to enjoy the meditation. Then count from one to five. When you reach the number five, open your eyes. You will feel wide awake, perfectly relaxed, and better than you did before.

Third Pair Meditation

In the third pair meditation you will activate the third and fifth chakras and look inward in the world of soul. Your designated intent will be "It is my intent to activate my third chakra pair and to look inward in the world of soul on the levels of the third and fifth chakras."

As soon as you're ready to begin, find a comfortable position with your back straight. Then use the standard method to relax and balance conscious and unconscious mental activity. Continue by activating and and centering yourself in the back of your heart chakra. Then split your attention and activate the front of your heart chakra. Once the front of your heart chakra has become active, set your intent. Then state "It is my intent to split my attention and to activate the back of my third chakra." Once the chakra is active, state "It is my intent to split my attention and activate the front of my third chakra." Take a moment to experience the activity of your third chakra. Then state "It is my intent to split my attention and to activate the back of my fifth chakra." Continue by stating "It is my intent to split my attention and to activate the front of my fifth chakra." Once both chakras are active, state "It is my intent to look inward, in the world of soul on the levels of the third and fifth chakras."

Take about fifteen minutes to enjoy the meditation. After about fifteen minutes, count from one to five. When you reach the number five, open your eyes. You will feel wide awake, perfectly relaxed, and better than you did before.

Below is a list of additional exercises which will enhance your awareness of chakra pairs and their functions.

1. First pair meditation: Look inward in the world of spirit on the levels of the first and third chakras.

2. First pair meditation: Look inward in the world of the lower mind on the levels of the first and third chakras.

3. Second pair meditation: Look inward in world of the chakras on the levels of the second and fourth chakras.

4. Second pair meditation: Look inward in the world of spirit on the levels of the second and fourth chakras.

5. Third pair meditation: Look inward in the world of the lower mind on the levels of the third and fifth chakras.

6. Third pair meditation: Look inward in the world of intellect on the levels of the third and fifth chakras.

Chapter Twelve

The Tao begot one.
One begot two.
Two begot three.
And the three begot the ten thousand things.
The ten thousand things carry yin and yang.
They achieve harmony by combining these forces.

—Lao Tzu, 42

Meridians and Minor Energy Centers

Complementing the functions of the chakras—and in some cases working in concert with them—is the system of meridians (nadis correspond to meridians in yogic nomenclature). The meridians are streams of energy that connect the chakras to one another and transmit unqualified energy throughout the human energy system. By transmitting prana the meridians support the higher and lower mind, keep the human energy system in balance, and help to maintain the integrity of the auric boundaries.

The word "nadi" comes from the Sanskrit root *nad* which means "hollow stalk." The word "meridian" is an English derivative of the Chinese word *jingxian*. Though there are differences between the systems of meridians and nadis, both ancient Chinese and Indian texts agree that these streams of energy are numerous.

Although our present knowledge of meridians comes to us from China and India, in 1990 the mummified remains of a Bronze Age man was found in the Austrian Alps. On his body tattoos were located directly upon known acupuncture points. Further investigation led to even more startling discoveries. Medical teams studying his connective tissue learned that the man suffered the effects of arthritis. The points highlighted by the tattoos were precisely those that a modern-day acupuncturist would stimulate to treat his condition.

Structure of the Meridians

Although functionally the meridians correspond to the veins and arteries of the circulatory system—which distributes blood and life-nurturing nutrients throughout the physical-material body—structurally they close-ly resemble currents of water or air found in the earth's oceans and atmosphere. While the veins and arteries have a precise structure (essen-tially long elastic tubes) with a consistent shape, surface texture, and car-rying capacity, meridians, in contrast, are streams of unqualified energy whose size, shape, and carrying capacity are regulated by the quantity of energy they carry, the condition of the first and seventh chakras, and the minor energy centers in the hands and feet and variations in pressure exerted by qualified subfields in their immediate environment. Their unique structure, or lack thereof, makes it possible for them to rapidly increase or decrease in size and carrying capacity, and even shift position if necessary, as the quality and quantity of prana flowing through them changes. Indeed, it is not unusual for the meridians to change position or to move from side to side as the volume of prana they carry changes and they react to shifting conditions in their immediate environment.

The shushumna, ida, and pingala meridians are a case in point. Ancient texts describe how these meridians located in the back of personal body space swell in size once the kundalini-shakti has been aroused, and how they unite structurally and functionally to become one mighty channel once the kundalini-shakti has reached the crown chakra.

Function of the Meridians

Individually and collectively, meridians have several important functions. They connect the organs of the human energy system and distribute unqualified energy from one part of the system to another. In this capacity they serve as bridges between one chakra and another, and between the chakras and the minor energy centers in the hands and feet.

Through extensions the major meridians connect the chakras above and below personal body space to the chakras within personal body space. This allows excess energy flowing through the higher and lower chakras to spill into the auras, which keeps them filled with prana, and the auric surfaces taut and resistant to intrusions of qualified energy.

The meridians help regulate pressure within the human energy field. They do this by expanding and contracting as the quantity of unqualified energy changes, and by shifting unqualified energy from one part of the human energy system to another as needed.

The meridians release toxins that have collected within energy bodies and their corresponding energetic vehicles. Toxic energy within an energy body or energetic vehicle will be absorbed into the system of meridians, which will transfer the toxins to the appropriate chakra, which will then expel the globules of toxic energy into the auric field surrounding it. These globules will then make their way to the auric surface and diffuse through its pores into the external environment.

In their final function, meridians allow unqualified energy that is ready to make the quantum jump to be transmitted from the splenic levels to the physical-material body and etheric double. The energy made available in this way will be used to charge the nerves and to integrate the functions of the physical-material body with their corresponding energetic vehicles so that all energetic vehicles, including the splenic bodies, will react synchronistically to environmental stimulus.

The Ruling Meridians

In the Tantric system of Yoga we are told that the shushumna, ida, and pingala serve as the ruling nadis, or meridians (see figure 12-1, p. 187). The shushumna-governor meridian originates at a position in personal body space that corresponds to the muladhara chakra and passes through the male pole of the seven traditional chakras on its way up to the crown. The ida and pingala originate on either side of the first chakra. The ida works its way up the left side of the shushumna-governor and passes through the left nostril. The pingala works its way up the right side of the shushumna-governor and passes through the right nostril. Both the ida and pingala join the shushumna-governor again in the region of the ajna center, the sixth chakra.

Although some ancient texts suggest that both the ida and pingala can deviate from their spinal course, all Tantric texts agree that the ida moves up the left side of the spine while the pingala moves up the right side.

The fact that the ida and pingala pass through the nostrils is noteworthy because it supports the idea, embraced by Yoga, that by regulating prana on each inhalation, it is possible to regulate the movement of energy through the human energy system. It also explains why the ajna center, while concerned primarily with finite consciousness, memory, and the development of paranormal abilities is considered an essential part of the system that regulates the transmission and transmutation of prana through the human energy field.

Chinese medicine teaches that the meridians carry chi (chi is identical to prana) through the body; and that over two thousand acupuncture points are located along the major meridians.

Below is a list of eight additional meridians that play an important role in maintaining the health and well-being of the human energy system.

1. **The Tu Mo:** The tu mo rises from a position within personal body space corresponding to the base of the penis or vagina and passes through the spine to the brain. It is called the governor and is the channel of control. It is identical to the shushumna nadi described in Yoga.

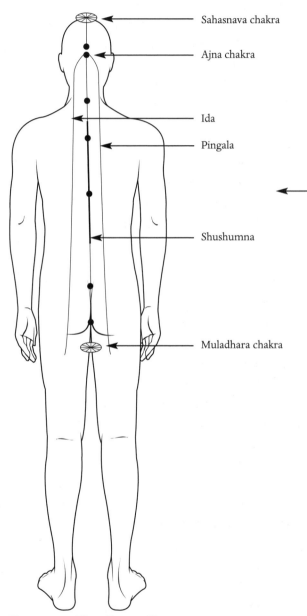

Sahasnava chakra

Ajna chakra

Ida

Pingala

Shushumna

Muladhara chakra

Figure 12-1 — The ruling meridians.

2. **The Jen Mo:** The jen mo rises from a position within personal body space corresponding to the base of the penis or vagina and passes through the stomach, chest, and neck before it reaches the brain. It is called the "conceptual" in some texts and is the channel of function.

3. **The Tai Mo:** The tai mo begins at a position within personal body space corresponding to the navel and makes a horizontal belt across the abdomen. It is called the belt channel.

4. **The Ch'ung Mo:** The ch'ung mo rises from a position within personal body space corresponding to the base of the penis or vagina and travels upward between the tu mo and jen mo channels to end at the heart. It is called the thrusting channel.

5. **The Yang Yu:** The two yang yu meridians are the masculine arm channels located in both arms. They link the shoulders with the centers in the palms, after passing through the middle fingers. Along with the yin yu they form the minor energy centers in the palms.

6. **The Yin Yu:** The yin yu are feminine arm channels that link the centers in the palms with the chest. They travel along the insides of each arm.

   The energy centers in the palms play a significant role in healing and in regulating pressure in the human energy system and are considered energy centers in their own right. They are often referred to as minor energy centers or minor chakras.

7. **The Yang Chiao:** The two yang chiao meridians rise from a central point in the soles of the feet and pass through the outer sides of the ankles and legs where they connect with additional meridians at the base of the penis or vagina. Along with the Yin Chiao meridians they form minor energy centers in the feet.

8. **The Yin Chiao:** The Yin Chiao meridians rise from a central point in the soles of the feet and pass through the inside of the ankles and legs where they connect with additional meridians at the base of the penis or vagina. They are called nega-

tive leg channels because they are yin in relation to the yang chiao meridians.

The centers in the soles composed of the yang chiao and yin chiao meridians are considered minor energy centers and they play a significant part in regulating pressure in the human energy system. Below you will find two exercises designed to enhance the function of the minor energy centers in the hands and feet and to stimulate the flow of unqualified energy through the major meridians.

Yin Yu-Yang Yu Meditations

The yin yu-yang yu meditation is designed to enhance the flow of prana through the circuit formed by the meridians converging in the hands, first on the right side of personal body space and then on the left. As the flow of prana through each circuit increases your minor energy centers will become more active and you will receive valuable information about their condition.

Your designated intent for this exercise will be "It is my intent to activate the energy centers in my palms." To begin, find a comfortable position with your back straight. Then use the standard method to relax and balance conscious and unconscious mental activity. Continue by activating and centering yourself in the back of your heart chakra. Once you're centered, split your attention and activate the front of your heart chakra. Then set your intent and state "It is my intent to split my attention and to project my second attention to the upper end of the yang yu meridian on the right side of personal body space." If there are no obstructions, the moment your second attention reaches the yang yu, the prana flowing through the meridian will carry it down the meridian to its terminus in the palm of the hand (see figure 12-2, p. 190). As soon as your second attention reaches the terminus, bring your emphasis to your second attention. Then move your second attention about an inch (three centimeters) diagonally down toward the base of your hand, using the prana that enters with each inhalation. This is the access point of the yin yu meridian in the right palm. If there are no obstructions caused by subfields of qualified energy, the moment your second attention finds the meridian, your attention will be carried up the inside of your arm by the prana flowing through the meridian to its terminus on the right side of your chest. Once the circuit has been completed, release your emphasis and your second attention. Remain centered in the back of the heart chakra and enjoy the enhanced flow of prana in your palm center and the yin yu and yang yu meridians.

When you're ready to proceed to the second part of this exercise, state "It is my intent to project my second attention to the access point of the left yang yu meridian." If there are no obstructions the moment you locate the access point with your attention it will be carried down to the meridian's terminus in the palm of the left hand. Bring your emphasis to your second attention. Then move your second attention one inch (three centimeters) diagonally down the palm, at a forty-five-degree angle away from your thumb. There you'll find the access point of the yin yu meridian. Let the prana flowing through the meridian carry your second attention to the terminus in the chest. Then release your emphasis and your second attention.

Take fifteen minutes to enjoy the effects of the exercise. Then count from one to five. When you reach the number five, open your eyes. You will feel wide awake, perfectly relaxed, and better than you did before.

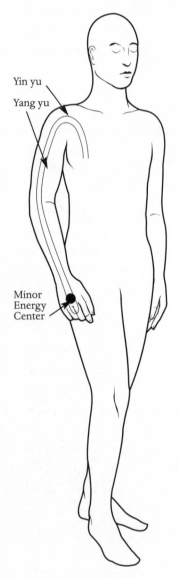

Yin yu
Yang yu

Minor
Energy
Center

Figure 12-2 — Minor energy
center located in the palm.

The Chiao Yang-Chiao Yin Meditation

In the chiao yin meditation you will enhance the flow of prana through the circuit formed by the meridians converging in the feet, first on the right side of personal body space and then on the left. As the flow of prana through each circuit increases your minor energy centers will become more active and you will receive valuable information about their condition.

Your designated intent in this exercise will be "It is my intent to activate the energy centers in my soles." To begin, find a comfortable position with your back straight. Then use the standard method to relax and balance conscious and unconscious mental activity. Continue by activating and centering yourself in the back of your heart chakra. Once you're centered, split your attention and activate the front of your heart chakra. Then set your intent and state "It is my intent to project my mental attention to the upper end of the chiao yang meridian, on the right side of personal body space." As soon as your second attention has been projected to the access point of the chiao yang, prana flowing through the meridian will carry it down to its terminus in the sole of the foot. Once your second attention reaches the terminus, bring your emphasis to your second attention. Then move your second attention diagonally back and inside about an inch (three centimeters). This is the access point of the chiao yin meridian (in the right sole). If there are no obstructions caused by subfields of qualified energy, the moment your mental attention finds the meridian, your attention will be carried up the inside of your ankle and thigh to a point an inch and a half (four centimeters) below the base of the spine on the inside of your leg. Once the circuit has been completed, release your emphasis and your second attention. Remain centered in the back of the heart chakra and enjoy the enhanced flow of prana in the sole center and the chiao yang and chiao yin meridians.

When you're ready to proceed, state "It is my intent to project my second attention to the access point of the left chiao yang meridian." If there are no obstructions, the moment your mental attention reaches the chiao yang, the prana flowing through the meridian will carry it down to its terminus in the sole of your foot. Once your second attention reaches the terminus, bring your emphasis to your second attention. Then move your second attention to the chiao yin access point on the sole of the foot diagonally across and back about an inch (three centimeters). The moment your second attention finds the meridian it will be carried up the inside of your ankle and thigh to a point about an inch and a half (four centimeters) below the base of your spine by the prana flowing through the meridian.

Once the circuit is complete release your emphasis and your second attention. Then take fifteen minutes to enjoy the effects of the exercise. After fifteen minutes count from one to five. When you reach the number five, open your eyes. You will feel wide awake, perfectly relaxed, and better than you did before.

Minor Energy Centers

Complementing the functions of the chakras, meridians, and auras is the system of minor energy centers in the hands and feet. Four minor energy centers exist in positions corresponding to the palms and soles. These centers should not be confused with the chakras, since both the structure and function of the minor energy centers are quite different. In fact, the minor energy centers are not structures, rather they are centers of activity created by the functional interaction of major meridians (one masculine and one feminine) located in the palms and soles. In the palms they are created through the interaction of the yang yu and yin yu meridians. (see figure 12-3, p. 193). In the soles they are created through the interaction of the chiao yang, and the chiao yin meridians

The minor energy centers have several functions that contribute to human health and well-being. In their first function the minor energy centers in the hands, along with the functions and aspects of mind, facilitate one's ability to manifest will and intent in the external environment. In the same way, the energy centers in the feet, along with the functions and aspects of mind, facilitate one's progress in the phenomenal world. These two functions, which are manifest on all phenomenal worlds and dimensions, mark an important and often overlooked convergence between the functions of the higher and lower mind and the minor energy centers in the hands and feet.

The minor energy centers, along with the first and seventh chakras, also regulate pressure within the microcosmic circuit. In addition, the minor energy centers influence the condition of the kandas—hubs where meridians emerge—and the system of meridians. If the minor energy centers are blocked, then the distribution of prana through the kandas and meridians will be disrupted. On the other hand, if the minor energy centers are functioning healthfully prana will radiate through the kandas into the meridians, and the meridians will distribute it throughout the human energy system.

Since the minor energy centers distribute prana, they are inviting targets for qualified subfields and the CECs within them. In fact, it is quite common for the minor energy centers to support thick layers of karmic sediment as well as extensions from the ego and attached qualified subfields, such as cords and controlling waves. The exercise that follows is de-signed to activate the minor energy centers so that prana can radiate through them more freely and they can more readily perform their prescribed activities.

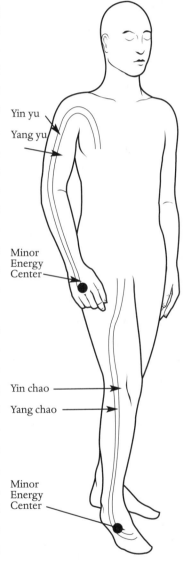

Figure 12-3 — Minor energy centers in palm and sole.

Pressure Meditation

Like the physical-material body, the health of the human energy field is dependent on the pressure within it. Although pranic pressure within the human energy system is dependent on the healthy function of the traditional seven chakras within personal body space and the minor energy centers in the hands and feet, it is the interaction of the first and seventh chakras and the minor energy centers that is most important.

Pranic pressure has an influence on polarity and gender identity. It also has an influence on the strength of surface boundaries and the energy system's ability to support vertical integration.

The exercise that follows is designed to keep pranic pressure within healthy parameters. In the exercise you will activate your first and seventh chakras and the minor energy centers in your hands and feet. Your designated intent in this exercise will be "It is my intent to restore pranic pressure in my energy system to its appropriate condition."

To begin, find a comfortable position with your back straight. Then use the standard method to relax and balance conscious and unconscious mental activity. Continue by activating and centering yourself in the back of your heart chakra. Once you're centered, split your attention and activate the front of your heart chakra. Then set your intent, split your attention, and activate the back of your first chakra. Continue by activating the front of your first chakra. Then split your attention once again and activate the back and the front of your seventh chakra.

After you've activated the first and seventh chakras, project your second attention to the chiao yang meridian on your right side. Then let prana stream your second attention down the meridian to your right palm. Once your second attention reaches your palm, bring your emphasis to it and project your second attention to the chiao yin. Let the prana stream your second attention to the meridian's terminus in the chest. Then repeat the same process with the chiao yang and chiao yin on your left side.

Once the centers in the palms have been activated and the chiao yang and chiao yin meridians have been cleared, project your second attention to the access point of the yang yu by your right thigh. Then let the prana stream your second attention down the meridian to the sole of your foot. Bring your emphasis to your second attention and project your second attention to the yin yu in your right sole. Then let the prana stream your second attention to the terminus in your thigh. Repeat the same process with the meridians and minor energy center on the left side. Then release your emphasis and second attention.

Take fifteen minutes to enjoy the meditation while pressure increases and prana fills your auric fields and strengthens your boundaries. After fifteen minutes, count from one to five. When you reach the number five, open your eyes. You will feel wide awake, perfectly relaxed, and better than you did before.

Chapter Thirteen

*Realize with a still mind your own true nature which is
the one pure, undivided Consciousness underlying the
restless mind which is composed of the whole universe
in all its diversity.*

—Tripura Rahasya, 70

Structure and Function of Chakras
Outside Body Space

The function of the human energy system is dependent as much on the activities of the chakras above and below body space as those within it. Unfortunately, until the present time there has been a lack of detailed information about the structure and function of the higher and lower chakras.

Some ancient Yogic texts have referred to seven chakras above personal body space that individually and collectively regulate the higher functions of human consciousness. Other texts have referred to seven chakras below personal body space that regulate the baser functions of human nature, but none of the texts offer much detail concerning the chakras' structures and functions.

In spite of the lack of extant material, we now know that there are one hundred and forty-two chakras (including the seven traditional chakras) that regulate the transmission and transmutation of unqualified energy in the higher and lower mind and on the splenic levels. Sixty-three higher

197

chakras are located above personal body space. These, along with the seven traditional chakras in personal body space, constitute the higher chakras. Complementing the higher chakras are seventy lower chakras located below personal body space. The remaining two chakras are the lower splenic and upper splenic chakras, which are located in personal body space between the second and third chakras.

In the past decade, as we've learned more about the structure and function of the the chakras above and below personal body space, it has become clear that the greater part of spirit, intellect, soul, and authentic human desire emerge from the dimensions above and below the frequencies of energy regulated by the traditional seven chakras. This shouldn't come as a total surprise. Both Yoga and Vedanta teach that human beings—who are essentially interdimensional beings—exist simultaneously in three collective fields of energy. The upper field of energy, which has the highest mean frequency, is associated with dimensions eight through seventy. The middle field of energy, with a lower mean frequency, is associated with dimensions one through seven, the splenic levels and the first seven dimensions below personal body space. The lower field of energy is associated with the dimensions with the lowest mean frequency, the eighth through seventieth dimensions below personal body space.

Since the collective field of maya surrounds all worlds and dimensions, including those above and below personal body space, in order to overcome karmic baggage it is not enough to activate the chakras and become fully conscious on the dimensions regulated by the chakras within personal body space. One must activate the chakras on the the higher and lower dimensions, overcome the attachments that karmic baggage creates, and bring the higher and lower dimensions on each world into conscious awareness.

Structure and Function of the
Higher and Lower Chakras

The sixty-three chakras above personal body space are located above the sahasrara chakra, beginning one and a half inches (four centimeters) above the crown. From that point they extend approximately eighteen feet (six meters) above the top of the head.

The seventy chakras below personal body space begin their descent downward just below the muladhara chakra. The first chakra below personal body space is located about three inches (eight centimeters) below the perineum and the remaining chakras extend downward approximately eighteen feet (six meters).

The structure of the chakras above and below personal body space are almost identical to the chakras within personal body space. The female end of each chakra is disk-shaped, with spokes or petals that continually spin around a central axis that serves as a vortex through which prana flows. As a chakra outside personal body space becomes more active, its rate of rotation will increase and it will glow more brightly. The more distant from personal body space, the more spokes the disk section will contain. Connected to the disk is a shaft or axle, which is substantially shorter than the chakras within personal body space, and located at the far end of the axle is the male pole of the chakra.

Although the higher and lower chakras regulate prana in the higher and lower dimensional fields, it is the eighth through thirteenth chakras and the first seven chakras below personal body space that regulate the energy associated with aspects of the higher and lower mind that transcend body consciousness. In the world of spirit this includes the intuitive mind, insight, catharsis, transcendent consciousness, and identification with the Self.

In the world of intellect this includes appropriate activity, dharma, Self- knowledge, and identification with the aspects of human awareness associated with the higher and lower mind.

In the world of the soul, this includes human emotion—unconditional joy—full participation with the external environment, and the expression of divine consciousness through creativity and the organs of expression.

In the world of the lower mind and the bodies of desire, these include authentic desires and the sensations and feelings that support them. It also includes appropriate activity that precludes attachment to the glittering and seductive aspects of the celestial planes.

The remaining chakras above and below personal body space regulate unqualified energy on the higher and lower dimensional fields. Like their counterparts in the middle field, excluding the splenic chakras, these chakras and the energy and consciousness that emerge from them can function without the support of the physical-material body, which means that one can function with conscious awareness while alive and during the transition between incarnations.

Therefore, if one becomes fully conscious of the higher and lower worlds, while functioning consciously in the middle world, it becomes possible to conquer death and its limitations. ". . . And there shall be no more death, neither sorrow, nor crying, neither shall there be any more pain: for the former things are passed away" (Revelation 21:4).

Indeed, life and death have never been mutually exclusive conditions or fields of activity. Aspects of life and death continually interact through the activities of the chakras above and below personal body space. It is precisely the synergy created by their mutual interaction that makes the higher and lower chakras so important in the process of overcoming karmic baggage.

In fact, fascination with death, and/or the inordinate fear of death, the inability to surrender completely during periods of intimacy, the need to justify one's existence, and/or the need to find something or someone to live for, all indicate that the functions of the chakras above and below personal body space have been disrupted and are not fully integrated with each other and the other organs of the human energy system.

Chakras Eight through Thirteen

While the seven traditional chakras, as well as the splenic chakras, and the first seven chakras below personal body space are needed to maintain health and well-being to regulate the higher functions of human consciousness, more chakras are needed. The first six chakras above personal body space perform this function in the worlds of spirit, intellect, soul, lower mind, and the world of the chakras. The main function of these chakras is to elevate human consciousness, awareness, emotion, feeling, and sensation above the mundane functions of life so that union with the Self becomes possible.

The eighth through the thirteenth chakras are located directly above the sahasrara chakra. The eighth chakra is situated two inches (five centimeters) above the crown and the ninth through thirteenth extend upward at approximately two-inch intervals (see figure 13-1, p. 202).

When the eighth through thirteenth chakras emerge into conscious awareness they can produce an unusual effect called "elongation." Elongation is a stretching sensation at the top of the head that is accompanied by the feeling that one has become taller or longer. Rather than being disturbing or disorienting, the experience can be quite pleasant, since it is prana radiating through the higher chakras and meridians that is responsible for the effect.

The collective functions of chakras eight through thirteen become even more important once one chooses to engage in a relationship based on appropriate activity (dharma), rather than a relationship based exclusively on the functions of gender and polarity. The shift in relationship based on dharma and appropriate activity will permit the eighth through thirteenth chakras to participate directly in the relationship. The mechanics of this union are simple to understand. In a traditional relationship the masculine partner will be assertive from the second chakra, meaning that energy will be asserted forward—and will be receptive by the fourth chakra, meaning that energy will be received or embraced, while the female partner will be receptive by the second chakra and will be assertive by the fourth chakra.

In a relationship that includes the eighth through thirteenth chakras, both partners will remain centered in the higher and lower mind, and prana emerging from the muladhara chakra will flow upward as far as the thirteenth chakra and beyond, rather than being diverted forward. By staying centered in the higher and lower mind, neither partner would polarize their energy system. In fact, there wouldn't be any push or pull in any of their interactions. As a result, prana would flow more freely and

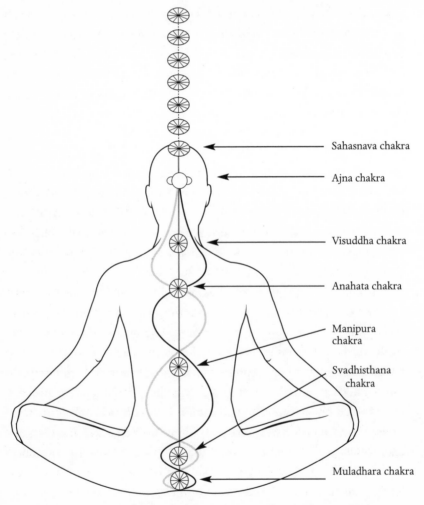

Sahasnava chakra

Ajna chakra

Visuddha chakra

Anahata chakra

Manipura chakra

Svadhisthana chakra

Muladhara chakra

Figure 13-1 — The eighth through thirteenth chakras extend upward from the crown of the head, and are spaced about 2 inches apart.

both partners would experience more pleasure, love, intimacy, and mutual joy within their relationship.

Moving Beyond the Seventh Chakra

To function with conscious awareness on the levels of the eighth through the thirteenth chakras, it is necessary to embrace appropriate activity. To embrace appropriate activity, three centers of awareness in personal body space must function together synchronistically: the head (awareness and will), the heart (emotion and love), and the generative organs (vitality and pleasure). If there is will without heart, or heart without pleasure, which is the precursor of joy and bliss, it will be difficult if not impossible to consistently embrace appropriate activity and become conscious on the levels of the eighth through the thirteenth chakras.

Exercise: Connecting Will, Love, and Pleasure

In the exercise below you will activate and balance the energy of the second, fourth, and sixth chakras within body space in the world of the lower mind, in preparation for your work with chakras eight through thirteen.

Your designated intent in this exercise will be "It is my intent to activate the second, fourth, and sixth chakras and to look inward on these dimensions in the world of the lower mind."

When you're ready to begin, find a comfortable position with your back straight, then use the standard method to relax and balance conscious and unconscious mental activity. Continue by activating and centering yourself in the back of your heart chakra. Then split your attention, activate the front of your heart chakra, and set your intent. To continue, split your attention again, bring your emphasis to your second attention, and activate the back of your second chakra. Then activate the front of your second chakra. Once the second chakra is active, continue by activating both the back and the front of your sixth chakra. Then state "On the level of the second chakra it is my intent to look inward in the world of the lower mind." Continue by saying "On the level of the fourth chakra it is my intent to look inward in the world of the lower mind."

Finally, state "On the level of the sixth chakra it is my intent to look inward in the world of the lower mind." Take fifteen minutes to enjoy the shift in consciousness.

Then count from one to five. When you reach the number five, open your eyes. You will feel wide awake, perfectly relaxed, and better than you did before.

You can enhance your ability to embrace appropriate activity by practicing the exercises below.

1. Activate the second, fourth, and sixth chakras and look inward in the world of the soul on all three dimensions.

2. Activate the second, fourth, and sixth chakras and look inward on the world of intellect on all three dimensions.

3. Activate the second, fourth, and sixth chakras and look inward in the world of spirit on all three dimensions.

4. Activate the second, fourth, and sixth chakras and look inward in the world of the chakras on all three dimensions.

Activating the Eighth through Thirteenth Chakras

After you've mastered the exercise above and embraced appropriate activity, you can take the next step by activating the eighth through thirteenth chakras. Your designated intent in this exercise will be "It is my intent to activate the eighth through thirteenth chakras and to look inward in the world of the lower mind."

To begin, find a comfortable position with your back straight. Then use the standard method to relax and balance conscious and unconscious mental activity. Continue by activating and centering yourself in the back of your heart chakra. Then split your attention, activate the front of your heart chakra, and set your intent.

After you've set your intent, split your attention and activate the back end of the eighth chakra. Then split your attention and activate the front of the eighth chakra. Continue by working upward, first activating the back and then the front of the remaining five chakras. After you've activated all six chakras you will look inward simultaneously on all six dimensions in the world of the lower mind by stating "On the dimensions of the eighth through thirteenth chakras it is my intent to look inward on the world of the lower mind."

Take fifteen minutes to enjoy the increased flow of prana and the enhanced consciousness you experience. Then count from one to five. When you reach the number five, open your eyes. You will feel wide awake, perfectly relaxed, and better than you did before.

Activating the Lower Chakras

There is a common misconception that being grounded means grounding yourself in the physical-material world by connecting with the earth. In fact, being grounded is an energetic process that can take place in only two ways: first by activating the splenic chakras and vertically reintegrating your splenic and upper splenic bodies, which will ground you in the physical-material world; and second, by grounding yourself in the lower seventy dimensions by activating the seventy chakras below personal body space, and reintegrating the communities of energy bodies on those dimensions.

The next meditation will provide you with a strong sense of grounding. However, the process of grounding is not complete until all seventy chakras below personal body space have been activated, and the communities of energy bodies on the lower seventy dimensions in the worlds of the higher and lower mind have been recollected and reintegrated.

Activating the First Three Chakras
Below Body Space

In this exercise you will activate the first three chakras below personal body space and look inward on the world of the lower mind. Your designated intent will be "It is my intent to activate the first three chakras below personal body space and to look inward, in the world of the lower mind."

To begin, find a comfortable position with your back straight. Then use the standard method to relax and balance conscious and unconscious mental activity. Once you're relaxed, activate and center yourself in the back of your heart chakra. Then split your attention, activate the front of your heart chakra, and set your intent. Continue by activating the seven traditional chakras in personal body space, beginning with the back of the first chakra and working upward, then working downward from the front of the seventh chakra to the front of the first chakra—excluding the fourth chakra, which is already active.

After you've activated the seven traditional chakras, state "It is my intent to split my attention and to activate the back of my first chakra below personal body space." Then state "It is my intent to split my attention and to activate the front of my first chakra below personal body space." Activate the second and third chakras below personal body space in the same way. Then state "It is my intent to look inward on the world of the lower mind on the levels of the first three chakras below personal body space."

Take about fifteen minutes to enjoy the meditation. Then count from one to five. When you reach the number five, open your eyes. You will feel wide awake, perfectly relaxed, and better than you did before.

You can experience the resonance of the first three chakras below personal body space in additional worlds by practicing the exercises below.

1. Activate the first three chakras below personal body space and look inward in the world of soul on all three levels simultaneously.

2. Activate the first three chakras below personal body space and look inward in the world of intellect on all three levels simultaneously.

3. Activate the first three chakras below personal body space and look inward in the world of spirit on all three levels simultaneously.

4. Activate the first three chakras below personal body space and look inward in the world of the chakras on all three levels simultaneously.

5. Activate the first three chakras below personal body space and look inward simultaneously on the worlds of spirit, intellect, soul, lower mind, and chakras.

Activating the First Seven Chakras Below Personal Body Space

In this exercise you will activate the first seven chakras below personal body space and look inward in the world of the lower mind. Your designated intent for this exercise will be "It is my intent to activate the first seven chakras below personal body space and look inward on these seven dimensions, in the world of the lower mind."

To begin, find a comfortable position with your back straight. Then use the standard method to relax and balance conscious and unconscious mental activity. Once you're relaxed, activate and center yourself in the back of your heart chakra. Then split your attention, activate the front of your heart chakra and set your intent. Continue by activating the seven traditional chakras in personal body space. Then state "It is my intent to split my attention and to activate the back of my first chakra below personal body space." Continue by stating "It is my intent to split my attention and to activate the front of my first chakra below personal body space." Activate the next six chakras below personal body space in the same way. Then state "On the levels of the first seven chakras below personal body space it is my intent to look inward in the world of the lower mind."

Take about fifteen minutes to enjoy the meditation, then count from one to five. When you reach the number five, open your eyes. You will feel wide awake, perfectly relaxed, and better than you did before.

You can experience the resonance of the first seven chakras below personal body space in additional worlds by practicing the following exercises.

1. Activate the first seven chakras below personal body space and look inward in the world of soul, on all seven levels simultaneously.

2. Activate the first seven chakras below personal body space and look inward in the world of intellect on all seven levels simultaneously.

3. Activate the first seven chakras below personal body space and look inward in the world of spirit on all seven levels simultaneously.

4. Activate the first seven chakras below personal body space and look inward in the world of the chakras on all seven levels simultaneously.

5. Activate the first seven chakras below personal body space and look inward in all worlds of the higher and lower mind on all seven levels simultaneously.

Part Four

Overcoming the Non-Self

Chapter Fourteen

The karmas carry the seeds of their own destruction in themselves.

—Ramana Maharshi, 3

The Amazing Aprana

In this chapter you will learn to use the Aprana to release subfields of qualified energy surrounding personal body space.

The aprana is a feminine form of prana that exists on the dimensions of the higher and lower mind and on the splenic levels. When it is used in conjunction with the mental attention and the intent of the higher and lower mind, it becomes an effective tool for removing karmic sediment from the auric field in the region between the surface of personal body space and the apranic boundary.

The aprana emerges from a position or boundary that surrounds personal body space in each world and dimension at a distance of approximately eight inches (twenty centimeters). The boundary or position from which the aprana emerges should not be confused with the surface of the auric fields. The apranic boundary is not a structure, but rather a departure boundary from which an energetic field—the aprana—emerges.

When the aprana on a particular world and dimension is active it tends to dislodge karmic baggage as it moves toward the surface of personal body space. The combination of the aprana with its feminine polarity emerging from outside personal body space and the prana emerging from the chakras is so powerful that when they are both active they will wrest control of the vital area between the surface of personal body space and the apranic boundary from the individual mind and ego.

In classical Yoga the pranas (including the aprana) are divided into two classes. One school of Yoga compares the pranas to the senses, but in the strictest sense the pranas refer to *streams* of unqualified energy. The traditional five streams or *airs* of unqualified energy include the prana, aprana, vyana, samana, and udana.

From classical Yoga we also learn that the aprana expels toxins and promotes the circulation of energy. When the aprana unites with prana, the life force, we are told that the spirit will be centered in the heart. This means that when the aprana with its feminine polarity is able to unite with the prana emerging from the chakras, not only will karmic baggage be released, but the Self will emerge through the higher and lower mind into conscious awareness.

Structure and Function of the Aprana

The aprana has no structure or distinct qualities, but it is possible to recognize it when it emerges from the apranic boundary by the way it stimulates the human energy system, increases vitality, expands awareness, and puts pressure on qualitative subfields.

The aprana can either move or remain static. When it is static it remains functionally dormant. Movement is normal and considered far healthier. The aprana on a particular world and dimension will become static when an inordinate accumulation of karmic energy extends outward from the surface of personal body space and intrudes into the apranic boundary. The addition of an enlarged ego on a particular world and dimension as well as the presence of cords and/or controlling waves can inhibit the movement of aprana even further. In some cases the movement of aprana can become fitful or selectively active on portions of the apranic boundary in a particular world and dimension.

The aprana's ability to emerge from the apranic boundary and move without disruption in the direction of personal body space is dependent on several factors including the quality and quantity of karmic sediment surrounding personal body space on a particular world and dimension, the size of the ego, its mean density, the degree to which the host has become attached to the individual mind and ego, and the presence of controlling waves and/or cords in the host's energy field.

Controlling waves and cords have a significant effect on the ability of the aprana to emerge and function healthfully for two reasons. First, they introduce qualified energy and CECs into the host's internal environment, and second, they remain attached to the perpetrator, which increases the density of all qualified energy in the host's energy field on the world and dimension on which the projections are located.

For anyone who is fortunate enough to have their energy bodies fully integrated and their energy system functioning healthfully, the aprana will remain continually active, providing them with a tool that can remove qualified energy that has intruded into the area between the apranic boundary and the surface of personal body space.

By paying attention to your breath, particularly your inhalation, it is possible to experience the aprana as it moves toward personal body space. As you observe the incoming breath you'll notice that it appears to be emerging from a boundary that may shift up and down, but that is always the same distance from personal body space, no matter how you move your head. This is the apranic boundary, and it surrounds personal body space at a distance of about ten inches (twenty-five centimeters) on all worlds and dimensions of the higher and lower mind and the splenic levels.

The aprana should not be confused with the prana that enters with each inhalation. It is a separate manifestation of shakti, which functions exclusively between the apranic boundary and the surface of personal body space. For this reason, the aprana shouldn't be used to remove karmic baggage in the form of intrusions that have entered personal body space. You should also take note: the aprana will not function in association with the functions and aspects of mind on any world or dimensions of the higher and lower mind, or the splenic levels. In addition, when removing karmic baggage you should never compel the aprana to enter personal body space on any dimension of the higher and lower mind, even if the qualified subfield you've chosen to release straddles it on both sides. To work with intrusions—qualified subfields within personal body space—other techniques are safer and more effective (see the seven step process in chapter sixteen).

If the buildup of karmic sediment around personal body space in a specific world and dimension has been kept at a minimum, the aprana will function healthfully, which means that the aprana will emerge as a continuous stream that will flow without the need for conscious support. Unfortunately, for most people the aprana has been blocked by a combination of karmic sediment, cords, and controlling waves, as well as the interference of the ego, particularly when the ego has become enlarged or has sent out extensions that have become attached to the outer layers of karmic sediment (see figure 14-1, p. 215).

Indeed, getting the aprana to function healthfully by flowing without disruption is in itself an important achievement that will enhance the overall health of your energy system. As you will learn, liberating the aprana is not a difficult process, although on dimensions where there is an inordinate amount of karmic sediment you may have to repeat the process described below several times before the aprana becomes active and flows smoothly over the entire surface of the apranic boundary.

Activating the Aprana

In the following exercise you will locate and activate the aprana in the world of soul on the level of the fourth chakra. Your designated intent will be "It is my intent to locate and activate the aprana in the world of soul on the level of the fourth chakra."

Begin by finding a comfortable position with your back straight. Then use the standard method to relax and balance conscious and unconscious mental activity. Once you're relaxed, activate and center yourself in the back of your heart chakra. Then split your attention, activate the front of your heart chakra, and set your intent.

When you're ready to continue, state, "It is my intent to look inward in the world of soul on the level of the fourth chakra." Then state, "It is my intent to locate and activate the aprana in the world of soul on the

level of the fourth chakra." Although the aprana can emerge from the entire apranic boundary when it has become active, in this initial exercise
focus your attention on the apranic boundary facing you.

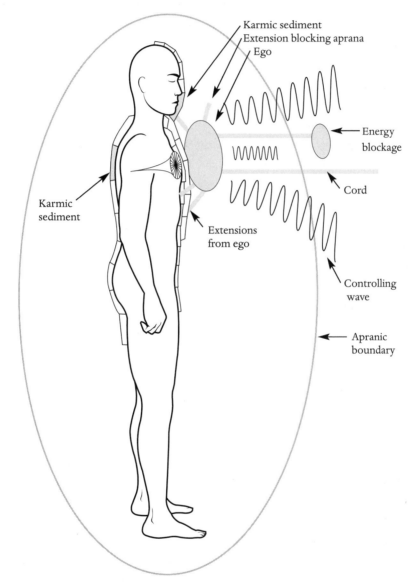

Figure 14-1 — The ego sends out extensions that may
become attached to karmic sediment.

Since you won't be removing karmic sediment in this exercise, as soon as you feel a slight pressure state, "It is my intent to release the aprana." Then take about fifteen minutes to enjoy the effects produced by the aprana. After fifteen minutes count from one to five. When you reach the number five, open your eyes. You will feel wide awake, perfectly relaxed, and better than you did before.

Normally, the aprana will emerge as soon as it has become active. If it doesn't, be patient. After a few moments you may feel a pop as the aprana frees itself from karmic baggage and moves toward the surface of personal body space.

If there is only minimal resistance from qualified energy there will be no pressure and barely any pop. If there is an inordinate amount of qualified energy the pressure may precede the pop and grow quite strong before the aprana begins to move toward the surface of personal body space. If there has been a buildup of karmic sediment it is normal for the pressure to continue for a short time, since the aprana will be squeezing karmic sediment against the surface of personal body space. If the pressure becomes too strong you can state, "It is my intent to release the aprana." This will release the aprana and relieve the pressure.

If there is no pop, or if the aprana does not become active and move toward personal body space, restate your intent and continue to be patient. If the aprana still doesn't become active, then try again at another time. Conditions may change and the qualified energy that has prevented the aprana from emerging may change state and/or become less dense, making it more likely that the aprana will become active and emerge from the apranic boundary.

If you feel pressure after you've returned to normal consciousness don't be concerned—it will quickly dissipate as soon as you've been distracted or centered your attention on something else.

To activate the aprana and to become aware of your karmic condition on more worlds and dimensions of the higher and lower mind, you can practice the exercises below.

1. Activate the aprana in the world of the lower mind, level of
   the third chakra.

2. Activate the aprana on the splenic level.

3. Activate the aprana in the world of intellect, level of the first chakra.

4. Activate the aprana in the world of the spirit, level of the seventh chakra.

Activating the Aprana on the First Seven Dimensions

In this exercise you will activate the aprana in the world of soul on the levels of the seven traditional chakras. Your designated intent will be "It is my intent to activate the aprana in the world of soul on the levels of the seven traditional chakras."

Begin by finding a comfortable position with your back straight. Then use the standard method to relax and balance conscious and unconscious mental activity. Continue by activating and centering yourself in the back of your heart chakra. Then split your attention, activate the front of your heart chakra, and set your intent. Continue by activating the back and then the front of the seven traditional chakras, excluding the fourth chakra, which you've already activated. After you've activated all seven chakras, state, "It is my intent to look inward in the world of soul, on the levels of the seven traditional chakras."

Once you've looked inward on the levels of the seven traditional chakras you can activate the aprana. Begin on the level of the first chakra by asserting, "It is my intent that the aprana emerge in the world of soul on the level of the first chakra." If there isn't an inordinate amount of karmic baggage or an enlarged ego, the aprana will emerge from the apranic boundary and move toward personal body space until it comes in contact with the outermost layers of karmic sediment on the level of the first chakra. Since you won't be releasing karmic energy in this exercise, as soon as you feel pressure, state, "It is my intent to release the aprana on the world of soul, level of the first chakra." Once you've released the aprana on the the level of the first chakra, state, "It is my intent that the aprana emerge in the world of soul on the level of the second chakra." Wait until you feel a slight pressure, then release the aprana and move to the level of the third chakra. Continue in this way, activating and releasing the aprana, on the levels of the third, fourth, fifth, sixth, and seventh chakras.

After you've activated and released the aprana on the seven dimensions within personal body space, release your second attention. Then take about fifteen minutes to enjoy the effects produced by the aprana. After fifteen minutes, count from one to five. When you reach the number five, open your eyes. You will feel wide awake, perfectly relaxed, and better than you did before.

To activate the aprana in additional worlds and dimensions you can practice the exercises below. By practicing them you will increase your skill and become more aware of your karmic condition.

1. Activate the aprana in the world of the lower mind on the levels of the seven traditional chakras.

2. Activate the aprana in the world of the intellect on the levels of the seven traditional chakras.

3. Activate the aprana on the levels of the upper splenic and splenic chakras.

4. Activate the aprana in the world of soul, level of the first three chakras below personal body space.

5. Activate the aprana in the world of the lower mind, level of chakras eight through thirteen.

Take note: Activating the aprana on worlds and dimensions where karmic baggage surrounding personal body space is inordinately dense, polarized, active, and/or where there is an enlarged ego with extensions, cords and/or controlling waves may be more difficult than you anticipate. To deal with these conditions you may have to strengthen your intent, stay more focused, or repeat the process several times until the aprana emerges from the apranic boundary and begins to move toward personal body space.

Selectively Activating the Aprana

For the aprana to release karmic baggage on a particular world and dimension it's not necessary to activate the aprana along the entire apranic boundary. In fact, you will find it far more efficient to activate the aprana only in front of the qualified subfield you've chosen to release. In the exercise below, in preparation for releasing karmic baggage you will activate the aprana in the world of intellect on the level of the fifth chakra, in the area facing you between the third and fifth chakras. Your designated intent in this exercise will be: "It is my intent to activate the aprana in the world of soul on the level of the fifth chakra, in the area facing me between the third and fifth chakras."

Begin by finding a comfortable position with your back straight. Then use the standard method to relax and balance conscious and unconscious mental activity. Continue by activating and centering yourself in the back of your heart chakra. Then split your attention, activate the front of your heart chakra, and set your intent. Continue by stating, "It is my intent to look inward In the world of soul on the level of the fifth chakra." Take a few moments to enjoy the shift in consciousness, then say, "It is my intent that the aprana emerge in the world of soul on the level of the fifth chakra, in the area facing me between the third and fifth chakras." Once the aprana has become active it will move toward personal body space. Let it continue to move until you feel pressure. Then state, "It is my intent to release the aprana." Take fifteen minutes to enjoy the effects produced by the aprana.

Then count from one to five. When you reach the number five, open your eyes. You will feel wide awake, perfectly relaxed, and better than you did before.

To selectively activate the aprana in additional worlds and dimensions, you can practice the exercises below. By practicing them you will increase your skill and become more aware of your karmic condition.

1. Activate the aprana in the world of spirit, level of the first chakra, in the area facing you between the first and third chakras.

2. Activate the aprana in the world of the chakras, level of the sixth chakra, in the area behind you between the fourth and seventh chakras.

3. Activate the aprana in the world of the lower mind, level of the second chakra, in the area facing you between the first and third chakras.

4. Activate the aprana in the world of spirit, level of the eighth chakra, in the area on your left side between the second and fifth chakras.

5. Activate the aprana on the level of the splenic chakra, in the area above the seventh chakra.

Releasing Karmic Energy

With the knowledge and skills you've acquired you're now ready to re-lease a subfield of karmic energy using the aprana. But take note: during the process you must stay centered in the back of your heart chakra and resist all forms of distraction, including thoughts, emotions, feelings, and the movement of qualified energy. In addition, you must resist the tendency to split your ego.

The process will proceed as follows: after you've located a suitable qualified subfield, you will activate the aprana in the appropriate world, dimension, and location. Once the aprana has become active and has put the subfield you've chosen under pressure, you will split your attention and project your second attention (which will emerge from the back of your heart chakra) directly behind the advancing aprana. The second at-tention will cover the back of the aprana like a thin veneer. Once it does, you will bring your emphasis to your second attention and gently push against the surface of the qualified subfield from behind the advancing aprana (see figure 14-2, p. 221). This will put the subfield under increased pressure. As the pressure increases, the pores of the surface membrane will expand. At a critical point they will become large enough for the aprana to pour through the surface boundary into the subfield. Since qualified energy and unqualified energy cannot occupy the same space at the same time, the qualified energy will be released permanently from your energy field.

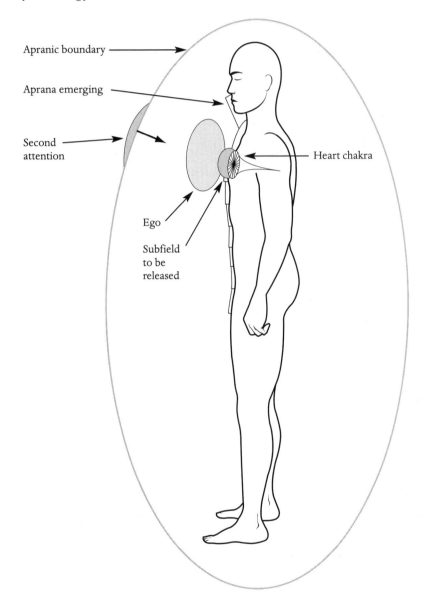

Apranic boundary

Aprana emerging

Second attention

Heart chakra

Ego

Subfield to be released

Figure 14-2 — The process of releasing karmic energy.

In some cases the qualified subfield you've chosen to release will be large enough to expand beyond the edges of your second attention. To prevent that from happening it will be necessary to expand your second attention by stating, "It is my intent to expand my second attention up, down, left, and right."

If you're already aware of a qualified subfield you wish to release, you can proceed directly to the next stage of the process. If not, then you must scan the area between the surface of personal body space and the apranic boundary to locate one (to review the technique for scanning, consult chapter seven).

The subfield that you choose to release in this exercise should be average sized with an average density, polarity, and level of activity, and it should be located between the surface of personal body space and the apranic boundary.

To begin the process, find a comfortable position with your back straight. Your designated intent will be: "It is my intent to release the qualified subfield which I have in mind (then specify world, dimension, and location), or specify (on the world and level where you feel heavy, pressure, discomfort, or pain)."

To continue, use the standard method to relax and balance conscious and unconscious mental activity. Then activate and center yourself in the back of your heart chakra. Once you're centered, split your attention, activate the front of your heart chakra, and set your intent. Then state your intent to look inward in the world and dimension where you've scanned or located the subfield: If you don't know the world and dimension, then state, "On the world and dimension where I feel (heaviness, discomfort, pressure or pain), it is my intent that the aprana emerge." Once you feel pressure, which will indicate that the aprana has made contact with the subfield you've chosen to release, state, "It is my intent to bring my second attention behind the advancing aprana." Then state, "It's my intent to bring my emphasis to my second attention." If necessary, extend your second attention up, down, left, and right, then gently push inward along the entire surface of your second attention. Stay attentive and don't let the aprana push qualified energy into personal body space.

Be sure not to split your ego or allow your attention to drift. Simply apply pressure as the aprana moves toward personal body space. If resistance becomes too strong hold your attention in place for a few moments. Then push again along the surface of the your second attention. When the pressure reaches the appropriate level, the aprana will penetrate the subfield and the subfield will be released.

As soon as the aprana penetrates the subfield's surface boundary, the pressure will abruptly cease and there will be a sense of relief, which is often accompanied by a pop that indicates that the qualified energy has been released and the aprana has replaced it.

Once the subfield has been released, release the aprana, your emphasis, and your second attention. Then count from one to five. When you reach the number five, open your eyes. You will feel wide awake, perfectly relaxed, and better than you did before.

Chapter Fifteen

*To the degree that you turn away from attachment to
the unreal your inner vision of Reality develops. If by a
steady practice of this kind, the mind comes under control and becomes aware as Consciousness-Self, you can
abide as the the Ocean of Bliss through living in the bit-
ter body.*

—Kaivalya Navaneeta, 50

Releasing Personas

Personas are complex subfields of qualified energy that express the will
and individual qualities of the CECs within them. Although personas
exist within the individual mind and ego, they can be projected through
the macrocosm from one human being to another. Personas that are projected through the macrocosm emerge from karmic sediment or from independent energy blockages and/or intrusions. When they emerge from
intrusions personas can be particularly disruptive, since they will be exceedingly dense, polarized and highly active, which means they will have
a high degree of penetrating power.

Personas in the microcosm can be found within the collective field of
maya on all worlds and dimensions, as well as in the splenic levels and
the functions and aspects of mind. In some cases, personas can become
trapped in energy bodies or energetic vehicles if an energy body or

energetic vehicle has been ejected from personal body space and has been contaminated by qualified subfields.

All personas contain at least one CEC, although most personas contain several. Even though the position of the CECs within personas may vary, all CECs within individual personas will be integrated into the individual mind and/or ego on the world and dimension on which they're located.

Personas can vary in size, shape, state, density, polarity, level of activity, and surface texture. In most cases, personas come in bunches, with the bunched personas corresponding closely to one another in size, shape, density, polarity, and resonance and/or mean frequency. Since personas in bunches have similar characteristics, it is extremely important to stay focused on your chosen persona when releasing it and not allow it to drift to one of the neighboring personas in its bunch.

Although a persona can be influenced by other personas within its immediate environment, the vast majority of personas tend to be quite stable for two reasons: first, they are integrated into the individual mind and ego, and second, pressure from neighboring karmic sediment tends to stabilize them.

Personas have a degree of sentience, which means they manifest individual will, finite consciousness, and desire, as well as a limited spectrum of unauthentic emotions, feelings, and sensations. In extreme cases (when the CECs in a persona are particularly tamasic) they will manifest one of the following qualities: need, obsession, craving, lust, and/or aversion, which can manifest as terror, dread, anxiety, nervousness, and panic.

Personas can also manifest self-limiting characteristics, such as fatigue, confusion, inattention, and indolence. Although personas are located within the microcosm, they remain part of the collective field of maya and cannot express authentic desires and/or emotions.

Not all personas have what are normally considered negative qualities, although it is important to remember that all personas block the effluence of the Self and disrupt the transmission and transmutation of prana through the human energy system. In fact, personas have qualities that range from extremely sattvic to extremely tamasic.

The qualities of a persona can emerge into one's conscious awareness in four ways. They can emerge when samskaras intrude into personal body space. They can emerge when outer layers of samskaras and/or vasanas expand. Expansion takes place when pressure exerted against a subfield within karmic sediment has weakened and the subfield is given room to express the will, awareness, emotions, feelings, and sensations of the CECs within it. Personas can emerge when their host becomes conscious of additional worlds and dimensions where subfields of karmic energy have been laid down as karmic sediment. Finally, personas can emerge when foreign subfields that have violently intruded into the microcosm or independent qualified subfields floating in the aura express their qualities through the individual mind and ego.

While the aprana can be used to release karmic baggage between the apranic boundary and the surface of personal body space, releasing personas can supplement the technique by making it possible to release samskaras, vasanas, and personas within the microcosm, both inside and outside personal body space on any world and dimension, including the splenic levels and the functions and aspects of mind.

Releasing samskaras and vasanas that have emerged as personas should not be difficult, since their size and shape makes them relatively easy to work with. Normally they are flat and elongated, and are restricted from becoming overly active by the pressure exerted by karmic sediment surrounding them. Some personas, particularly independent subfields, can be more challenging to release since they can be more irregularly-shaped and will have less restriction put on their movement by subfields in their immediate environment.

Projected Personas

Personas, particularly those that are located within personal body space, can be projected from one individual to another. When a persona has been projected it can become trapped in the target's energy field, particularly if the target has become attached to their individual mind and ego on the world and dimension on which the projection has taken place. If the target accepts the qualities of the persona it will be integrated into their individual mind and ego. Although personas projected in this way can become part of the target's karmic baggage, and even integrated into their individual mind and ego, the persona will remain connected to the perpetrator via a thin cord of qualified energy. Personas that remain attached to the perpetrator will remain under the influence of the perpetrator and subject to the vagaries of their will, desire, and/or aversion.

Personas that are projected but remain connected to the perpetrator are called cords, and cords can be particularly debilitating for the host, since qualified energy can be projected though the cord by the perpetrator long after the initial penetration. Besides making the host chronically insecure, the intrusion of qualified energy through the cord can polarize the host's energy field, making it more feminine and receptive and therefore more reactive.

It's not uncommon for cords to keep their host under the control of the perpetrator for years after the original projection has taken place. In fact, the pathological connection created and maintained by the cord accounts for the anti-Self feelings, irrational fear, and inner turmoil that can plague the host for years after the initial penetration has taken place. It also explains why the host's condition can deteriorate years after his or her energy field has been penetrated by the cord.

Children are particularly prone to this type of violation since they are dependent on adults and don't have the tools necessary to protect themselves against energetic intrusions, particularly from people they trust and/or who exercise authority over them.

In the case of sexual abuse this is clearly evidenced. In sexual abuse the victim is penetrated twice. The first penetration is physical. The second penetration is energetic in the form of a cord. Although the physical penetration is abhorrent, the symptoms caused by the physical penetration are almost always temporary. It is the energetic penetration that is responsible for the most enduring and debilitating symptoms, including the disruption of boundaries and the introduction of dense, highly polarized qualified energy into the host's energy field. In addition to the cord, large numbers of CECs will be projected into the host's energy field, either as part of the initial projection or as part of subsequent intrusion through the cord, and these CECs can coalesce into subordinate personas.

In the host's energy field, subordinate personas will often come into conflict with the dominant persona by radiating rage, insecurity, Self-loathing, and a host of anti-Self and antisocial sensations, feelings, emotions and ideas, which can produce irrational fear (particularly of the perpetrator), self-doubt, and depression.

Dominant and Subordinate Personas

The individual mind as a functional unit contains a dominant persona and one or more subordinate personas. The dominant persona is composed almost entirely of samskaras carried from one lifetime to another. The ego supports the dominant persona by acting as a lens through which the dominant persona can focus its attention and by filtering information received by the centers of consciousness in the higher and lower mind.

Subordinate personas can either support or oppose the dominant persona. Although most subordinate personas exist on dimensions hidden within the human unconscious—particularly the splenic levels and the dimensions regulated by the higher and lower chakras—it is not unusual for subordinate personas to emerge into conscious awareness through dreams, and phobias, and through one's fantasy life—particularly through sexual fantasies. When subordinate personas emerge and oppose the dominate persona, they can undermine their host's well-being and the stability of their relationships. In some cases, especially those that are life threatening, or when the host temporarily releases his or her inhibitions under the influence of alcohol or stimulants, subordinate personas can make an unexpected and dramatic appearance.

Members of the same family tend to have personas that are quite similar—even identical—since parents and other relatives attached to the individual mind and ego tend to project qualified energy at people they want to influence—particularly children and dependents. In the process of acculturation we see a similar process at work. Through their traditions and

institutions, all cultures make demands on children and dependents that
will inevitably restrict the flow of prana through a developing child's energy system. Indeed, the acculturation process invariably involves, toler-
ates, and even encourages the projection of qualified subfields, often in
the form of personas, from those in authority to those who are subordinate to them.

The fact that personas can be integrated into the individual mind and
ego and then counterfeit the activities of the higher and lower mind and
their functions and aspects makes them very disruptive. In energy work,
however, it is their very strength that undermines them and makes it possible to release personas permanently by using the seven-step process.

Releasing Personas

When a persona penetrates the human energy field or emerges from
karmic sediment into conscious awareness, its host can react to it in three
ways. She or he can contract, in order not to have a conscious experience
of the persona or to be affected by its qualities. Although contraction and
denial may control the persona, it will disrupt the flow of prana and the
synchronistic function of the human energy system on the world and dimension in question. In addition, contraction will cause the CECs in the
persona to react by projecting qualified energy into the external environment. Projections of this sort will have a disruptive effect on relationships
by projecting the needs and desires of the CECs contained within the
persona toward people with whom the host interacts.

The host's second choice is to surrender his or her will to the will of
the CECs within the persona and to integrate the qualities emerging
from the persona into their individual mind and ego. This choice is inher-
ently dangerous because the subordinate persona may be strong enough
to vie with the host's dominant persona for control. A conflict of this sort
may lead to obsessive-compulsive behavior and passive or aggressive anti-
Self behavior.

The host's final choice is to remain centered in the higher and lower
mind, take responsibility for the persona and observe it, while remaining

detached from its qualities. If the host chooses to remain centered in the higher and lower mind, the persona will expand and appear to grow increasingly stronger, creating the false impression that it will overwhelm the dominant persona and the higher and lower mind. Of course, this is energetically impossible, since the corresponding field of prana will expand along with the persona. As both fields expand, they will be forced to interact, and it is precisely this interaction that makes it possible to release personas from the human energy field.

Indeed, as the persona continues to expand, the qualified energy in it will become less dense and the pores in its surface boundary will grow larger. When the pores become large enough, prana from the corresponding field of the higher and/or lower mind will pour through the surface membrane. Once unqualified energy penetrates the persona, all qualified energy, as well as all of the persona's functions—individual will, finite awareness, emotions, feelings, and/or sensations—will be permanently released from the host's energy field and the empty space would be filled by the prana that released it.

The Seven-Step Process

Releasing a persona is a seven-step process, which must be followed in the order presented below.

Step one is **Awareness**. In step one the host becomes aware of the persona (size, shape, density, and location) they wish to release. Step two is **Acceptance**. In step two the host suspends judgment and accepts the qualities that emerge from the persona. Step three is **Enjoyment**. In step three the host goes beyond acceptance and enjoys the qualities emerging from the persona. Step four is **Identification**. In step four the host identifies with the persona by suspending attachment to their dominant persona (but not the higher and lower mind) while actively embracing the qualities of the persona. Step five is **Participation**. In step five the host participates with the persona by letting the qualities of the persona suffuse their personality, no matter how negative and/or unpleasant they may be. Step six is **Becoming**. In step six the host abandons the internal script that normally inhibits their activities and internalizes the intent of the persona. Step seven is **Permission**. In step seven the host becomes the persona and gives him- or herself permission to perform the activities that emerge as a function of the persona's intent, desire and/or will.

Awareness

Each persona has a unique resonance that differs from its neighbors and from personas within its bunch. Therefore, the most reliable way to become aware of a persona is to isolate it by its qualities. For example, if you are depressed you can use your intent to isolate the persona responsible for your depression so that the persona will emerge from the background field of karmic baggage. The more specific you make your intent, the better it will be. You might assert, for example "It is my intent to become aware of the persona, in the world of soul, level of the fourth chakra that makes me feel depressed."

After you've isolated the persona with your intent you can focus your mental attention on it. The prana emerging from your mental attention will activate the qualified energy in the persona increasing its vibration so that it will expand. As it expands, it will become less dense making the persona easier to accept.

Once you become aware of a persona, it is important to remain focused on it to the exclusion of everything else. Only then can you proceed to the next step, Acceptance.

Acceptance

Once you've become aware of a persona you must accept it by taking responsibility for it and accepting its qualities. This means you must abandon any attempt to change the persona, deny it, and/or bury it in your subconscious. It also means that you've stopped thinking about it and must abandon any attempts to understand it.

By accepting the persona it will expand even further, and by accepting the qualities that emerge from the persona without rejecting it, denying it, or attempting to change it, you will prepare yourself for the next step in the process, enjoyment.

Enjoyment

To enjoy a persona you must step outside duality by giving up your attachment to the concepts of good and bad and right and wrong. This means you must abandon judgment and give up your aversion to the qualities of the persona, no matter how negative and disturbing they may be.

Like a lion in the wild that kills to eat, the persona you've chosen to release is simply acting in accord with its nature. Judging a lion for killing to sustain itself is obviously absurd. In the same way, judging a persona for having qualities is absurd and only complicates the process of releasing it.

Indeed, releasing a persona is not a war of good against evil. It is a technique designed to restore your energy field to its natural state of well-being. Recognizing this is crucial and will make enjoyment far easier.

As soon as you begin to enjoy the persona it will expand downward toward the second chakra. As the persona expands and becomes less dense, prana expanding along with it will be reflected off its surface, making the persona glow. This, in turn, will make it easier for you to take the next step in the process, identification.

Identification

By identifying with the persona you go beyond passive enjoyment to active participation with the persona and its qualities. In taking this important step you signify your faith in the power of the higher and lower mind—and the prana that is their dynamic aspect—to release the persona.

As soon as you take on the qualities of the persona it will expand upward to the sixth chakra. This gives the persona room to express its will. In the process, prana emerging from the sixth chakra will expand and be reflected off the persona's surface, isolating the persona even further from its bunch. By isolating the persona from its bunch, you facilitate participation, which is the next step in the seven-step process.

Participation

As soon as you've identified with the persona you can move to the next step in the process, which is participation. In participation, you give your-

self permission to enjoy the individual qualities of the persona. To enjoy
the individual qualities of the persona, you must go beyond an abstract
relationship with the persona. You must make it real by letting go of the
concept of "I-thou."

Indeed, it is only after you've embraced the persona and enjoyed its individual qualities that it will expand backward into the masculine part of
your energy field. As the persona expands backward it will become less
dense and its surface boundary will become more porous. This will allow
the seven chakras within personal body space to become more active so
that prana can continue to expand along with the persona and you can
choose to become the persona, which is the next step in the process.

Becoming the Persona

By becoming the persona, you actively accept and substitute the intent of
the persona (which you've chosen to release) for the intent of your dominant persona. This will allow your chosen persona to become dominant,
at least temporarily.

Once you've become the persona by taking on its qualities, any dis-
tinction or separation between you and the persona will be eradicated.
This will allow the persona to expand forward. As the persona expands
forward, the feminine poles of the chakras will become active and prana
will expand forward along with the persona. With prana expanding forward you will be ready for the next step in the process, permission.

Permission

It is not enough to become the persona. Without giving the persona permission to perform the activities it finds pleasurable the process will not
become real, and the persona will not expand forward beyond your energy field into the external environment. In fact, giving the persona permission to act is the ultimate act of faith in the Self and the functions of
the higher and lower mind. It is by giving your permission that the Self
becomes the doer, and the Self, through the aegis of the higher and lower
mind and the human energy system, can release the persona.

In the final step of the process, the subfield you've chosen to release will expand forward beyond your auric boundary. Prana will expand along with it, and when the pores in the persona's surface boundary become large enough, prana will pour into the persona. Since it is impossible for prana and qualified energy to occupy the same space—on the same world and dimension—at the same time, the persona and CECs within it will be released and all that will remain will be the prana that filled the space occupied by the persona.

Finding a Persona to Release

To release a persona, you must locate one and isolate it from its bunch. After you've isolated it, you must remain focused on it while you shift your relationship to the persona during the seven steps required to release it. Adding to the challenge will be the resistance and/or interference of neighboring subfields in the persona's bunch.

Bunches are groups of personas with a similar resonance and almost identical structure (long, thin, and narrow) that are pressed together and held in place by pressure from neighboring subfields. It is not uncommon for subfields within a bunch to expand while you're releasing a persona. When they expand they can obscure the qualities emerging from your chosen persona and cause it to move or shift erratically. Therefore, it is essential to remain focused and not to drift, because once you've become distracted you'll find it is exceedingly difficult to refocus on your designated persona and release it.

There are two methods for locating a persona. The first is to identify a persona by tracing symptoms emerging from a persona back to their cause. To locate a persona in this way you will use the standard method to relax and balance conscious and unconscious mental activity. Then you will activate and center yourself in the back of your heart chakra, split your attention, and activate the front of your heart chakra. Once you've activated the front of your heart chakra you will look inward to the world, level, and location where the symptoms originate by stating "It is

my intent to look inward on the world and dimension where the symptoms I have in mind have emerged."

If there isn't a symptom or group of symptoms that lead you back to a
persona, it will be necessary to perform a scan. You've already performed
this type of scan in chapter eight. You may want to review the information in that chapter before you proceed.

Before you perform a scan take note: samskaras form the deepest layers of karmic sediment and free floating personas can be active and hard
to control, therefore, you will find it easier, at least initially, to work with
a vasana on the outer surface of karmic sediment, particularly one that is
ready to emerge as a persona.

Releasing a Persona

In the exercise below you will locate a vasana ready to emerge as a persona in the world of soul, level of the fourth chakra, and scan it for size,
shape, state, density, polarity, level of activity, and surface texture, as well
as any emerging sensations, feelings, and emotions. After you've located
a suitable vasana and scanned it you will isolate it from its bunch. Then
you will release it, using the seven-step method described earlier. Your
designated intent will be: "It is my intent to release the persona I've
scanned in the world of soul, level of the fourth chakra."

To begin, find a comfortable position with your back straight. Then
use the standard method to relax and balance conscious and unconscious
mental activity. Continue by activating and centering yourself in the back
of your heart chakra. Then split your attention, activate the front of your
heart chakra, and set your intent. Once you've set your intent, look inward in the world of soul on the level of the heart chakra. Then split
your attention and project your second attention to the surface of karmic
sediment facing you, on the world of soul, level of the heart chakra.
When you're ready to continue, bring your emphasis to your second attention and activate your scanning tool.

If a vasana is ready to emerge as a persona, it will manifest individual
will, finite awareness, and a limited spectrum of emotional energy. Since

you will conduct the scan on the world of soul, level of the heart chakra, the emotional energy that will emerge will be pain or one of its variants: sadness, melancholy, despair, and so forth. In some cases, what may emerge is an emotion that denies your right to feel, express, and/or resolve emotional energy, such as shame, embarrassment, or humiliation.

To conduct your scan, make up and down overlapping strokes with your scanning tool until you locate the desired persona. Then scan the persona and record its qualities. When you've completed your scan, release your scanning tool, return your emphasis to the back of your heart chakra, and release your second attention.

When you're ready to release the persona, state, "It is my intent to become aware of the vasana I've chosen to release." This will isolate the persona from its bunch so that the persona begins to expand and manifest its qualities.

To accept the persona, state, "It is my intent to accept the persona I've chosen to release." By accepting the persona and suspending judgment the persona will continue to expand. Continue by stating, "It is my intent to enjoy the persona I've chosen to release." Enjoying the persona will allow the persona to expand downward to the second chakra. Shift your awareness along with the persona as it expands downward. Then state, "It is my intent to identify with the persona." By identifying with the persona and taking on its qualities, the persona will expand upward to the sixth chakra, making the persona larger and less dense. Continue by stating, "It is my intent to enjoy the qualities of the persona." By enjoying the qualities of the persona you will become receptive to it and the persona will expand backward into the masculine part of your energy field. Continue to shift your awareness, then state, "It is my intent to become the persona." By becoming the persona you will identify exclusively with the persona. With no separation between you and the persona, the persona will expand forward and become less dense and more porous. In the final step, state, "It is my intent to perform the activities of the persona." By giving yourself permission to perform the activities of the persona, the persona will expand forward beyond the surface of your auric field. Prana will continue to expand along with the persona, and when the pores within the persona's surface boundary become large enough prana will pour through, releasing the persona.

Once the persona has been released, return your emphasis to the back of your heart chakra and release your second attention. Then count from one to five. When you reach the number five, open your eyes. You will feel wide aware, perfectly relaxed, and better than you did before.

Chapter Sixteen

For the ignorant person, this body is the source of end-less suffering, but to the wise person, this body is the source of infinite delight.

—Yoga Vasishtha

Energy Bodies and Corresponding Vehicles

Energy bodies and energetic vehicles on all worlds and dimensions serve as the Self's vehicles of awareness, cognition, assimilation, sensation, and expression.

Although it is a commonly held belief that there are five energy bodies, the etheric, astral, mental, and spiritual bodies, plus the physical body to which they correspond in structure and function, in fact this is not the complete picture. Human beings are divine beings, not created in the image of God, but God manifest as the Self.

In each world and dimension, including the splenic levels and the functions and aspects of mind, human beings have a community of energy bodies or energetic vehicles through which the Self can emerge and participate. In the higher and lower mind and their functions and aspects, there are one hundred and forty dimensions in each world, and in the world of the chakras and its functions and aspects there are one hundred and forty two (including the splenic levels).

The splenic levels are separate fields of activity with their own energetic vehicles. The functions and aspects of mind interpenetrate the worlds of the higher and lower mind as well as the splenic levels, and have energetic vehicles that serve a role similar to the ones performed by the energy bodies and energetic vehicles of the higher and lower mind and the world of the chakras.

Although prana has no qualities and each energy body and corresponding energetic vehicle is composed of prana—in the three states or gunas: solid, liquid, and gaseous—the frequencies of energy transmitted and transmuted by a particular energy body and energetic vehicle is restricted to one third of the energetic spectrum, which means an energy body or energetic vehicle can only transmit and transmute prana that corresponds to qualified energy that is either tamasic, ragistic, or sattvic.

Energy bodies and energetic vehicles originally emerged from universal consciousness by way of the tattvas, along with the worlds and dimensions of the phenomenal universe, and they do not suffer death when the physical-material body and etheric double die at the end of each incarnation. As they evolve though linear-sequential time, energy bodies and energetic vehicles maintain their structural integrity and do not experience any essential changes. They are infinite, although not eternal like the Self.

The communities of energy bodies and their corresponding energetic vehicles have a strong and enduring connection to personal body space on their particular world and dimension, and they will not leave it unless they are compelled to do so. Even when they are ejected by a shocking or traumatic event, they will be drawn back to it unless they are blocked by karmic sediment, energy blockages (called intrusions), and/or attachment to the individual mind and ego. This intimate relationship will prove exceedingly useful when it comes to recollecting and reintegrating energy bodies and energetic vehicles.

Energy Bodies

Each energy body is composed of unqualified energy in a solid and gaseous state, regardless of whether it exists on the world of soul, intellect, or spirit.

The size and shape of an energy body corresponds closely to the physical-material body. Its internal structure is quite different, however. Instead of containing a collection of tissues and organs, it consists of a large cavity filled entirely with unqualified energy, and a surface boundary that surrounds the cavity and corresponds to physical skin.

The surface of each energy body is a smooth elastic membrane that appears solid when viewed under normal perspective. However, when viewed under greater magnification the surface turns out to have a complex inner structure consisting of luminescent fibers that crisscross each other in every imaginable direction. The mosaic of luminescent fibers creates a tightly woven, lattice-like structure, much like felt, which is porous, flexible, and exceedingly strong.

Surrounding each energy body is an auric field that is a reservoir of unqualified energy, and surrounding the auric field is another membrane of unqualified energy that has the same inner structure as the surface of an energy body. This surface membrane, known as the auric boundary, separates the internal environment (the microcosm) from the external environment (the macrocosm).

As long as an energy body remains vertically integrated (fixed in personal body space), its size and shape will correspond to the size and shape of the physical-material body. However, energy bodies don't have internal organs that correspond to the skeletal system, and if they suffer a shocking or traumatic event their shape can become distorted. In fact, when an energy body has been ejected from personal body space, its shape can become so distorted that it may be difficult to distinguish it from large complex subfields.

In extreme cases, when an energy body has been ejected from personal body space and has become contaminated by qualified energy, it can intrude into the space occupied by another sentient being. This can distort its shape even further and make it even more difficult to recognize and locate.

Normally, energy bodies fixed within personal body space resist the intrusion of qualified subfields because prana flowing into them creates a powerful field that protects them. Once an energy body has been ejected from personal body space, however, the situation changes dramatically. An energy body may continue to resist intrusions, but sufficiently dense and polarized CECs will be able to penetrate it, weakening the surface boundary even further, and making it increasing likely that there will be additional intrusions.

Bodies of Desire

On the dimensions of the lower mind, human beings have energetic vehicles called "bodies of desire." Bodies of desire are the same size and shape as energy bodies and are composed of prana in a solid and gaseous state. As vehicles of divine consciousness, bodies of desire perform many of the same functions and suffer many of the same problems as energy bodies. In fact, if a body of desire has tilted out of personal body space or been ejected, there will be a disruption—similar to that suffered by an energy body—in the ability of the vehicle to function synchronistically with bodies of desire on its dimension and with neighboring energy bodies and energetic vehicles.

On each dimension of the lower mind there exists a community of energetic vehicles (bodies of desire). The frequencies of energy transmitted and transmuted by each vehicle is restricted to one third of the energetic spectrum. This means that a body of desire can only transmit and/or transmute prana, which corresponds to qualified energy that is either tamasic, ragistic, or sattvic.

The primary function of the bodies of desire is to enable the Self to participate in the world of the lower mind. They do this by regulating the four primary desires that as fields of unqualified energy emerge through the lower mind.

To understand why fields of desire emerge through the lower mind, you must understand the relationship of paramatman and jivamatman. Paramatman refers to the the supreme Self, Atman. *Para*, in Sanskrit means "higher, universal, or supreme." It can also refer to aspects that are transcendental. It is commonly used in conjunction with Atman and/or Brahman. In the Sankhya philosophy, the precursor to Yoga, it refers to perusha, the supreme consciousness. Paramatman is the absolute or eternal condition of each human being, which is a priori union with the Self.

Jivamatman refers to the conditional or individuated Self, which is composed of the higher and lower mind and their functions and aspects. It is the jivamatman and its desires that motivate human beings to act and to be incarnated into a physical-material body (and etheric double). The four desires that emerge from jivamatman through the bodies of desire are artha, kama, dharma, and moksha.

Artha denotes wealth. Since it is considered an economic necessary to amass wealth, particularly for householders, it is considered a positive value.

Kama denotes pleasure and/or the desire for pleasure. It is important not to forget that both Christian and Vedantic texts state that God, universal consciousness, created the universe for his pleasure. In the *Bhagavad Gita* (the most revered Vedantic text), desire is put at the center of living and is equated with the life force. Indeed, Vedanta never taught that pleasure should be suppressed or denigrated as anti-Self or antispiritual. It teaches, in fact, that the opposite is true; that at the deepest levels of being it is jivamatman that dictates an individual's desires and aspirations.

Dharma is the third authentic desire that emerges from the lower mind. In Sanskrit, dharma means "that which holds together"—in essence, that which prevents worldly relationships from dissolving into chaos.

Dharma has two applications. There is dharma that is common to all mankind, collective dharma, and there is individual dharma that applies to each human being.

Collective dharma is righteousness or spiritual duty and is related specifically to appropriate activity and Self-realization. Individual dharma is the particular path of appropriate activity that leads a person back into conscious union with the Self.

Moksha is the fourth authentic desire to emerge from the lower mind. It denotes spiritual freedom and liberation from karmic attachment. Of the four desires, the desire for moksha is the highest. Advaita Vedanta, the vedantic school of nondualism, teaches that jnana (knowledge) that comes from direct experience is the most direct way to achieve moksha. Since moksha is the true state of each human being, it is experienced once ignorance has been banished by direct experience.

Romana Maharshi declared that ignorance is nothing more than attachment to the "I idea." Jainism, as usual, is more detailed. It tells us that moksha is the highest state of separation or detachment. Saivism equates moksha with bliss, and Yoga equates it with the state of nirvakalpa-samadhi, the state of unparalleled isolation and stillness.

World of the Chakras

In the world of the chakras, human beings have energetic vehicles called "chakra bodies." Chakra bodies are the same size and shape as the physical-material body, and are composed of prana in a solid and gaseous state. Chakra bodies exist on all one hundred and forty-two dimensions, including the splenic levels.

On each dimension of the higher and lower mind—as well as the splenic levels—there exists one chakra and three chakra bodies. The chakra regulates the entire spectrum of unqualified energy on its particular dimension in the worlds of the higher and lower mind. The field of activity for each chakra body corresponds to qualified energy in the collective field of maya, which is either tamasic, ragistic, or sattvic. If even one chakra body on a particular dimension has not been vertically integrated, then the chakra will be unable to function healthfully within its entire range of activities.

Indeed, when the three chakra bodies on each world are vertically integrated, the chakra they support will remain active, regardless of external conditions on the worlds of the higher and lower mind and splenic levels, and qualified energy will be prevented from accumulating as karmic sediment in the area surrounding personal body space on all worlds, on the dimension supported by the chakra.

Functions and Aspects of Mind

Functions and aspects of mind are known respectively as koshas, indyrias, and pranas; and manas, chitta, buddhi, and amankara. Structurally, all functions and aspects of mind are the same size and shape as the physical-material body, and, like the energy bodies and energetic vehicles to which they correspond, the functions and aspects of mind must be vertically integrated in order to function healthfully.

The functions and aspects of mind are active on all one hundred and forty-two dimensions. Each energetic vehicle that participates in a functional community (function of mind), or community of identity (aspect of mind), functions within the tamasic, ragistic, or sattvic part of the energetic spectrum.

The energetic vehicles that compose the functions and aspects of mind function synchronistically with one another and with the chakra bodies, bodies of desire, and the energy bodies of the higher and lower mind. Collectively, they allow a human being to emerge into the external environment and participate by interacting with both unqualified and qualified fields of energy.

Individual functions and aspects are particularly susceptible to intrusions of qualified energy, since it is through the functions and aspects of mind that one makes contact with external objects, energy fields, and other sentient beings—and the CECs and qualified subfields within them.

Splenic Bodies

On the splenic levels, human beings have energetic vehicles called "splenic bodies." The structure and function of the splenic bodies correspond closely to the structure and function of the energy bodies in the higher and lower mind, and the bodies of desire. If vertical integration has been disrupted there will be a corresponding disruption in the ability of the splenic bodies and the splenic chakras to function healthfully. This, in turn, will make it more difficult for the physical-material body and etheric double to function synchronistically with the energetic vehicles of the higher and lower mind, the chakra bodies, and their functions and aspects.

The primary function of the splenic bodies is to permit the Self to interact through the physical-material body and the etheric double with the physical-material universe.

The field of function for each splenic body corresponds to qualified energy in the collective field of maya that is either tamasic, ragistic, or sattvic. The splenic bodies' field of activity includes physical sensation, awareness, sexual vitality, motivation, desire, physical assimilation, evacuation, sleep, security, and physical well-being.

To remain grounded and balanced in the physical-material world and to integrate the functions of the higher and lower mind with the physical-material body and the etheric double, it is essential to have the splenic chakras active and the splenic bodies vertically integrated and functioning synchronistically.

The Function of Energetic Vehicles

Individual energy bodies and their corresponding energetic vehicles—with the exception of the splenic bodies—are infinite, which means they continue to exist indefinitely. The primary function of each energy body and energetic vehicle is to serve as a vehicle through which the Self (Atman) can emerge and participate in the phenomenal universe. Since human beings are Self-aware and sentient on all worlds, levels, and dimensions simultaneously, it is through human beings and their energetic vehicles that Atman (the Self) can experience its reflection in its fullness.

Energy bodies function and cooperate with one another, and they form synchronistic communities which correspond functionally to five broad areas of human activity: soul, intellect, spirit, desire, and power.

The Spirit

Although it is generally assumed that the source of consciousness is spirit, the world of spirit is not the the source or even the highest level from which consciousness can emerge. The source of consciousness is the Self (Atman).

Although the Self is the cause, and spirit is one of its effects, it is from the world of spirit that human beings experience the state of transcendental consciousness, insight, catharsis, and intuition. In fact, it is through the experience of spirit that one transcends the limitations imposed by the finite mind and the collective field of maya. Raising the kundalini-shakti to the crown chakra is one of these experiences; so, too, is activating the higher and lower chakras and recollecting and reintegrating the energy bodies in the world of spirit.

In fact, as karmic baggage on the spiritual world is released and spiritual awareness is developed, one will experience more prana emerging through the world of spirit and will become less reactive to qualified sub-fields. This, in turn, will prevent the individual mind and ego from providing counterfeit spiritual experiences, or from offering false or misleading interpretations of authentic experiences in the world of spirit. In fact, once vertical integration in the world of spirit is complete, one will recognize that she or he is an interdimensional being whose primary purpose for being incarnated is to follow their dharma and seek reunion with the Self.

The Intellect

The communities of energy bodies in the world of intellect serve as the Self's vehicle of finite human consciousness, memory, ideation (inductive and deductive reasoning), self-awareness, cognition, and assimilation. In addition, they focus the awareness of the higher mind, which can then emerge into the external environment via the functions and aspects of mind.

When the communities of energy bodies in the world of intellect are functioning healthfully, awareness of both the microcosm and the macrocosm will be complete, and discernment on these levels will remain unobstructed. Karmic energy will have little effect on finite human consciousness, and reactivity to outside stimuli will be negligible. Both inductive and deductive reasoning will function properly, and human consciousness will no longer be subject to an avalanche of conflicting thoughts, ideas beliefs, attitudes, and concepts.

Understanding and belief will give way to observation and discernment, and on the world of intellect, one will become the observer of the movie of their mind.

The Soul

The communities of energy bodies associated with the soul serve several important functions. First and foremost, they serve the Self as vehicles of sensation, feeling, and emotion in the world of soul. In this capacity, the energy bodies that compose the soul serve as a bridge between the physical-material body and etheric double, and the community of energy bodies that compose the intellect.

Through the synchronistic function of the energy bodies on the world of soul and the human energy system, human beings experience emotions, feelings, and sensations.

The authentic emotions of anger, fear, pain, and joy emerge as functions of the community of energy bodies in the world of soul. Anger emerges when there has been a disruption of intimacy, fear when survival is threatened, pain when rights are threatened, and joy when individual relationship supersedes the authentic desire for moksha (transcendence).

Without the energy bodies in the world of soul there would be no human affection and care. Empathy would cease to function, and without empathy, human relationship and love would be unable to provide a basis for transcendence.

Bodies of Desire

The bodies of desire that compose the lower mind are primarily concerned with the four authentic desires that motivate a person to incarnate in a physical-material body (see "Bodies of Desire" above).

When the bodies of desire are vertically integrated and functioning healthfully the barrage of counterfeit desires presented by the individual mind and ego and the projections of both physical and nonphysical beings in the world of the lower mind, will be revealed for what they are and rejected as non-Self. Craving, lust, obsession, need, and their variations will no longer be able to cause conflict or disrupt relationship. Indeed, desire and its flip-side, fear, will lose their power to compel one to identify with the individual mind and ego. Hence, one will find it easier to choose appropriate activity and to follow dharma.

Authentic desires make it possible to grow, learn, prosper, and transcend. In addition, they provide the motivation to seek pleasure, human love, intimacy, joy, and bliss, as well as to trust in the process of Self-realization. Without the bodies of desire, life as we know it would be impossible, and relationships would deteriorate into utter chaos. In fact, authentic desires provide a structure through which human beings can interact appropriately within the context of human relationship.

Unlike unauthentic desires that cause attachment, authentic desires create no need or compulsion, nor do they motivate a person to act obsessively. Therefore, they cannot attach a person to the individual mind and ego or to the phenomenal universe. In fact, by resisting the desires of the individual mind and ego and remaining centered in the bodies of desire, one will experience the pleasure and Self-centered awareness that emerge as a function of their synchronistic activity.

Splenic Bodies

On the physical-material and etheric levels, the splenic bodies serve as the Self's vehicles of feeling, sensation, vitality, and activity, but take note: the physical-material body and etheric double emerge from the collective field of maya. Without the splenic bodies there wouldn't be any authentic vehicles through which one could experience physical well-being, fatigue, hunger, digestion, sexual vitality, etc.

The splenic bodies vitalize the nerves of the physical-material body by providing it with prana. In addition, the splenic bodies and the bodies of desire serve as the Self's vehicles of pleasure. Since pleasure evolves into human love—and love into intimacy, joy, and bliss—in order to transcend the mundane world, the splenic bodies must be vertically integrated and functioning healthfully.

Chakra Bodies

The energetic vehicles known as chakra bodies serve as the Self's vehicles of consciousness in the world of the chakras. In this capacity they serve as bridges between the higher and lower mind (and their functions and aspects) and the human energy system.

There is virtually no extant information from Yoga, Vedanta, and Tantra that can shine light upon the relationship between the chakras and the chakra bodies. However, it is clear from observation that each chakra has a relationship with three chakra bodies, and that each chakra body functions within a part of the energetic spectrum that corresponds to qualified energy which is either tamasic, ragistic or sattvic .

While the chakras provide prana to energy bodies and energetic vehicles, the chakra bodies bring this power and its potential into conscious awareness. Vertically integrating the chakra bodies, therefore, is an act of becoming that awakens one to the dormant power in their higher and lower mind and integrates that power into their identity. The power emerging from the communities of chakra bodies is manifest as the innate, and normally unconscious, ability to overcome the force of qualified energy (in the form of karmic baggage).

When the chakra bodies are integrated the power of qualified subfields and energetic projections will be more than matched by the power of prana emerging through the human energy system. In fact, when the chakra bodies are fully integrated prana will suffuse the human energy field, making it increasingly difficult for karmic baggage to disrupt the flow of prana or to create a counterfeit mind that can usurp the functions of the higher and lower mind.

Functions and Aspects of Mind

The energetic vehicles that compose the functions and aspects of mind provide the Self with vehicles to externalize sensation, feeling, emotion, and conscious awareness. They also provide the Self with a means to recognize, integrate, and assimilate fields of energy that express the same or similar functions in the external environment. It fact, it is primarily through the activities of the functions and aspects of mind that one accumulates, integrates, and assimilates knowledge of their surrounding environment.

The functions of mind accumulate knowledge by emerging into the external environment and making contact with objects, beings, and energy fields. Once contact has been made, the functions assimilate that knowledge and make it available to the centers of consciousness in the human energy field, including the aspects of mind.

It is the aspects of mind that use knowledge accumulated and assimilated by the functions of mind and the centers of consciousness in the higher and lower mind to form an identity. An identity is essential for processing and classifying the almost-infinite quantity of information bombarding a human being simultaneously on all worlds and dimensions. In fact, wisdom and Self-knowledge, which allow one to perform appropriate activity and follow dharma, are to a large extent dependent on the functions of the aspects of mind that process and integrate this never-ending stream of information.

The vague sense of appropriateness, often nothing more than a gut feeling, can only emerge through the synchronistic function of the aspects of mind and the corresponding energetic vehicles in the higher and lower mind. Intuitive insight emerges from its source (universal consciousness) and is transmuted into something that the aspects of mind can recognize. These insights that emerge from the aspects of mind are consistent and reliable, and permit one to make appropriate decisions and perform appropriate activities with confidence.

Disruption of the Energy Bodies
and Corresponding Vehicles

Under normal conditions, when energy bodies and energetic vehicles are vertically integrated no qualified energy can disrupt their functions or activities. However, their functions or activities can be disrupted when qualified energy intrudes into personal body space and an energy body or energetic vehicle is dimpled, tilted, or ejected. An intrusion can be caused by a differential in polarity, the inordinate buildup of vasanas or samskaras, or the intrusion of qualified energy. In any case, the severity of the intrusion will determine the effect. When the intrusion is mild it will cause stress, when it is moderate it will cause shock, and when it is intense it will cause trauma.

Stress will destabilize an energy body or energetic vehicle and disrupt its ability to remain vertically integrated. When stress is mild, it will cause dimpling. When it is more severe, it will cause the energetic vehicle to tilt outside personal body space.

Shock will cause an energy body or energetic vehicle to be temporarily ejected from personal body space.

Trauma is such a violent event and has such a disruptive effect on the human energy field that it will cause an energy body or energetic vehicle to be ejected from personal body space and will prevent it from returning until the qualified energy blocking its return is released.

Projections

A number of different energetic projections, including controlling waves, cords, and personas can disrupt the vertical integration of one or more energy bodies or energetic vehicles.

Controlling waves are projected at the host's energy field by another human being who seeks to control and/or change an aspect of the host's personality. This type of projection can be projected from any direction. When the projection is projected, and enters the host's energy field from the front, the perpetrator will have expectations that have not been fulfilled. When the projection is projected and enters the host's energy field from behind, the perpetrator will be trying to regain something that they perceive they have lost. People unsure of their position will project a controlling wave from either the right or left side of the host's energy field.

Cords are projected at the front of the host's energy field by another human being.

Personas are projected by another human being or nonphysical being, and can enter the host's energy field from any direction.

Stress

Stress is caused by the intrusion of qualified energy—particularly karmic sediment—into personal body space. When there has been an intrusion that causes stress, one or more energy bodies and/or energetic vehicles will be dimpled or will tilt out of personal body space.

Karmic sediment can intrude into personal body space in several ways. It can intrude when there has been an inordinate buildup of samskaras and/or vasanas, when a controlling wave or cord has intruded into personal body space, or when there has been an intrusion of one or more highly active nonphysical beings, personas, and/or foreign energy bodies. In addition, the human energy field can be stressed when one passes through a dense and/or active external atmosphere, or when one becomes intimate with someone whose energy field carries an inordinate amount of karmic energy or whose energy bodies are tilting or drifting outside personal body space. Since stress does not cause the ejection of an energy body or an energetic vehicle, it will have the least disruptive effect on the human energy field.

The effects of stress are usually temporary, but they can become chronic when one associates with someone who continually projects qualified energy into their energy field, or when controlling waves projected at the host contain an inordinate number of CECs or are supported energetically by the perpetrator.

Shock

Shock will have a more severe effect on the synchronistic function of the human energy field than stress. In a shocking experience, one or more energy bodies or energetic vehicles will be ejected from personal body space. Surprise is an essential element in shock. In fact, the greater the surprise, the greater the impact shock will have upon an energy body or energetic vehicle.

A shocking experience is caused by the sudden, violent intrusion of dense, highly active, qualified energy into personal body space. A shocking experience will lack intent, however, and it is the lack of intent that differentiates shock from trauma and cushions the host from the more egregious effects that are caused by a traumatic experience.

Although shock will cause an energetic vehicle to be ejected, it is the intent of the perpetrator (which is lacking in a shocking experience) to control, change, manipulate, dominate, or harm their target, which will prevent the immediate return of the ejected energy body and/or energetic vehicle.

Shock can disrupt the normal function of the host's energy field in two ways: by ejecting an energy body and/or energetic vehicle, and by setting up a fear-aversion pattern that can disrupt the flow of prana and make it increasingly difficult to remain centered in the higher and lower mind.

In some cases, a pattern of this type can become habitual and can cause the host to contract in fear whenever there is a reminder of the shocking event.

Trauma

A traumatic experience will have the most disruptive effect on the synchronistic function of human energy field. Trauma is caused by an energetic intrusion that is sudden, violent, and supported by the intent of the perpetrator. In a traumatic event dense polarized energy, in the form of waves, cords, and/or personas containing particularly tamasic CECs, will be intentionally projected into the host's energy field. Since CECs contained within projections of this kind are highly polarized, even if they are subsequently ejected but not permanently released from personal body space, they will make repeated attempts to penetrate the host's energy field in order to get as close as possible to a source of unqualified energy—the chakras, the three hearts, and the minor energy centers.

What differentiates trauma from shock more than anything else is intent. In a shocking experience, there will be no conscious intent by the perpetrator to do damage or to maintain control over the host. The shock is the result of convergence caused by energetic patterns played out by partners in polar relationship.

Although trauma has an immediate effect on the human energy field, most people will recognize it by its second and third generation symptoms. These symptoms include the disruption of self-control, trust, personal power and self-esteem. In addition to these symptoms, trauma can cause a loss of vitality, chronic fatigue, depression, anxiety, a loss of motivation, sexual dysfunction, creative blocks, and boundary problems.

Unfortunately the very symptoms, particularly second and third generation symptoms that emerge through the chain of cause and effect, can obscure the true nature of the traumatic event and its first generation symptoms. This can cause additional problems when it comes to diagnosis and treatment.

First generation symptoms caused by trauma include:

1. The disruption to one or more surface boundaries.

2. The loss of pressure in one or more auric fields.

3. The intrusion of qualified energy into personal body space.

4. The rapid loss of energy in the field of activity that has been traumatized and remains under duress.

5. The ejection of one or more energy bodies or energetic vehicles from personal body space.

The first generation symptoms cited above generally go unnoticed unless they are accompanied by physical violence and/or abuse. Second and third generation symptoms quickly follow, however, and these invariably make an impact on the host's awareness, emotions, feelings, or sensations.

It is important to note that as long as ejected energy bodies and/or energetic vehicles remain outside personal body space, the chain of cause and effect will remain intact and symptoms will continue. In order to overcome the effects of a traumatic experience, intrusions of qualified energy must be released and the ejected energy bodies and/or energetic vehicles must be recollected and reintegrated by a skilled practitioner.

Chapter Seventeen

This above all, to thine own self be true; And it must
follow, as the night the day, Thou canst not then be false
to any man.

—William Shakespeare

The Ejection and Recollection
of Energy Bodies

In order to experience the pleasure, intimacy, joy, and bliss that emerge
from the Self and to ensure that qualified energy cannot intrude into personal body space, all energy bodies and energetic vehicles must be vertically integrated.

Unfortunately, stress, shock, and trauma can disrupt vertical integration. The disruption of vertical integration is called "fragmentation."
Fragmentation, which is caused by the full or partial ejection of one or
more energy bodies or energetic vehicles, is such a serious problem it
must be addressed in a timely and effective manner if one expects to overcome the residual effects of karmic baggage and the collateral problems
karmic baggage creates in the human energy field.

Fragmentation

Fragmentation can take place on any world or dimension, at any time,
during any phase of a person's life, including the nine months between

257

conception and birth. It can be accompanied by sexual abuse, physical abuse, verbal abuse, and/or neglect, although in some circumstances it may not be accompanied by any tangible abuse on the physical-material plane—or at least any conscious memory of it.

Fragmentation is caused by the violent intrusion of dense qualified energy into personal body space on one or more dimensions. An intrusion can take place once and dissipate quickly, or it can be sustained and become a chronic condition.

Fragmentation has become so common—especially among people who have been the victims of violence and/or abuse or have been in relationships with substance abusers or people who are inordinately attached to them, seek to control them, change them, or manipulate them—that overcoming fragmentation by the recollection and reintegration of energy bodies and their corresponding energetic vehicles has become an essential part of energy work and a precondition for reexperiencing uninterrupted pleasure, intimacy, joy, and bliss.

Although the ejection of one or more energy bodies and/or energetic vehicles will disrupt the activities of the higher and lower mind, one must recognize that fragmentation serves a higher purpose. That purpose is to protect an energy body or energetic vehicle from being penetrated or otherwise damaged by CECs and the dense, qualified energy that accompanies them.

Although it is extremely rare for an energy body to be damaged by CECs—even those that are exceedingly dense and violent—it remains a remote possibility, and one that should be consistently avoided. Fortunately, the response of the human energy field to an energetic intrusion is so rapid when penetration is imminent that there is virtually no danger unless, contrary to the dictates of intuition, one engages in spiritual activities that prevent an energetic vehicle from moving out of harm's way.

Note: because the danger is real, one should never use force to hold an energy body and/or an energetic vehicle in personal body space, or any other position for that matter. It is essential to respect the centers of consciousness within each energy body or energetic vehicle, and permit it to move, particularly when movement is necessary to safeguard its integrity.

When a single shocking experience has caused an energy body to be ejected, fragmentation will last for a relatively short time. The distance an energy body will drift, as well as how long it will remain outside personal body space, will depend on whether the shock was caused by the inordinate buildup of samskaras and vasanas, whether a controlling wave or cord has pushed vasanas and samskaras into personal body space, or whether there has been a violent projection of qualified energy and CECs into the host's energy field. It will also depend on the condition of the host's energy field and the likelihood that there will be a subsequent intrusion.

Other factors that will have an influence are the presence of additional controlling waves and/or cords on the same dimension and the host's relationship to the individual mind and ego.

A shocking condition can be exacerbated when an ejected energy body has been outside personal body space for an extended time or the host has become identified with the intrusive energy. Shock will give way to trauma when an ejected energy body or energetic vehicle is kept permanently outside personal body space or if one or more of the conditions cited below have been met:

1. If the penetration of qualified energy is part of a pattern that makes the victim feel chronically insecure.

2. If an intrusion causes a fundamental breakdown in trust or it disrupts the victim's world view to the extent that she or he begins to distrust their perceptions, gut feeling, or intuition.

3. If there is conscious intent behind the projection, and the perpetrator wants to permanently control, possess, and/or change the host.

4. If external boundaries have been disrupted by channeling, etc., and CECs have been given access to personal body space on the world and dimension where the energy body or energetic vehicle has been ejected.

5. If a foreign energy body has usurped the position of the ejected energy body and/or energetic vehicle.

Preparation for the Recollection
of an Energy Body

In the case of severe or chronic stress, an energy body or energetic vehicle will pivot out of position, which means that a portion of the energy body will vacate personal body space. In the most common scenario, an energetic vehicle will pivot at the neck and/or pelvis, in either a straight back-and-forth or side-to-side movement (figure 17-1, p. 261). The movement of an energetic vehicle under duress is not limited exclusively to these two directions, however. An energy body or energetic vehicle can pivot in any direction in order to protect itself from an intrusion of qualified energy.

When an energy body does pivot, movement will be in the direction of the intrusive energy—if the projection is from the front the energy body will pivot backward, if the projection is from the left the energy body will pivot to the right.

When an energy body or energetic vehicle has been ejected, it will remain as close as possible to personal body space, unless there is an additional threat or the initial intrusion is inordinately dense and violent. Indeed, the distance that the energetic vehicle will pivot or drift, or the length of time it will remain outside personal body space—as well as the ebb and flow of its movements—will depend on the violence of the projection, the threat of additional projections, the state of the qualified energy, and CECs within the projection (how tamasic, ragistic, or sattvic they are) and the type of intrusion (energy blockage, energy body, persona, cord, or controlling wave).

If the host, after being shocked or traumatized, consciously or unconsciously substitutes the functions of an intrusion for the functions of an ejected energy body or energetic vehicle, then the CECs within the intrusion will create a counterfeit will, with a counterfeit agenda, which will conspire to keep the ejected vehicle out of personal body space. This, in turn, will make recollecting and reintegrating the energy body or energetic vehicle significantly more difficult.

Before an ejected energetic vehicle can be recollected and reintegrated, personal body space must be prepared for its return. This is accomplished by releasing the intrusive energy that has usurped the position of the ejected vehicle. In some cases, karmic sediment along the surface of personal body space must be released as well. In addition to removing intrusive energy, the energetic vehicle must be located, recollected, and cleansed of qualified energy, if necessary. Only then can it be reintegrated.

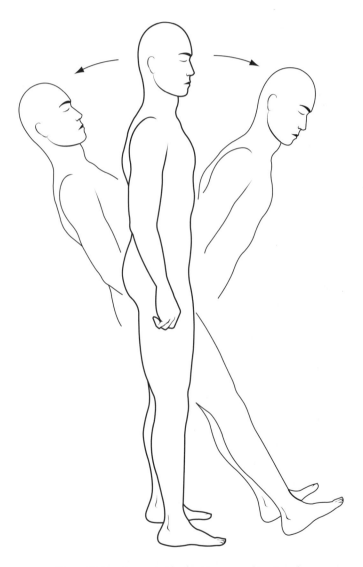

Figure 17-1 — An energy body may respond to stress by tilting out of personal body space.

Success in these initial steps will depend on the practitioner's knowledge, skill, and perseverance.

What are Intrusions?

Personal body space is designed to accommodate the appropriate energy body and/or energetic vehicle, and nothing more. If an energetic vehicle has tilted out of personal body space or has been ejected, qualified sub-fields, and the CECs within them, will fill the empty space almost as soon as it appears.

It is interesting to note that more than two thousand years ago Jesus addressed this phenomena when he declared "Now when the unclean spirit goes out of a man, it passes through waterless places, seeking rest, and does not find it. Then it says, 'I will return to my house from which I came'; and when it comes it finds it unoccupied, swept and put in order. Then it goes, and takes along with it seven other spirits more wicked than itself, and they go and live there" (Matthew, 12:43–45).

Even if there hasn't been a violent intrusion of qualified energy, the vacuum created by the ejection of an energetic vehicle will generate a polar relationship between the vacuum and the qualified energy surrounding it. The vacuum will become feminine in relationship to the surrounding karmic sediment and this polar relationship will facilitate the intrusion of qualified energy into personal body space.

Symptoms of Intrusions

By usurping the position of an energetic vehicle, intrusions polarize pre-existing energy blockages, bumpy strings, vasanas, and samskaras in the auric field surrounding personal body space, making them more dense and active on the world and dimension where fragmentation has taken place. This will cause *armoring*, which can lead to discomfort, pain, and physical disease. Back pain and/or abdominal pain, migraines and cramps are common symptoms caused by intrusions. Second generation symptoms of armoring include shortness of breath, exhaustion, sinusitis, memory loss, emotional and/or mental distress, and physical disease.

Intrusions are often accompanied by localized burning on the surface of personal body space or a popping sensation that occurs when intrusions are in the process of filling personal body space. Popping can occur in clumps, or appear only once as an isolated event. Popping can begin as soon as an energetic vehicles is ejected, or only later, after a new energetic balance has been achieved.

Structure and Behavior of Intrusions

Intrusions are composed of qualified subfields that fill personal body space vacated by a tilting or ejected energy body and/or energetic vehicle. They can be found on all worlds and dimensions, including the functions and aspects of mind. Given enough time, intrusions—regardless of their original form, whether vasanas, samskaras, personas, etc.—will take on a uniform quality and function as a singular subfield (unless acted upon by an outside force) because pressure will increase its overall density.

In some cases, particularly when an energy body or energetic vehicle has remained outside personal body space for an extended time or there has been an inordinate buildup of karmic baggage surrounding personal body space, on a particular dimension, intrusive energy will spill into the auric field. This energy will be more dense and polarized than the samskaras surrounding personal body space, and must be released prior to the main body of the intrusion—otherwise the process of reintegration will be disrupted.

Scanning for Intrusions

Intrusions should be scanned before they're released to determine their qualities and condition. When scanning intrusions, it is important to be precise, and, whenever possible, to include the guna in your intent. In the exercise below you will scan for an intrusion on the world of soul, level of the second chakra, in the tamasic part of the energetic spectrum. If you don't locate an intrusion on this particular dimension then change your designated intent and scan for an intrusion on another dimension on the same world and in the same part of the energetic spectrum.

Your designated intent for this exercise will be "It is my intent to scan for an intrusion on the world of soul, level of the second chakra, tamasic."

Begin by finding a comfortable position with your back straight. Then use the standard method to relax and balance conscious and unconscious mental activity.

To continue, activate and center yourself in the back of your heart chakra. Then split your attention, activate the front of your heart chakra and set your intent. Continue by stating "It is my intent to look inward in the world of soul, level of the second chakra, tamasic." Then split your attention and project your second attention to a position outside personal body space, to the left of your fourth chakra. Bring your emphasis to your second attention and activate your scanning tool. Then make up-and-down, overlapping strokes that extend into personal body space.

You'll quickly discover that there is a distinct difference between intrusive energy and an energy body and/or energetic vehicle. Your scanning tool will penetrate an intrusive energy once it's entered personal body space, but it will not penetrate an energy body. In fact, if the energy body on the world dimension and part of the energetic spectrum you are scanning is vertically integrated, then your scanning tool will not penetrate personal body space. This knowledge will help you determine if an energy body is tilted, and how far, or if it has been ejected from personal body space.

If you meet resistance along the front surface of personal body space, continue scanning from the left to the right until you're satisfied that the energy body or energetic vehicle is fixed in position. If there is a lack of resistance and your scanning tool penetrates personal body space, then scan the intrusion and record your findings.

When you're satisfied with what you've found, release your scanning tool, return your emphasis to the back of your heart chakra, and count from one to five. When you reach the number five, open your eyes. You will feel wide awake, perfectly relaxed, and better than you did before.

The following is a list of additional worlds and dimensions where you can scan for intrusions.

1. World of spirit, level of the sixth chakra, ragistic.

2. World of intellect, level of the first chakra, sattvic.

3. Upper splenic level, tamasic.

4. World of the lower mind, level of the first chakra below body space, ragistic

5. World of spirit, level of the twelfth chakra, sattvic.

Removing Intrusions

Before you can recollect and reintegrate an energy body or energetic vehicle, you must remove all intrusive energy from personal body space as well as any external extensions, but it is important to recognize that intrusive energy cannot safely be pushed out of personal body space—it must be released permanently.

The most effective way to release intrusive energy and extensions is to isolate the personas within them and release the personas using the seven-step technique you learned in chapter fifteen.

Isolating Intrusions

To release personas within intrusions and extensions you must first isolate them from their bunch. You can do this by using the first two steps (awareness and acceptance) of the seven-step process. Take note, the intrusive energy will be more dense than karmic sediment and may require more attention to isolate. It will also take more time for individual personas to emerge, expand, and express their qualities.

As soon as you've isolated a subfield within the intrusion, treat it like a persona and release it by completing the seven-step process. Once the subfield has been released, move on to the next subfield, isolate it, and release it. After the majority of intrusive energy has been removed the density of the intrusion will decrease sharply and you can proceed to recollecting and reintegrating the ejected energy body and / or energetic vehicle.

Recollecting, Cleansing, and
Reintegrating Energy Bodies

The next step in the process of recollecting and reintegrating an energy body or energetic vehicle is to locate it. This is far easier than you might imagine, since the length of time an energy body has been outside personal body space, and the distance it has drifted have only a minor impact on the process.

There are two ways to locate an energetic vehicle. If it is still in your energy field you can scan for it. If it has drifted beyond your auric boundary you can locate it using your mental attention and intent.

A scan will require the usual set-up. You will designate your intent, center yourself in the higher mind, create a scanning tool, etc. Then you will make broad overlapping strokes, working inward from the surface of your auric field toward the surface of personal body space.

In the world of the lower mind the surface of the auric field will extend about eight inches (twenty centimeters) from the surface of personal body space. In the world of soul the surface of the auric field will extend to about eighteen inches (forty-six centimeters). In the world of intellect it will extend about eight feet (two and a half meters), and in the world of spirit it will be about twenty-six feet (eight and a half meters).

Take note: if the energy body has been under duress while it's been outside personal body space, its shape may have become distorted. Therefor, the only reliable way to recognize it will be by its resonance, which will be both familiar and have a sense of appropriateness to it. This means that if the energy body you have in mind is someone else's energy body, or is a qualified subfield that you've mistaken for your own, the resonance will feel wrong, and it won't feel appropriate to recollect and reintegrate it.

To locate an energy body or energetic vehicle that has drifted outside your auric field using your mental attention and intent, it is essential to designate your intent as precisely as possible. If your intent is to locate an energetic vehicle in the world of soul, level of the fourth chakra, in the ragistic part of the energetic spectrum, your intent will be "It is my intent to locate and recollect my ejected energy body or energetic vehicle in the world of soul, level of the fourth dimension, ragistic." As soon as you've set your intent, your higher mind will locate the energy body and project your second attention to the part of the energy body closest to personal body space.

Recollecting Energy Bodies and Energetic Vehicles

Once you've located the energy body you have chosen to recollect and reintegrate, project your second attention to its trailing end so that you can push it. Bring your emphasis to your second attention, expanding it up and down and to the right and left. Combine the appropriate prana with your second attention and then gently push the energy body toward personal body space. It is important to remain focused. Regardless of how far the energy body has drifted, the combination of the second attention and prana will be sufficient to push the energy body back into personal body space.

In some cases, the closer the ejected energy body or energetic vehicle comes to personal body space, the more resistance it will encounter from layers of karmic sediment. It is important not to let your resolve weaken in the face of opposition. If you remain steadfast, the energy body will return to personal body space and you will sense a pop as it becomes fixed in position.

If you feel renewed pressure on the energy body after it has been reintegrated, you will have to release additional layers of karmic sediment from the auric field surrounding personal body space. You can easily do this by using the aprana (see chapter fourteen).

Cleansing Energy Bodies and Energetic Vehicles

If an energy body or energetic vehicle has been outside the protective umbrella of personal body space for an extended length of time, it can be contaminated by qualified subfields, making it more difficult to recollect and reintegrate. To determine if an energetic vehicle has become contaminated it will be necessary to scan its interior for qualified sub-fields, cords, and controlling waves.

The appropriate time to conduct a scan for contaminants is after an ejected vehicle has been located, but before it has been recollected and reintegrated.

As soon as you've located contaminants, you can proceed by isolating and releasing them as personas. Stay focused and continue the process until all the subfields have been released—this can be done in more than one session.

If a particular subfield within a contaminated energetic vehicle will not expand into a persona, abort the process and choose a subfield that is not under as much pressure. Once a sufficient number of subfields have been released, even the most tamasic subfield will have enough room to expand so that it can be released.

If care is not taken it is possible to inadvertently reintegrate an energy body that has been contaminated. If that happens, symptoms will inevitably surface, including anti-Self and antisocial feelings that emerge from contaminants within the energy body or energetic vehicle. To cor-rect the situation, you will have to remove the contaminants while the energy body is in personal body space by using your intent to project your mental attention inside the energy body, so that you can isolate the personas and release them using the seven-step method.

Reintegrating Your Energy Bodies and Energetic Vehicles

Once an energy body or energetic vehicle has been recollected, it must be reintegrated vertically, so that its surface is congruent with the surface of personal body space. Congruence is the final step in the process of rein-tegration, occurring once the surface of an energy body or energetic vehicle that has been reintegrated is in the same position as the surface of personal body space.

Congruence is important for several reasons. It permits the reintegrat-ed vehicle to function synchronistically with other energy bodies and energetic vehicles. It facilitates the uninterrupted flow of prana through the vehicle, which prevents it from being dimpled, tilted, or ejected from personal body space. It allows the Self to emerge in its fullness. It releases vast amounts of prana into the surrounding auric field. It inhibits qualified subfields from forming new karmic sediment. Finally, the uninterrupted flow of prana that radiates into the auric field and beyond, once a vehicle is congruent, will protect the functions and aspects of mind from the interference of projections of qualified energy and qualified subfields.

To determine if a reintegrated energy body is congruent you will have to scan the surface of personal body space on the world and dimension in question to discover whether it is uniformly taut, or if there is a gap between it and the surface of the energetic vehicle in question. If you determine that there is a gap between the energetic vehicle and personal body space you can use the aprana to release the karmic sediment that has intruded into personal body space.

As soon as the recollection and reintegration process is complete and congruence has been achieved, you will experience a sense of satisfaction, greater inner strength, and an increased flow of prana that will last as long as the energy body remains fixed in personal body space.

Chapter Eighteen

He has completed his voyage; he has gone beyond sorrow. The fetters of life have fallen from him, and he lives in full freedom.

—The Dhammapada, 7:90

Giving Up the I Idea

In the preceding chapters you learned to strengthen your boundaries, to overcome karmic baggage, and to bring your energy field into a state of radiant good health by recollecting and reintegrating the energy bodies and their corresponding energetic vehicles. In the process, you've been able to enhance your level of pleasure, human love, intimacy, and joy— but the final goal of Self-realization, which is experienced as sat (eternal life), chit (all knowledge, which comes from within), and ananda (bliss) will remain a distant dream unless you're ready to give up the mistaken notion that you are an individual separate from universal consciousness.

Giving up this mistaken notion means giving up the idea that you and everyone else are separate beings, living in a dualistic universe with separate identities that emerge from the the individual mind and ego. Ramana Maharshi, the twentieth-century master of Jnana Yoga (the Yoga of knowledge) declared "The thought 'I am this body of flesh and blood' is the one thread on which are strung the various other thoughts. Therefore, if we turn inward, inquiring 'Where is this "I"? all thoughts (including the 'I' thought) will come to an end and Self-knowledge will then spontaneously shine forth" (*The Teachings of Romana Maharshi*, 9).

Giving up the "I" thought and identification with individual mind and ego begins with detachment; detachment becomes a way of life with the development of discernment; and discernment becomes the stepping stone to transcendence with the development of (seeded) samadhi.

One develops detachment by consistently choosing to remain centered in the higher and lower mind so that appropriate activity becomes a way of life. The great Indian master Pantanjali declared that "Non-attachment (detachment) is self-mastery. It is freedom from desire . . ." (vs. 15).

Once one has chosen to remain centered in the higher and lower mind, one will recognize the true nature of the individual mind and ego. This will mark the beginning of discernment.

Discernment, in the strictest sense, is the ability to distinguish the difference between what is real and what is only apparently real or illusory. The Self, which is eternal, is always real because it is the same in the beginning, the middle, and the end. The higher and lower mind are real because they will remain the same as long as the phenomenal universe exists, and because they are not subject to the Hermetic principles of mind, cause and effect, rhythm, correspondence, vibration, polarity, and gender. On the other hand, the collective field of maya and the individual mind and ego are only apparently real because they evolve and involve through linear-sequential time and are not the same in the beginning, the middle, and the end.

Once one is able to discern the difference between what is real and what is apparently real, it naturally follows that one will choose to embrace what is real. By making that choice one will experience seeded samadhi.

Samadhi comes from the Sanskrit root *sam*, which means, "with, or together." Once one has achieved a state of seeded samadhi, identification with the individual mind and ego will come to an end and one will experience authentic fields of energy and consciousness directly. In regard to samadhi, Pantanjali declared "Just as the naturally pure crystal assumes shapes and colors of objects placed near it, so the Yogi's mind, with its totally weakened modifications, becomes clear and balanced and attains the state devoid of differentiation between knower, [what is] knowable and knowledge. This culmination of meditation is samadhi" (*Yoga Sutras*, 1:41).

Once detachment, discernment, and seeded samadhi have been mastered, the Self (Atman) will emerge into conscious awareness through the third heart. In the final act of surrender, samadhi will be turned inward, and union with the Self will become complete and irreversible.

Relationship with the Self, Atman, begins with seeded samadhi. In seeded samadhi the Self emerges through the energy bodies and energetic vehicles of the higher and lower mind and experiences union with the fields of energy, objects, and beings with which it comes in contact. You've already experienced seeded samadhi by centering yourself in the back of your heart chakra, activating one or more chakras, and looking inward in the worlds of the higher and lower mind. You've even enhanced this experience by reducing your karmic baggage and by recollecting and reintegrating your energy bodies and energetic vehicles.

However, Self-realization is not complete until seeded samadhi has been replaced by nirvakalpa samadhi (seedless samadhi), and intimacy and union with the Self (universal consciousness) replaces union with objects, fields of energy, and/or individual beings.

It's Your Choice

More than two thousand years ago Jesus recognized that the crux of the human predicament wasn't simply the inordinate buildup of karmic baggage or the disruption of the synchronistic function of the energy bodies and the human energy system. Through his ability to discern energy fields, the Nazarite observed that the root of the problem was choice and commitment. He recognized that human beings choose to be attached to the individual mind and ego, and even defend their attachment. Why else would Jesus have declared that "Nothing [but your own choice] can separate you from the love of God" (universal consciousness)?

Granted, the original choice described in "the biblical fall from grace" took place lifetimes ago, and since then you've collected additional karmic baggage. Nonetheless, the simple fact remains: you still have free will. You can change your mind at any time of your choosing, give up attachment to the individual mind and ego, and once again experience union with the Self. It doesn't matter how long you've been attached to the individual mind and ego, or how vehemently you've rejected the Self in the past. Free will is a fact of life. It can't be lost, stolen, or forfeited—not even by blaspheming the name of the lord.

Indeed, the conflict created by attachment to the individual mind and ego can only be resolved by choice and commitment, not by energy work, miracles, or lifestyle changes. Though you may desire union with the Self and may even experience the yearning of the third heart (Atman) for Self-realization, neither will be sufficient to take you beyond seeded samadhi unless you recognize that it is impossible to serve two masters. Either you choose the Self and as a condition of that choice commit yourself to act appropriately and to remain centered in the higher and lower mind, or you don't. If you don't, you will remain attached to the individual mind and ego and continue to be reactive to qualified subfields that make an impact on your energy field.

It is choice that leads one to the path of Self-realization and to a recognition that life and consciousness emerge from the Self, but it is commitment to the path and the final goal of Self-realization that enables one to overcome the inertia of the individual mind and ego so that union with the Self becomes one's moment-to-moment experience.

From Friendship to Union

The relationship one has with the Self once one has committed oneself to the path of Self-realization is unique and like no other relationship one has previously experienced. In the *Bhagavad Gita,* Krishna declares that a person in such a relationship will be "... free of ego, indifferent to pain and pleasure .... always satisfied, self-restrained, firmly resolved ... liberated from ... [the] ... anxieties of joy, anger, and fear ... impartial, pure, capable, detached, untroubled, who renouncing all undertakings is ... full of love ..." (*Bhagavad Gita*, 12).

In the Song of Solomon, that unique relationship is likened to the relationship between a young woman and her beloved king, "As the lily among the thorns, so is my love" (the committed lover declares), ". . . As the apple tree among the trees of the wood so is my beloved . . . I sat down under his shadow with great delight, and his fruit was sweet to my taste. He brought me to the banqueting house, and his banner over me was love. Stay with me . . . comfort me . . . for I am sick of love" (Song of Solomon 1:2–5).

These poetic expressions of love and devotion are echoed throughout devotional, spiritual literature. In fact, commitment to the Self and the experience of union that accompanies it can be an overwhelming experience. Ramakrishna describes the moment in this way: "When divine bliss is attained, a person becomes quite intoxicated with it; even without drinking wine, he looks like one fully drunk" (*Sayings of Sri Ramakrishna*, 939–40).

What happens when one finally commits oneself to the Self and the path of Self-realization may not always be so joyful. One's experience will depend on whether one has developed detachment, cultivated discernment, and achieved seeded samadhi. If attachment to the individual mind and ego remains strong, if there is a lack of discernment and/or if seeded samadhi is a rare or even frightening experience, then the Self will be seen as a threat and there will be a backlash from the individual mind and ego when it emerges into conscious awareness.

If, on the other hand, detachment, discernment, and seeded samadhi have been consistently cultivated, then when the Self emerges from the right side of the heart it will bring with it the hoped-for benefits—i.e., freedom, truth, and bliss.

For those who have cultivated detachment, discernment, and seeded samadhi, relationship with the Self will evolve in predictable stages. In the first stage, the Self will emerge as a reliable and indulgent friend. Friendship will not last long, however, since universal consciousness cannot fully emerge within the context of friendship or any reciprocal human relationship

In the second stage, friendship will evolve into love, and the desire for union will replace the simple desire for contact and friendship. In this stage one will see individuality and individual rights for what they are, manifestations of the individual mind and ego and obstacles to union with the Self.

In the third stage, indulgence will end. The Self will emerge in its fullness. If detachment is not complete and the individual mind and ego retain enough power to disrupt union when it occurs, the Self will withdraw. For the individual in the middle of the struggle it can be a tortuous period of inner turmoil as the individual mind and ego vie with the Self for influence and control. If one's commitment is strong enough, then one will move to the next stage in the process. If one's commitment is not strong enough, then one will identify with the outrage and resentment that the individual mind and ego throw up in in their defense.

In the fourth stage, one will grow tired of the struggle and the tempest will subside. Commitment will grow and one will recognize that they are not separate and have never been separate from the Self. This recognition will be accompanied by a growing desire to experience uninterrupted union with the Self.

In the final stage, the last remnants of the individual mind and ego will be subdued. Union will become permanent, and one will finally recognize that they are not an individual seeking the Self. They are, in fact, the Self seeking to emerge through the vehicles of the higher and lower mind and their functions and aspects. At that moment of total recognition duality will be abolished, Self-realization will be achieved, and sat chit ananda will become one's permanent experience.

Glossary

Advaita: Advaita can be defined as nondualism. It is the dominant view of Vedanta, particularly the Upanishads. Advaita teaches that the universe and all that is contained within it emerges from universal consciousness in the same way that a dream and everything contained within it emerges from human consciousness.

This ancient point of view is echoed by Hermetics, the foundation of western metaphysics, whose first principle states "The All is mind; the universe is mental."

Ahamkara: *See:* Aspects of Mind.

Aprana: The aprana is a feminine form of prana that emerges from the higher and lower mind and the splenic levels. When it is used in conjunction with the mental attention and the intent of the higher and lower mind, it becomes an effective tool for removing karmic sediment from the auric field, in the region between the surface of personal body space and the apranic boundary.

Apranic Boundary: The apranic boundary surrounds personal body space at a distance of eight inches (twenty centimeters) on the worlds and dimensions of the higher and lower mind. When the apranic boundary is not inordinately burdened by karmic sediment and the movement of the aprana is not obstructed, then unqualified energy emerging from the apranic boundary will keep the surface of personal body space free of karmic sediment and will safeguard the integrity of the human energy field.

Appropriate Activity: Appropriate activities are actions in accord with one's personal dharma (purpose). They promote the flow of consciousness and prana in the higher and lower mind and their functions and aspects.

Artha: *See:* Authentic Desires.

Astral Plane: The traditional term used in western metaphysics to designate the world of soul. In the microcosm, the world of soul includes the
functions of emotion, feeling, and sensation.

Aspects of Mind: The manas, buddhi, chitta, and ahamkara are known as
the aspects of mind. Aspects provide a human being with both a coherent structure and an identity through which the higher and lower mind
and splenic levels can function synchronistically.

   The manas grasps or takes hold and separates an object, being,-or energy field in the external environment. The buddhi analyzes and compares it after it has been separated from its environment. The chitta confers a value on what has been isolated by the manas and analyzed by the
buddhi. The ahamkara is the decision maker. It distills the information it
receives from the other aspects of mind and uses it to create and support one's view of themselves and their relationships.

Atman: Atman is the Self (divine consciousness), the one singularity from
which the phenomenal universe emerges and continues to owe its existence. It is from Atman that life, bliss, and knowledge emerge and must
someday return.

   Atman emerges into one's conscious awareness from the third heart,
on the right side of the chest.

Attachments: Attachments emerge from karmic baggage and connect a
person to objects, fields of consciousness and energy, and other sentient
beings. Attachments emerge into one's conscious awareness as patterns
of thought, feeling, and behavior, and keep one busy with activities that
merely serve to perpetuate the pattern. Patterns of activity created and
perpetuated by one's karmic baggage are ultimately Self-defeating and
antagonistic to Self-awareness and freedom of Self-expression.

Auric Fields: The auric fields are reservoirs of unqualified energy composed of an inner cavity surrounded by a thin surface boundary. Auric
fields surround personal body space on each world and dimension.
They extend the human energy field beyond personal body space as far
as twenty-six feet (eight meters), and they form a boundary between the
human energy field, the microcosm, and the external field of energy,
the macrocosm.

Authentic Desires: The Vedic texts, which are the basis of ancient Yoga,
teach that there are four essential desires, which are functions of the

bodies of desire. Through their synchronistic functions they motivate a human being to be incarnated into a physical body. The four authentic desires are a normal function of life on earth and shouldn't be confused with desires for specific things that create attachment and emerge through the individual mind and ego.

The four desires are artha, kama, dharma, and moksha. Artha is the desire for material comfort or wealth. Kama is the second desire, which denotes both pleasure and the desire for pleasure. In the *Bhagavad Gita* desire is put at the center of living and is equated with the life force.

Dharma literally means "that which holds together," in essence, that which prevents worldly relationships from dissolving into chaos. Dharma has two applications: shared dharma, which is righteousness or spiritual duty—righteousness in this context can be equated with appropriate activity—and individual dharma, the specific path of appropriate activity, which will lead a person back into conscious union with the Self.

Moksha denotes transcendence, which is spiritual freedom and liberation from karmic attachment. Of the four desires moksha is the highest.

Authentic Emotions: Anger, fear, pain, and joy are the four authentic human emotions. They are regulated by the chakras and emerge when the flow of energy through the chakras is restricted because of fear or contraction. Anger, the authentic human emotion with the lowest mean frequency, is regulated by the second chakra, fear is regulated by the third chakra, pain by the fourth chakra, and joy by the fifth chakra.

Avatars: Avatars manifest universal consciousness in human form. Their mission on earth is to restore and maintain balance in the collective field of consciousness and energy. There are a handful of avatars in every generation—all of whom are associated with Vishnu, the second god of the Hindu godhead. It is Vishnu who is responsible for preserving the phenomenal universe.

Bhagavad-Gita: The *Bhagavad-Gita* is considered the most authoritative part of the Upanishads. The *Gita* is essentially a dialogue between the avatar Krishna and Prince Arjuna. In the *Gita*, Krishna explains the basic principles of Yoga and dharma.

Bliss: Bliss is the permanent condition of universal consciousness. Bliss exists outside time-pace—therefore, it cannot be influenced by anything in the phenomenal universe. It is the condition of all avatars, bodhisatvas, and jivamuktis. When one experiences bliss as their permanent condition, one has achieved the state of Self-realization.

Bodhisatvas: Masters born in union with Atman. They have a physical-material body but remain centered in universal consciousness and detached from the "I" and the individual mind and ego.

Bodies of Consciousness: Within the field of unqualified consciousness, paramatman, there are bodies of consciousness that serve as a blueprint for the energy bodies in the field of unqualified energy, jivamatman. Although composed entirely of unqualified consciousness, bodies of consciousness have the same structure and functions as bodies composed of unqualified energy.

Bodies of Desire: The lower mind is composed of energetic vehicles called bodies of desire. Bodies of desire are the same size and shape as the bodies of consciousness and energy to which they correspond. The Vedic texts teach that there are four essential desires, which are functions of the bodies of desire. The four desires are artha, kama, dharma, and moksha. *See:* Authentic Desires.

Body Space, Personal: Personal body space is the space on the nonphysical planes that corresponds to the space occupied by a human's physical-material body. On the worlds of the higher and lower mind, their functions and aspects, the world of the chakras, and splenic levels, this space is occupied by an energy body or an energetic vehicle.

Boundaries: *See:* Auric Fields; Surface Boundaries.

Buddhi: *See:* Aspects of Mind.

Bumpy Strings: *See:* Complex Subfields.

CECs (Conscious Energy Concentrations): At the core of all qualified subfields in both the macrocosm and the microcosm are conscious energy concentrations, or CECs. CECs are nonphysical beings (entities) that exist in the collective field of maya and in all subfields of qualified energy. In the external environment they can be found in atmospheres, pool, and waves. In the human energy field they can be found in karmic sediment (samskaras and vasanas), bumpy strings, personas, energy blockages, cords, controlling waves, and independent blockages. In addition, large numbers are concentrated in the individual mind and ego. At the present time (the Kali Yuga), CECs exist in numbers far exceeding the number of living creatures that exist in the physical-material universe.

Although the cognitive ability of CECs as well as their ability to act and express themselves is severely limited, they do have the individual will to fulfill their needs, a form of finite consciousness, rudimentary emotions and feelings, and the ability to express these qualities through time/space on the world and dimension on which they exist.

Center: In all fields of activity one's center is located on the level of the heart. For the developing person it will be the human heart, for the developed person it will be the heart chakra, and for the transcendent person it will be Atman (the Self), which emerges from the right side of the heart chakra.

Chakras: In Sanskrit, the word chakra means "wheel." The chakras appear as brightly colored disks, each spinning rapidly at the end of what looks like a long axle or stalk. The wheel portion is about three inches in diameter (eight centimeters), and perpetually moves or spins around a central axis.

The main function of the chakras is to keep the Self, universal consciousness, connected to the worlds and dimensions of the phenomenal universe. In this capacity the chakras serve as vortexes through which prana can enter the phenomenal universe. In addition to serving as vortexes, the chakras transmit and transmute prana into different frequencies or pitches.

Chakras, Splenic: The splenic chakra is located by the spleen on the left side of personal body space and the upper splenic chakra is located directly across from it. Both the splenic chakra and the upper splenic chakra have the same structure as the traditional chakras.

Prana emerging through the splenic chakras supports the activities of the splenic bodies. When the splenic bodies are vertically integrated and the splenic chakras are functioning healthfully one will be fortified against the coercive and seductive activities of the individual mind and ego that condemn the normal human activities such as eating, working, and participating in intimate relationships.

Chakras, Traditional: There are seven traditional chakras described in the texts of Tantra and Vedanta. All are located in personal body space. As a structural and functional group, they are responsible for regulating life on the dimensions dedicated to feeling, emotion, finite human consciousness, relationship, and psychic well-being.

Chi: Chi is the word used by Taoist and Oriental metaphysicians to designate unqualified energy. Chi or ki, as it is sometimes called, is identical to prana.

Chitta: *See:* Aspects of Mind.

Companion Chakras: Companion chakras are two chakras that have complementary functions and which coordinate their activities. Their relationship affects the well-being of both chakras and the energy bodies or energetic vehicles that they support.

The first pair of chakras in partnership consists of the first and third chakras. Their partnership is based on the complementary roles they play in stability, security, and joy of existence.

The second pair of chakras in partnership consist of the second and fifth chakras. Their partnership is based on the complementary roles they play in regulating Self-expression and joy.

The third pair of chakras in partnership consists of the fourth and sixth chakras. Their partnership is based on the complementary roles they play in recognizing and securing basic human rights.

The functional partnership between the first and seven chakras and the minor energy centers in the hands and feet is based on the role they play in regulating pressure in the human energy system.

Complex Subfields: Given enough time, independent qualified subfields can combine with other qualified subfields with similar resonance to form complex subfields such as bumpy strings, vasanas, samskaras, cords, controlling waves, and personas.

Complex subfields can vary in size and shape depending on the number of CECs in the subfield and the amount of qualified energy surrounding them. If complex subfields and the CECs within them are integrated, they will become part of the host's karmic sediment and will eventually manifest their qualities through the host's individual mind and ego.

Controlling Waves: These are complex qualified subfields which are polarized and highly active. They contain at least two CECs and are projected from the functions of mind, the koshas, indyrias, and pranas. Controlling waves tend to put pressure on qualified subfields and/or karmic baggage already present in the target's energy field on the level from which the wave is projected. The increased pressure caused by controlling waves is the most common source of stress and stress-related symptoms.

Cords: Cords are complex subfields that contain at least two CECs and are projected from one sentient being to another. They are normally highly polarized and extremely active. Cords are a manifestation of dependency, need, or desire that can border on obsession.

Consciousness: Consciousness is one of the five building blocks of the phenomenal universe. The other four include energy, matter, time, and space. In the natural world the manifestation of consciousness is more or less limited. In the animal world consciousness becomes more centralized and complex, reaching its fullest development in man who can manifest consciousness, emerging from the Self, through the vehicles of spirit, intellect, soul, lower mind, and body.

Boundaries: *See:* Surface Boundaries.

Designated Intent: The intent serves the same function in the higher and lower mind as a software program does in a computer. Software programs function by instructing a computer to perform a particular task or series of tasks. The intent functions in the same way by programming the higher and lower mind to perform a particular task or series of tasks.

The designated intent is composed of three elements: class, type, and location. Class designates the class of work to be performed during the procedure. Type designates the type of structure or object to be scanned, released, activated, recollected and/or reintegrated. Location designates the specific locale, world, dimension, or field of activity, and/ or organ of the human energy system, energy body, or corresponding energetic vehicle where the work will take place.

Dharma: Dharma has two applications: shared dharma, which is common to all mankind, and individual dharma, which is specific to each human being. Shared dharma is righteousness or spiritual duty. Individual dharma is one's individual path to enlightenment. By following dharma, one does what is appropriate by choosing only those actions that promote the flow of unqualified energy through their energy system.

Ego: The human ego is a multiworld, multidimensional field of qualified energy that complements the individual mind. Elements of the ego are located within the human energy field on all worlds and dimensions of the higher and lower mind, the world of the chakras, the physical world, the splenic levels, and their functions and aspects.

The ego's structural and functional center on each world and dimension is approximately four inches (ten centimeters) in front and in back of the heart chakra. Qualified subfields that compose the ego on each dimension have been pressed together by their mutual attraction and shared polarity. This gives the ego the look of a misshapen ball. Extensions connect the ego to qualified subfields, objects, and living beings in both the microcosm and the macrocosm. These cord-like structures are continually changing, sometimes growing stronger or weaker, even changing size, polarity, and state as conditions in the environment surrounding the ego change.

Emotions: There are four authentic human emotions: anger, fear, pain, and joy. Authentic emotions emerge when energy moving up the shushumna-governor meridian has been blocked or restricted by karmic baggage or projections. When energy moving by the second chakra has been blocked anger emerges, by the third chakra fear emerges, by the fourth chakra pain emerges, and by the fifth chakra joy emerges.

Energy Bodies and Energetic Vehicles: Energy bodies (and energetic vehicles) on all worlds and dimensions serve as the Self's vehicles of awareness, cognition, assimilation, sensation, and expression. All energetic bodies and vehicles are composed of prana and are the same size and shape as the physical body to which they correspond .

Energy bodies (and energetic vehicles) originally emerged from universal consciousness (the Self) by way of the tattvas, along with the worlds and dimensions of the phenomenal universe.

Eternal Time: Eternal time is the same as the ever-present now. In eternal time there is no past or future. There is no space or events either, which means that in eternal time everything is united into one singularity that has no qualities.

Etheric Plane: *See:* Splenic Levels.

Functions of Mind: Energy bodies in the higher and lower mind interact with the phenomenal universe through the three functions of mind, known in Sanskrit as the koshas, indyrias, and pranas. Although their primary function is to serve as vehicles of consciousness and energy, functions of mind can extend beyond their surface boundaries and make contact with objects, beings, and fields of energy in both the collective field of maya and the field of unqualified energy. Koshas function as an extension of human awareness. Indyrias perform the same function as the koshas in the fields of emotion and feeling. The energetic functions through which the koshas and Indyrias operate are known as the pranas.

Gunas: In Sanskrit, the word *guna* means "quality or attribute." In Yoga, the gunas are used as a shorthand to describe the character of subfields from the collective field of maya. Since most qualified subfields aren't pure, but contain more than one CEC, the quality of a particular subfield, or its guna, can be thought of as the mean frequency or resonance of all CECs and qualified energy within the field. There are three traditional gunas, which are used to describe the qualities of qualified subfields: sattva, rajas, and tamas.

Hermetic Principles: Hermetics is the foundation of Western metaphysics. We are told that Hermetics was given to humankind by Thoth, the Egyptian god of wisdom, whom the Greeks called Hermes Trismegistrus. There are seven Hermetic principles: The Principle of Mind, The Principle of Correspondence, The Principle of Vibration, The Principle of Polarity, The Principle of Rhythm, The Principle of Cause and Effect, and The Principle of Gender.

Higher and Lower Mind: The worlds of spirit, intellect, and soul comprise the higher mind. Of these three, the world of spirit has the highest mean frequency, the world of intellect has a lower mean frequency, and the world of the soul has the lowest mean frequency. The fourth world is the world of the lower mind, which has a lower mean frequency than the worlds of the higher mind. Complementing the higher and lower mind are the world of the chakras, the splenic level, and the functions and aspects of mind.

Human Energy Field: The human energy field or jivamatman is the collective field of unqualified energy. It contains both energy bodies and energetic vehicles as well as the human energy system which supports it. The main function of the human energy field is to serve universal consciousness as a vehicle of cognition, expression, and assimilation.

Human Energy System: It is the human energy system that transmits and transmutes prana (unqualified energy) through the human energy field. Contained within the human energy system are the chakras, meridians, auric fields, the minor energy centers in the hands and feet, and the kandas, which are hubs from which meridians emerge.

Ida, Pingala, and Shushumna: In the Tantric system of Yoga, we are told that the ida and pingala serve as the ruling nadis, or meridians. The ida and pingala originate on either side of the first chakra. The ida works its way up the left side of the shushumna-governor meridian and passes through the left nostril. The pingala works its way up the right side of the shushumna-governor and passes through the right nostril. Both the ida and pingala join the shushumna-governor again in the region of the ajna center, the sixth chakra. Once the kundalini-shakti has been raised to the crown chakra the ida and pingala merge with the shushumna to create one large meridian through which the aroused kundalini can flow.

Inappropriate Activities: Inappropriate activities are those activities that are motivated by karmic baggage and emerge from the individual mind and ego. Inappropriate activities disrupt the flow of prana and disrupt relationship and intimacy. By engaging in inappropriate activities one becomes more attached to the phenomenal universe, making it increasingly difficult for one to follow dharma and achieve union with universal consciousness.

Individual Mind and Ego: The individual mind and ego are composed of karmic baggage laid down as sediment in the human energy field. Although they can collectively counterfeit the functions of the higher and lower mind, the individual mind and ego are not a structural part of the human energy field. In fact, neither have a definite structure that defines them. Rather, they are an evolving community of CECs, qualified subfields, and qualified energy.

Since the seeds of the individual mind and ego are carried from lifetime to lifetime as samskaras, what is developed anew in each incarnation is the sense of "I" (or individuality), which is manifest consciously as one's personality or dominant persona.

Indryias: *See:* Functions of Mind.

Intrusions: Intrusions are qualified subfields that have intruded into personal body space. Qualified subfields can intrude into personal body space in four ways. They can intrude when there has been an inordinate buildup of samskaras or vasanas, when a controlling wave or cord has intruded into personal body space, when there has been an intrusion of one or more highly active nonphysical beings, personas, or foreign energy bodies, and when one passes through a dense or active external atmosphere or becomes intimate with someone whose energy field carries an inordinate amount of karmic energy.

Intellect: The consciousness of the Self emerges through the vehicles of intellect as awareness. Awareness is not mind as one normally conceives of it. Awareness does not think, have attitudes, worry about the future, or dwell on the past. Awareness remains centered in the ever-present now. Therefore intellect can be viewed as. "The awareness of Self emerging through the higher and lower mind."

Intent: Intent emerges through the vehicles of the higher and lower mind when they have been fully integrated into personal body space. Intent is manifest as appropriate activity. It is the will of the higher mind manifested passively through the functions of authentic spirit, intellect, soul, or desire.

Jainism: An ancient religion of India that stresses aestheticism, nonviolence, and reverence for life. Like all great eastern religions, Jainism accepts the doctrine of reincarnation, karma, and the inevitable enlightenment of all human beings.

Jivamatman: Refers to the individual self, which is composed of spirit, intellect. soul, and authentic desire. All dimensional fields in the field of jivamatman are composed entirely of unqualified energy. Although jivamatman serves as a vehicle for universal consciousness, its ability to perform this function can be disrupted by projections and the inordinate buildup of karmic baggage.

Jivamukti: The term refers to enlightened human beings. In Sanskrit, *jiva* means "embodied soul," mukti knowledge of the Self. Therefore a jivamukti is one who has achieved knowledge of the Self via direct uninterrupted union.

Kali Yuga: *See:* Yugas.

Kama: *See:* Bodies of Desire.

Kandas: The kandas are hubs from which the major meridians emerge. One kanda is located at the base of the spine and the other is located about two inches (five centimeters) forward from the back of the heart chakra. Though the kandas (which function like mathematical points) occupy no space, they do perform an important organizational function by facilitating the transmission and transmutation of prana throughout the human energy system.

Karma: Karma is an aggregate of subtle matter that accumulates in the human energy field and veils the consciousness of the Self and everything that emerges from it. The word karma comes from the ancient Sanskrit root *kri*, "to act," and it signifies an activity or action.

Karma has eight functional aspects: it obscures comprehension, it obscures awareness, it produces counterfeit feelings (emotions and sensations), it deludes a person (veils the truth), it is age-determining, it defines personality by creating personas, it determines status and, therefore, psychic well-being, and it disrupts personal power. The first four aspects are obstructive, the remaining four are not—though they are Self-limiting—since they obstruct the flow of unqualified energy (prana), through the human energy system.

Much like gravity, the polarity karma creates between the cause and its effect attracts a person to objects, fields of qualified energy, and living beings (based on past actions), and then, using qualified energy, binds them to the object, field of energy, or living being to which they are attracted.

Karmic Baggage: Karmic baggage is the total amount of qualified (karmic) energy that has accumulated in a human being's energy field during this lifetime and previous incarnations.

Karmic baggage not only causes suffering and disease, it limits awareness by creating attachment to the external world of phenomena (maya). Karmic baggage does this by disrupting the vertical integration of energy bodies and energetic vehicles and by disrupting the transmission and transmutation of unqualified energy (prana) through the higher and lower mind and the human energy system.

Koshas: *See:* Functions of Mind.

Kundalini-Shakti: The word "kundalini" comes from the Sanskrit root *Kundala*, which means coiled. In Hindu mythology the Kundalini-sakti is often personified as the Devi (Goddess Kundalini) or anthromorphosized as a coiled sleeping snake.

As a manifestation of unqualified energy, kundalini emerges as the serpent power, which lies dormant at the base of the spine. When the the serpent power is aroused it begins to move upward through the shushumna-governor meridian to the crown chakra at the top of the head.

Linear Sequential Time: Linear sequential time has become a feature of western culture since the time of Sir Isaac Newton. It is distinguished from linear time and eternal time by virtue of the fact that science considers it an objective reality, like energy, space, and matter. By virtue of its definition, linear sequential time can exist only on the physical-material plane and in qualified fields of consciousness and energy.

Lower Mind: *See:* Bodies of Desire.

Mahatattva: Yoga teaches that there are thirty-six tattvas (steps in evolution), which are responsible for the incredible diversity of the phenomenal universe, both on the subtle and physical-material planes.

Manas: *See:* Aspects of Mind.

Maya: In Sanskrit, the word *maya* means "The appearance of reality." The world of maya is composed of qualified consciousness, qualified energy, and subtle matter in either a solid, liquid or gaseous state. It is only the collective field of maya that is subject to change, and which evolves and involves through linear-sequential time.

Meridians: The meridians are streams of energy that connect the chakras to one another. In addition to connecting the chakras, they transmit unqualified energy throughout the human energy system. By transmitting prana the meridians support the higher and lower mind, keep the human energy system in balance, and help to maintain the integrity of auric boundaries.

Minor Energy Centers: Four minor energy centers exist in the human field—one in each palm and one in each sole. The minor energy centers are not structures like chakras—rather, they are centers of activity created by the functional interaction of major meridians, one masculine and one feminine. In the palms they are created through the interaction of the yang yu and yin yu meridians. in the soles they are created through the interaction of the chiao yang and the chiao yin meridians.

Minor energy centers have two principle functions. They facilitate the movement of prana through the chakras and meridians and along with the meridians they maintain the pressure within the human energy field.

Moksha: *See:* Essential Desires.

Nadis: *See:* Meridians.

Nonphysical Beings: *See* CECs (Conscious Energy Concentrations).

Para: Para refers to what is higher, universal, or without second. Parabrahman is the supreme being. Paramatman refers to the supreme Self.

Paramatman: Refers to the supreme Self. Para means higher, universal or supreme. It can also refer to that which is transcendental. It is used in conjunction with Atman or Brahman. In the Sankhya philosophy—the precursor to Yoga—it refers to perusha, the supreme consciousness.

Personal Body Space: The space on the higher and lower dimensions which corresponds to the space occupied by the physical-material body. On the worlds of the higher and lower mind, their functions and aspects, the world of the chakras, and splenic levels, this space is occupied by an energy body or an energetic vehicle. The surface of the personal body space on a particular world and dimension stays strong and firm and will resist the intrusion of qualified energy as long as the energy body or corresponding energetic vehicle contained within it remains fixed in position (vertically integrated).

Personas: Personas are self-contained personalities composed of qualified energy and subtle matter. They emerge from karmic baggage and can usurp the functions of the higher mind on their dimension. In extreme cases they can grow strong enough to compel a person to obsessively fulfill their needs and desires.

Perusha: Perusha emerged along with prakriti as a function of the fourth tattva. It represents the primordial consciousness from which all subsequent consciousness emerged, including the individualized consciousness of paramatman. According to the Sankhya system, perusha represents pure consciousness, which is unattached and unqualified.

Pingala: *See:* Ida and Pingala.

Polarity: All qualified subfields are polarized either masculine or feminine. Masculine subfields are assertive. Feminine subfields are receptive. The polarity of a qualified subfield will be determined by the number of CECs within it, its density level of activity, and its polar relationship to neighboring subfields. The more CECs of a particular gender in a subfield, the more polarized it will be.

Subfields of qualified energy that are masculine will display enhanced personal will and penetrating power—the ability to penetrate the human energy field. Subfields that are feminine will compel their host to become more reactive and receptive to external subfields.

Prakriti: Prakriti emerged along with perusha as a function of the fourth tattva. It was from this primordial dynamic force that unqualified energy as it is known today evolved—including the kundalini-shakti, prana in its different forms, and the aprana. It was also from this primordial force that joy emerged into the microcosm and through joy, intimacy, human love, and pleasure.

Prana: Prana is a form of unqualified, nonphysical energy. It emerged from Prakriti and serves as the foundation of everything that exists and which moves, breathes, and takes up space. In the human energy field the microcosm prana serves as the foundation of the higher and lower mind and the subtle energy system.

Pranas: The pranas are the third function of mind. Along with the koshas and indyrias, they function within all worlds and dimensions of the higher mind. There are two types of pranas, incoming and outgoing. Pranas provide a medium for koshas and indyrias, and they extend vitality and power into the external environment via pranic extensions that emerge as a function of the intent of the higher and lower mind.

Qualified Energy: Qualified energy is energy that emerges from the collective field of maya. In contrast to unqualified energy, it causes attachment to fields, objects, and living beings. Given the right circumstances, qualified energy will coalesce into subfields that have the qualities of size, shape, density, polarity, surface texture, and color.

Qualified Subfield: A subfield of qualified energy contains at least one CEC, is composed of an internal cavity, and is surrounded by a surface boundary. Qualified subfields can be found in both the microcosm and the macrocosm. In the microcosm they are the principal component of karmic baggage and the individual mind and ego.

Rajistic Energy: *See:* Gunas.

Samadhi: Samadhi comes from the Sanskrit root *sam*, which means "with or together." Samadhi can be likened to union or intimacy. In samadhi one experiences the inner qualities of things with which one is intimate. There are two common types of samadhi. In seeded samadhi, identification with the individual mind and ego will come to an end and one will experience authentic fields of energy and consciousness directly. Once seeded, samadhi has been mastered and the Self (Atman) has emerged into conscious awareness through the third heart, the experience of samadhi can be turned inward. When it has, and union with the Self has become complete and irreversible, samadhi becomes seedless.

Samskaras: *See:* Complex Subfields.

Satchitananda: The natural condition of the Self: eternal life (sat), all knowledge (chit), and bliss (ananda).

Sattvic Energy: *See:* Gunas.

Self: The Self, universal consciousness, or Atman is the root of a person's spirit, soul, intellect, and body, as well as everything else in the phenomenal universe. It is the foundation of what you are now and what you were before you began identifying with the "I" and the individual mind and ego. The Self is alive and aware. It is the source of human life as well as the wellspring of bliss, joy, love, and pleasure, which animates it.

Shakti: Shakti represents the divine feminine. In Hindu mythology Shakti is the consort of Shiva—the third member of the godhead and the destroyer of the world. Saivism sees Shakti as vibration, which in a dormant form exists within universal consciousness. After it emerges via the tattvas, Shakti in the form of dynamic, creative energy, or prakriti (the primordial form of prana) begins to function as the driving force of evolution, the movement toward diversity. In the future, after evolution has come to an end, Shakti in the form of prana will become the driving force for involution, the movement toward union with universal consciousness.

Shiva: Shiva represents the divine masculine. In Hindu mythology he is the third member of the godhead the destroyer of the world. In Kashmir Saivism it is Shiva who represents universal consciousness. In that form Shiva symbolizes the union of divine consciousness and vibration.

Shiva and Shakti: It is the eternal dance of Shiva and Shakti (i.e., consciousness and energy) that serves as the foundation of both the physical and nonphysical universe.

Shock: Shock occurs whenever projections or karmic baggage exert enough pressure on a body or vehicle of energy to temporarily eject it from personal body space.

Shushumna-Governor Meridian: The shushumna (governor) meridian originates at a position in personal body space, which corresponds to the muladhara chakra. It then passes through the male pole of the seven traditional chakras on its way up to the crown chakra and beyond. Extensions of the shushumna connect the lower chakras, below personal body space—and the higher chakras, above personal body space with the seven traditional chakras.

Soul: The soul is an essential part of the higher mind and is composed of energy bodies and energetic vehicles known as functions and aspects, which are supported by the human energy system. The soul contains one hundred and forty dimensions and expresses itself through the four authentic emotions: anger, fear, pain, and joy.

Spirit: The spirit is the highest world within the higher mind. Contained within it are one hundred and forty dimensions. As a functional part of the higher mind it emerges as the *knower* within the field of knowledge. This means that universal consciousness emerges through the energy bodies and energetic vehicles of the human spirit as knowledge. The world of spirit is composed of energy bodies and energetic vehicles known as functions and aspects. Like the other worlds within the higher mind, the world of spirit is supported by the human energy system.

Splenic Bodies: Human beings have two splenic bodies that are the same size and shape as the physical-material body to which they correspond. Within the higher mind the splenic bodies are responsible for sensation and feeling. When the splenic bodies are vertically integrated and the splenic chakras are functioning healthfully, one will be fortified against the coercive and seductive activities of the individual mind and ego that condemn the normal activities of the physical-material world—such as eating, working, and participating in intimate relationships.

Splenic Chakras: *See:* Chakras, Splenic.

Splenic Levels: The splenic levels correspond to the etheric plane. There are two splenic levels which serve as a bridge between the nonphysical worlds of the higher mind and the physical-material universe. Primarily concerned with feeling and sensation, the two splenic bodies are supported by two splenic chakras and their corresponding meridians and auric fields.

Standard Method: A method used to relax and balance conscious and unconscious mental activity. In the standard method the physical-material body is relaxed by alternately contracting and releasing tension in the musculature.

Subfield: A qualified field of consciousness and/or energy with distinct characteristics which a person may unconsciously radiate or deliberately project through the larger field of qualified energy or become attached to, when a foreign field enters his or her internal environment.

Surface Boundaries: There are three types of surface boundaries that safeguard the human energy field and the organs, energy bodies, and energetic vehicles contained within it: the surface of personal body space, the apranic boundary (which surrounds the higher and lower mind) and the surfaces of the auric fields.

    All boundaries are composed of prana—in the case of surface boundaries, luminescent strands of prana that appear solid and crisscross each other in every imaginable direction.

Surface of Auric Fields: From the surface of personal body space on each dimension, the auric fields extend outward in all directions, from about two inches (five centimeters) to more than twenty-six feet (eight meters). The surface of the auric fields separate one's field from the external environment. Since the auric fields are flexible structures, as a person develops spiritually by removing karmic baggage, recollecting, and reintegrating energy bodies and energetic vehicles and activating the human energy system, the auras will grow larger, and the boundaries surrounding them will expand and become more taut (like the surface of a full balloon).

Surface of Personal Body Space: Personal body space is the space on each world and dimension that corresponds to the space occupied by the physical body in the physical-material world. The surface of personal body space on a particular world and dimension is composed of luminescent fibers that crisscross each other in every imaginable direction. This makes the surface porous, flexible, and extremely strong.

Tamasic Energy: *See:* Gunas.

Tantra: Tantra is an ancient school of Oriental thought that views unqualified energy (prana) and consciousness as essentially the same. In Tantric iconography, Shiva, who represents consciousness, and Shakti, who represents unqualified energy, are depicted in an eternal embrace. Tantrics, because of their insight, sought to raise their energetic vibration by participating in the activities of the world, rather than adopting an aesthetic lifestyle.

Tattvas: Tattvas are evolutionary steps through which the phenomenal universe emerges, evolves, and then involves from the original cause, universal consciousness. Yoga teaches that there are thirty-six tattvas that are responsible for the incredible diversity of the phenomenal universe, both in the macrocosm and the microcosm.

Three Hearts: As interdimensional beings, humans have three hearts: the human heart on the left side of the chest, the heart chakra in the center, and Atman, on the right side. The human heart reflects unqualified energy, the heart chakra transmits and transmutes it, and Atman is the doorway through which divine consciousness emerges into human awareness as unqualified energy, prana.

Trauma: Trauma occurs whenever a body or vehicle of energy is ejected from personal body space and is prevented from returning to its original position. Trauma can create permanent problems in the human energy field. A trauma usually occurs when an individual has collected an inordinate amount of karmic baggage on a particular dimensional field and then suffers a strong and/or sustained projection.

Universal Consciousness: *See:* The Self.

Unqualified Energy: Unqualified energy radiates from the universal consciousness (the Self) into the hierarchy of fields that compose the phenomenal universe. In one form or another, it forms the foundation of the phenomenal universe as well as the higher and lower mind. It fills all available space and connects everything on all dimensions. Everything that exists has a form and occupies space, including objects, beings, emotions, and feelings that emerge from unqualified energy and owe their existence to unqualified energy that supports it and provides it with a medium through which it can move and express its particular vibration or resonance.

Unqualified energy, in the form of prana—although an essential element of consciousness—emerges as an apparently separate force by way of the tattvas.

Vasanas: *See:* Complex Subfields.

Vedanta: The Sanskrit name given to a collective body of material that forms the core of Yoga, Tantra, and Hinduism. The major schools of Vedanta are advaita, visistadvaita, and dvaita. Advaita is the school of nondualism which sees Brahman and the phenomenal universe as one.

Visistadvaita is conditional nondualism, which views the phenomenal universe as conditionally real and separate from Brahman as long as it exists, and Dvaita is a form of dualism that sees Brahman and the phenomenal universe as fundamentally different and separate from one another.

Vedanta has had a material influence on Buddhism, Jainism, and Sufism, and the Western metaphysical tradition. Traditional Vedanta is composed of the *Upanishads*, the *Bhagavad Gita*, and the *Brahma-Sutras*.

Vertical Integration: Bodies and vehicles of energy are vertically integrated when they fully occupy personal body space on their particular dimension. When a body or vehicle is vertically integrated it will resist the intrusion of qualified subfields and will function synchronistically with corresponding bodies to express the will, desire, and intent of the higher and lower mind.

World of the Chakras: The world of the chakras interpenetrates and supports the worlds of the higher and lower mind as well as the splenic levels and the functions and aspects of mind. On each dimension, in the world of the chakras, there exists a community of chakra bodies. Like the energy bodies to which they correspond, chakra bodies are the same size and shape as the physical-material body.

Chakra bodies have a close relationship to the system of chakras, and for a chakra to function properly the chakra bodies of its dimension must be free of karmic baggage and vertically integrated.

Yoga: In Sanskrit, the word Yoga means union. In popular usage, it means both a method for achieving union with the Self (Atman) and the experience of personal liberation or Self-realization. There are many schools of Yoga, including dualistic schools, schools of qualified dualism, and nondualistic schools.

Four Yogas were described in the *Bhagavad Gita*: Raja Yoga, Karma Yoga, Bhakti Yoga, and Jnana Yoga.

Tantra and Vedanta have two somewhat different interpretations of what constitutes Yoga. Vedanta (the method of Shankara and Pantanjali) tend to see Yoga, union with the Self, as Samadhi. In Samadhi, Atman (the Self) is isolated from Prakriti (Shakti) and/or Maya. Tantra, as well as Yoga Marga on the other hand, see Yoga as the assimilation of Shakti or Maya into its source, the Self.

Yogic Breath: The Yogic breath is a synthesis of three basic breaths and is often called the "complete breath." The three breaths are the abdominal breath, mid-breath, and upper breath. In the abdominal breath the abdomen is expanded and stretched downward; in the mid-breath air and prana, having filled the chest cavity, expand to fill the rib cage and the shoulders. In the nasal breath, air and prana fill the nasal passages and continue upward, filling the head. The Yogic breath was developed to enhance the level of prana in the human energy field and is a basic part of pranayana, the Yogic science of breath.

Yugas: Yugas are epochs in the history of mankind. Hindu mythology teaches that there are four yugas. Mankind has lived through three yugas already, the Satya, Trea, and Dwapara, and now lives in the Kali Yuga.

In each succeeding yuga, the collective field of maya becomes more dense. Pleasure, love, intimacy, and joy diminish and people find it increasingly difficult to remain centered in the higher and lower mind.

Index

To Write to the Author

If you wish to contact the author or would like more information about this book, please write to the author in care of Llewellyn Worldwide and we will forward your request. Both the author and publisher appreciate hearing from you and learning of your enjoyment of this book and how it has helped you. Llewellyn Worldwide cannot guarantee that every letter written to the author can be answered, but all will be forwarded. Please write to:

Keith Sherwood

c /o Llewellyn Worldwide Ltd.

P.O. Box 64383, Dept. 0-7387-0354-0

St. Paul, Minnesota 55164-0383, U.S.A.

Please enclosed a stamped, self-addressed envelope for reply, or $1.00 to cover costs. If outside U.S.A., enclose international postal reply coupon.

Many of Llewellyn's authors have websites with additional information and resources. For more information, please visit our website: http:/ / www.llewellyn.com.